Family Law Agreements

Family Law Agreements

George Jamieson

Tottel Publishing, Maxwelton House, 41–43 Boltro Road, Haywards Heath, West Sussex, RH16 1BJ

© Tottel Publishing 2005

A CIP Catalogue record for this book is available from the British Library.

ISBN 1 84592 004 X

Project management and typesetting by The Partnership Publishing Solutions Ltd

Printed and bound in Great Britain by CPI Bath

Nuptiae sunt coniunctio maris et feminae et consortium omnis vitae, divini et humani iuris communicatio.

Marriage is the joining of male and female and a partnership for all of life, a sharing of divine and human law.

Modestinus D23.2.1

Huwelick ofte Echt is een verzameling van man ende wijf tot een gemeen leven, mede-brengende een wettelick gebruick van mal-kanders lichaem.

Marriage is a joining together of man and wife to a common life, permitting the lawful use of each other's body.

Hugo De Groot, Inleidinge tot de Hollandsche Rechtsgeleerdheid, I.5.1

Preface

This book is based on my material in the 'Separation Agreements' section of *Butterworths Scottish Family Law*. I have retained, but expanded, the original material with a view to assisting practitioners draft and enforce family law agreements. I have included a number of additional topics, which I considered were relevant to family law agreements, but I have not attempted to be comprehensive. For example, I have not considered bankruptcy, assignation of rights under family law agreements, or the law of unjustified enrichment in the context of cohabiting couples, or other persons living together.

I am grateful to all those who helped me, in their various ways, with the preparation of this book, including Lucy Ancelin of the Council of Europe for supplying me with copies of the unpublished papers of the Council of Europe Fifth European Conference on Family Law held at The Hague, 15-16 March 1999 relating to registered partnerships and statutory cohabitation in Europe, which I used in writing chapter 13.

I am especially grateful to Kimberly McCourt and Mandy Gardner, Crestlink Ltd, Glasgow, for their dedication and skill in typing the manuscript.

I remain responsible for the final text, and any errors in it, in which the law is stated at 12 July 2004. References to the Civil Partnership Act 2004, however, are stated at 18 November 2004, the date of its Royal Assent.

George Jamieson
Paisley
December 2004

Contents

Preface   vii
Note on references to Scottish Ministers   *xvii*
List of abbreviations   *xix*
Table of statutes   *xxv*
Table of statutory instruments   *xxxi*
Table of European legislation   *xxxv*
Table of conventions, treaties and other international instruments   *xxxvii*
Table of cases   *xxxix*

Chapter 1   Giving advice   1
1.   Women and men   1
       Marriage versus cohabitation   1
              The woman's position   1
              The man's position   2
              Marriage agreements   2
              Cohabitation agreements   3
       Separation   3
       Action of separation   4
       Reconciliation   4
2.   Sexual minorities   5
       Persons of the same sex   5
       Transsexuals and hermaphrodites   5
3.   Succession   7
4.   Taking title to heritable property   8
5.   Free movement of persons in the European Economic Area   8

Chapter 2   Acting for the client   12
1.   Taking instructions   12
      Identifying what the solicitor can do to help   12
      Terms of engagement letter   13
      Fees   13
      Negotiating agreements   13
      Mediation and arbitration as alternatives to negotiation   14
      What to do where the 'agreement' has already been reached   14
      Capacity to contract   15
      Drafting the agreement   15
2.   Professional responsibility   16
      Duty to give objective advice   16
      Conflict of interest   16
      Sale of the matrimonial home   17
      Investment advice   17
3.   Money laundering   18
      Proceeds of Crime Act 2002   18
      Money Laundering Regulations 2003   19
4.   Data protection   19
      Data protection principles   19
      Registration with Information Commissioner   21

Chapter 3   Drafting, executing and registering family law agreements   22
1.   Drafting the agreement   22
      Style   22
      Structure   24
      Paragraphs, clauses or sections   25
      Numbering   25
      The language of obligations and accessory obligations   25
      The rules of grammar   26
      Punctuation   28
2.   Execution of the agreement   29
      Requirements   29
      Testing clause   31
3.   Registration   31

Chapter 4   Agreements in contemplation of, or during, marriage   34
1.   Terminology   34
2.   Purpose   34
3.   Exclusion of child's right to legitim   36
4.   Gifts and inheritance tax   36
5.   Assurance policies   36

Chapter 5   Separation agreements   38
1. Marriage and separation agreements   38
2. Scope and form of the agreement   40
3. Practical and legal considerations   41
4. Contract and property law considerations   41
5. Taxation: maintenance   42
6. Stamp duty land tax   42
7. Legal Aid: recovery or preservation of property   43
8. Revocation of the agreement   44

Chapter 6   Cohabitation agreements   46
1. Present or contemplated cohabitation   46
2. Past cohabitation   47
3. Same sex couples   48

Chapter 7   Parenting and surrogacy agreements   49
1. Parents and their children   49
    Parents   49
    Children   49
    Acquisition of parental responsibilities   50
    Exercise of parental responsibilities and rights   50
    Recognition of parental responsibilities and rights of persons not habitually resident
        in Scotland   51
2. Guardians, legal representatives and children's property   52
3. Adoption and surrogacy arrangements   53
4. Private fostering of children   54
5. Enforceability and effect of surrogacy and other arrangements for care by persons
    other than child's parents   54
6. Parenting agreements   55
7. Parenting agreements as authentic instruments and enforceable agreements in the
    European Union   56

Chapter 8   Aliment and financial provision   59
    Introduction   59
1. Creating maintenance obligations   59
    A fundamental distinction   59
    Unilateral obligations   60
2. Variation of aliment and periodical allowance   60
    Aliment   60
    Periodical allowance   61
3. Agreements post-decree to vary aliment or periodical allowance   62
    Aliment   62
    Periodical allowance   62

Chapter 9   Child support and its effects on separation agreements   64
Introduction   64
1.   Jurisdiction: non-benefit cases   64
2.   Jurisdiction: non-benefit cases – children   66
3.   Jurisdiction: benefit cases   67
4.   Jurisdiction: written maintenance agreements made before 5 April 1993   68
5.   Variation of agreements for aliment payable by non-resident parent   68
6.   Child Support Act 1991 and agreements about maintenance   69
7.   Significance of date of registration of agreement for aliment payable by non-resident parent   70
8.   Exclusion of CSA jurisdiction   70
9.   Practical considerations   70

Chapter 10   Pension sharing and earmarking   72
1.   Earmarking orders   72
2.   Pension sharing   72
3.   Actuarial and practical advice   73
4.   Investment advice   74

Chapter 11   Same sex marriage   76
1.   Existing position   76
2.   Effect of Civil Partnership Act 2004   79
3.   Same sex marriage in Europe   80
4.   Same sex marriage in North America   80

Chapter 12   Civil partnerships in the United Kingdom   82
Introduction   82
1.   Civil partnerships as registered partnerships in the United Kingdom   82
Definition   82
Consequences   83
2.   Overseas relationships as civil partnerships in the United Kingdom   84
3.   Family law agreements in relation to civil partnerships   86

Chapter 13   Registered partnerships and statutory cohabitation in Europe   88
1.   Registered partnership   88
The Nordic countries   88
The Netherlands   88
Germany   89
2.   Statutory cohabitation   89
France   89
Belgium   90
Spain   90

Chapter 14   Authentic instruments: enforcement within Europe of maintenance obligations contained in family law agreements   92

Introduction   92

1. Overview of legal provisions relating to authentic instruments   93

Applicable legal provisions   93

Territorial scope   94

Substantive provisions concerning authentic instruments   95

The conditions which establish a document as an authentic instrument   96

Procedure for registration of an authentic instrument in Scotland   97

Stage 1: Application to the Scottish Ministers   97

Applications under the Brussels and Lugano Conventions   98

Applications under the Council Regulation on Jurisdiction and Judgments   99

Stage 2: Procedure in the Sheriff Court   100

Stage 3: Further appeal   104

Powers of the sheriff and Court of Session on appeal   104

Partial enforcement   105

Legal Aid and costs   106

2. Transmitting Scottish authentic instruments abroad for enforcement   107

3. Service of documents in connection with enforcement of authentic instruments   108

4. European Enforcement Order   108

Chapter 15   Diligence, enforcement and protective measures   110

1. General considerations   110

2. Payment of money under agreements registered for execution   111

3. Payment of maintenance under registered European authentic instruments   112

4. Letters of inhibition   113

5. Letters of arrestment   115

6. Adjudication   115

7. Civil imprisonment for non-payment of aliment   116

8. Protective measures in respect of foreign family law agreements   116

Proceedings in other jurisdictions   116

Registered authentic instruments for maintenance   117

Chapter 16   Challenging family law agreements   118

1. Common law challenge   118

2. Statutory challenge   118

Chapter 17   Resolving disputes   120

Introduction   120

1. Measures for reducing the possibility of post-agreement disputes   120

Drafting techniques   120

Contract out of the right of retention   120

Anticipate disputes and draft accordingly, even if this involves more words   121

Draft the agreement as clearly as possible and define expressions if necessary   121
Remember the obligations accessory to the main ones   122
Build dispute resolution mechanisms into the agreement, if possible   122
The solicitor's duty to give objective advice   122
2.   Methods of resolving disputes   123
The five principal methods   123
Negotiation   123
Mediation   124
Conciliation   126
Arbitration   126
Litigation   127
When it is appropriate   127
Suspending charges for payment and recalling inhibitions proceeding on registered agreements   127

Chapter 18   Extracts from relevant legislation and international instruments   129
1.   United Kingdom   131
Acts of Parliament   131
Statutory instruments and Scottish statutory instruments   147
Acts of sederunt   154
2.   European Community legislation   161
3.   International treaties   171
4.   Council of Europe recommendation   187

Chapter 19   Style family law agreements   188
Style 1   Separation agreement (continuing after divorce)   188
Style 2   Separation agreement (terminating on divorce)   203
Style 3   Pension sharing agreement (pension arrangement)   208
Style 4   Pension sharing agreement (state scheme rights)   215
Style 5   Arbitration agreement for aliment   221
Style 6   Cohabitation agreement   232
Style 7   Parental responsibilities and conciliation agreement   239
Style 8   Provisions in a separation agreement referring to a separate parenting agreement   246
Style 9   Parenting agreement: legitimate children   248
Style 10   Parenting agreement: homosexuals couples   253
Style 11   Provisions in a separation agreement referring to a separate agreement on aliment for children   258
Style 12   Separate agreement for aliment for the children   260

Appendix 1   Applications and appeals   263
1.   Authentic instruments   263
2.   Final appeals   266

Appendix 2   Case law on the Brussels and Lugano conventions   268

Index   269

Note on references to Scottish Ministers

The Scotland Act 1998 (Transfer of Functions to the Scottish Ministers etc) Order 1999 (SI 1999/1750), amended by SI 2000/1563 and subsequent Orders SI 1999/3321, SI 2000/1563, SI 2000/3253, and SI 2001/954, transferred various statutory functions to the Scottish Ministers. More generally, the Scotland Act 1998, ss 53, 54, transferred all devolved functions to the Scottish Ministers. Accordingly, any reference in this book to the 'Scottish Ministers', if not found in the original, pre-Scotland Act 1998 legislation (whether primary or subordinate), has been made with reference to the devolution of these functions from the Secretary of State to the Scottish Ministers.

List of abbreviations

1968 Convention	See reference to 'Brussels Convention'
1971 Protocol	Protocol on the interpretation of the 1968 Convention by the European Court, signed at Luxembourg on 3 June 1971
Accession Convention (1978)	Convention on the accession to the 1968 Convention and the 1971 Protocol of Denmark, the Republic of Ireland and the United Kingdom, signed at Luxembourg on 9 October 1978
Accession Convention (1982)	Convention on the accession of the Hellenic Republic to the 1968 Convention and the 1971 Protocol, signed at Luxembourg on 25 October 1982
Accession Convention (1989)	Convention on the accession of the Kingdom of Spain and the Portuguese Republic to the 1968 Convention and the 1971 Protocol, signed at Donostia – San Sebastián on 26 May 1989
Accession Convention (1996)	Convention on the accession of the Republic of Austria, the Republic of Finland and the Kingdom of Sweden to the 1968 Convention and 1971 Protocol, signed at Brussels on 29th November 1996
AC	Law Reports, Appeal Cases
AJFL	Australian Journal of Family Law
AJIL	American Journal of International Law
All ER	All England Law Reports

APS	Act of the Parliaments of Scotland 1424–1707 (Short titles given by the Statute Law Revision (Scotland) Act 1964)
aps	Act of the Parliament of Scotland 1999 – date
Bankton	*Institute of the Laws of Scotland* (1751–1753)
Bell's *Comm*	*Bell's Commentaries on the Law of Scotland* (7th edn, 1870)
Brussels Convention	Convention on jurisdiction and the enforcement of judgments in civil and commercial matters, signed at Brussels on 27 September 1968
CA or CA (EW)	Court of Appeal (England and Wales)
CCMR 1997	Act of Sederunt (Child Care and Maintenance) Rules 1997, SI 1997 No 291
Ch D or Ch	Law Reports, Chancery Division
CJJ Act 1982	Civil Jurisdiction and Judgments Act 1982
CJJ Order 1993	Civil Jurisdiction and Judgments (Authentic Instruments and Court Settlements) Order 1993, SI 1993 No 604
CJJ Order 2001	Civil Jurisdiction and Judgments Order 2001, SI 2001 No 3929
CJJ (AIACS) Order 2001	Civil Jurisdiction and Judgments (Authentic Instruments and Court Settlements) Order 2001, SI 2001 No 3928
CSA	Child Support Agency
CSA 1991	Child Support Act 1991
CSA 1995	Child Support Act 1995
Civ PB	Green's Civil Practice Bulletin
Council Regulation on Jurisdiction and Judgments	Council Regulation (EC) 44/2001 of 22 December 2000 on jurisdiction and the recognition and enforcement of judgments in civil and commercial matters
Council Regulation on Service of Judicial and Extra-judicial Documents	Council Regulation (EC) 1348/2000 of 29 May 2000 on the service in the Member States of judicial and extra-judicial documents in civil or commercial matters

Cruz, Real and Jenard Report	Report by Mr Martinho de Almeida Cruz, Mr Manuel Desantes Real and Mr P Jenard on the 1989 Accession Convention (OJ C 189/35, 28.7.1990)
D	Dunlop (Court of Session Reports 1838–1862)
Durie's Decisions	Durie's Decisions of the Court of Session 1621–1642
EC	European Community
ECR	European Court Reports
EEA	European Economic Area
EFTA	European Free Trade Association
EHRR	European Human Rights Report
EJIL	European Journal of International Law
ELR or Edin LR	Edinburgh Law Review
EU	European Union
Erskine, *Institute*	*Institute of the Law of Scotland* (8th edn, 1871)
Erskine, *Principles*	*Principles of the Law of Scotland* (21st edn, 1911)
Evrigenis and Kerameus Report	Report by Professors Evrigenis and Kerameus on the 1982 Accession Convention (OJ C 298, 24.11.1986), p 1
F	Fraser (Court of Session Reports 1898–1906)
FC	Faculty Collection (1752–1825)
FLR	Family Law Reports
FL(S) Act 1985	Family Law (Scotland) Act 1985
Fam LB	Green's Family Law Bulletin
FLR	Green's Family Law Reports
GWD	Green's Weekly Digest
HL	House of Lords
HR & UKP	Human Rights and United Kingdom Practice
ICQL	International and Comparative Law Quarterly
IFL	International Family Law
JC	Justiciary Cases

JETS	Journal of the Evangelical Theological Society
JLS	Journal of Law and Society
JLSS	Journal of the Law Society of Scotland
JR	Juridical Review
Jenard Report	The Reports by Mr P Jenard on the 1968 Convention and the 1971 Protocol (OJ 1979 C59/1 and C/59/66)
Jenard and Möller Report	Report on the Lugano Convention by Mr P Jenard and Mr G Möller (OJ C189, 28.7.1990, p 57)
LS Gaz	Law Society Gazette (England and Wales)
Lugano Convention	Convention on jurisdiction and the enforcement of judgments in civil and commercial matters, concluded at Lugano on 16 September 1988
M	Macpherson (Court of Session Reports 1862–1873)
Mor	Morison's Dictionary of Decisions (1540–1808)
McGlashan on Aliment	McGlashan, *The Law and Practice in Actions of Aliment* (1837)
Maastricht Treaty	Treaty on European Union, signed at Maastricht on 7 February 1992
Maxwell Committee Report	Scottish Committee on Jurisdiction and Enforcement. Chairman: The Honourable Lord Maxwell. Scottish Courts Administration 1980 (Edinburgh University Law Library KK3 Scot)
NILR	Netherlands International Law Review
NIPR	Nederlands Internationaal Privaatrecht
NJ	Nederlandse Jurisprudentie
OCR 1993	Act of Sederunt (Sheriff Court Ordinary Case Rules) 1993, SI 1993 No 1956
OJ C	Official Journal of the European Communities, Communications Series
OJ L	Official Journal of the European Communities, Legislation Series
QB	Law Reports, Queen's Bench Division

P&D	Law Reports, Probate and Divorce
R	Rettie (Court of Session Reports 1873–1898)
RCS 1994	Act of Sederunt (Rules of the Court of Session 1994) 1994, SI 1994 No 1443
Rev Crit DIP	Revue Critique de droit international privé
S	Shaw (Court of Session Reports 1821–1838)
SC	Session Cases
SCLR	Scottish Civil Law Reports
SCOLAG	Scottish Legal Action Group Legal Journal
Sh Ct Rep	Sheriff Court Reports
SLAB	Scottish Legal Aid Board
SLT	Scots Law Times
SLT (Notes)	Scots Law Times (Notes)
SLT (Sh Ct)	Scots Law Times (Sheriff Court Reports)
Schlosser Report	Report by Professor Schlosser on the 1978 Accession Convention (OJ 1979, C59/71)
Stair	*Institutions of the Law of Scotland* (2nd edn, 1693)
Treaty of Amsterdam	Treaty amending the Treaty on European Union, the Treaties establishing the European Communities and certain related Acts, signed at Amsterdam on 2 October 1997
Treaty of Athens	Treaty of Accession of the Czech Republic, Estonia, Cyprus, Latvia, Lithuania, Hungary, Malta, Poland, Slovenia and Slovakia to the European Union, signed in Athens on 16 April 2003
Treaty establishing the European Community	Treaty Establishing the European Community, signed at Rome on 25 March 1957
WLR	Weekly Law Reports
W&S	Wilson & Shaw's Appeal Cases 1824–1834

Table of statutes

Numbers on the right-hand side are to paragraph numbers. Those paragraph numbers in **bold** indicate where an Act is set out in part or in full.

PARA

Administration of Justice (Scotland)
  Act 1972
    s 1(1), (1A) 19.05
    3 .... 19.05, 19.06
    4 .... 19.05
Adoption and Children Act 2002
    s 50 .... 7.06, 12.03
    53A(1) 7.06
    111 .... 7.08
    112 .... 7.03
    123 .... 7.13
    133 .... 7.13
    144(4) 7.06, 12.03
    Sch 3
      para 30 .... 7.06
Adoption (Scotland) Act 1978
    s 12 .... 7.05
      (1)-(4) 7.04
    38 .... 7.06
      (1) 7.06
    39(1) 7.06
    47 .... 7.06
    50, 50A 7.13
    51, 52 .... 7.13
Adults with Incapacity (Scotland) Act 2000
    s 1(6) 2.11
Age of Legal Capacity (Scotland) Act 1991
    s 1(1) 2.10, 6.04, 7.02
    2(4A) 9.07
    (5) 6.04

PARA

British Nationality Act 1981
    Sch 6 .... 14.03
British Overseas Territories Act 2002
    s 1(2) 14.03

Child Abduction Act 1984
    s 6 .... 7.20, 19.09
Child Support Act 1991 .... 5.12, 8.04, 9.01,
  9.02, 9.06, 9.14, 9.16, 12.03,
    .... 12.08
    s 1 .... 9.02
    3 .... 9.02
      (3) 9.02
    4 .... 9.02, 9.03, 9.08, 9.09, 9.10,
            9.11, 9.15, 9.18
      (1) 9.02, 9.14
      (10) 9.05, 9.06, 9.08, 9.09,
           9.10, 9.11, 9.13, 9.14
      (11) 9.08
    6 .... 9.08, 9.09, 9.11, 9.13
      (1) 9.08
      (3) 9.08, 9.13
    7 .... 9.07, 9.08, 9.09, 9.10,
         9.11, 9.14, 9.15, 9.18
      (1) 9.07, 9.08, 9.14
      (10) 9.09, 9.10, 9.11, 9.13, 9.14
    8 .... 8.04, 19.01
      (1), (2) 9.03
      (3) 9.03
      (3A) 9.09

PARA

s 8(5) 9.04, 9.04, 9.05, 9.06, 9.09
  (6)-(9) 9.03
  (10) 9.02
9 .... **18.18**, 19.01
  (1), (2) 9.14
  (3) 9.09, 9.14
  (4) 5.12, 9.14
  (5) 8.04, 9.12, 9.13, 19.01
  (6) 9.13, 19.01
10 .... **18.18**
  (2) 9.11, 9.18
  11(d) 9.03
  18(6), (7) 9.03
  29 .... 9.02
  44(1) 9.16
  (2A) 9.16
  55(1) 9.01
Sch 1
  para 10(3) 9.03
Sch 5
  para 8(4) 15.01, 15.03
Child Support Act 1995 .... 9.01
  s 18(8) 9.01
Child Support, Pensions and Social
  Security Act 2000 .... 9.01
Children (Scotland) Act 1995 .... 1.04
  s 1(2) 7.02
  2(2) 7.04, 7.17
  (3), (6) 7.20
  (7) 7.02
  3(1) 1.04
  (5) 7.04, 7.15, 7.17
  (6) 7.15
  4 ...... 1.04, 1.18, 7.03, 19.06, 19.07
  5 .... 7.15
  6(1) 5.12, 7.04, 7.16
  7 .... 1.18
  (1), (2), (5) 7.09
  8 .... 1.18
  (1)-(5) 7.09
  10(1) 7.11
  11 .... 19.07
  (1) 7.04
  (2) 1.11, 7.03, 7.04, 7.05, 7.10
  (7) . 5.12, 7.04, 7.17, 15.01, 17.20
  (11) 7.03
  13 .... 1.11

PARA

s 14(3) 7.07, 7.12
  15(1) 7.01, 7.02
  (5) 7.11
  86 .... 7.05
  (1) 7.05
Civil Evidence (Family Mediation)
  (Scotland) Act 1995
  s 1(1) 17.14
  (2) 17.14, 17.15
  (7) 17.15
  (8) 17.14, 17.20
  (9) 17.14
  2 .... 17.16
  (1) 17.14, 17.16, 17.17
  (2), (3) 17.16
  (4) 17.17
Civil Evidence (Scotland) Act 1988 .. 17.21
  s 9 .... 17.21
Civil Imprisonment (Scotland) Act 1882
  s 4 .... 15.17
Civil Jurisdiction and Judgments
  Act 1982 .... 5.11, 14.07, 14.31, 15.23
  s 2(5) 8.05
  5 .... 8.05, 14.13, 14.14, 14.31,
                     15.05, 15.07, **18.07**
  (1) 14.10
  (2) 14.22
  6 .... **18.08**
  (3) 14.24
  7 .... **18.09**
  8 .... **18.10**
  11 .... **18.11**
  12 .... 14.20, 14.31, **18.12**
  15 .... **18.13**
  18 .... 14.20, 14.31
  (7) 14.03
  27(1) 15.19, 15.20
  (2) 15.19, 15.20, 15.21
  39 .... 14.03
  41 .... 14.07
  (7) 14.07
  48(2) 14.01
  50 .... 14.01
Sch 1 .... 14.02
Sch 3C 14.02
Sch 8 .... 8.05

PARA

Civil Partnership Act 2004 ...... 6.01, 11.05,
　　11.06, 12.01, 12.02, 12.03, 17.15
　s 1(1)(a) 12.02
　　(3) 12.02
　　84(1) 1.16, 12.02
　　115(1)-(3) 12.03
　　125 .... 12.03
　　204 .... 12.04
　　　(2) 12.06
　　205 .... 12.04
　　206 .... 11.07, 12.04, 12.06
　　207 .... 12.04
　　208 .... 12.04, 13.02
　　115(2), (3) 12.08
　　128 .... 12.10
　　206 .... 13.08
　　217 .... 12.03
　　238 .... 12.03
　　245 .... 12.03
　Sch 21 ...... 11.06, 12.04, 12.05, 13.08
　Sch 27
　　para 74, 76 .... 12.09
　Sch 28 .... 12.09
　　para 9 .... 12.03
　　　20 .... 12.03
　　　22 .... 16.02
　　　23 .... 16.04
　　　25-28 .... 12.03
　　　59 .... 17.15
Confession of Faith Ratification
　Act 1690 .... 1.12
　s 1 .... **18.01**
Conjugal Rights (Scotland)
　Amendment Act 1861
　s 6 .... 1.09, 12.08, **18.04**
Court of Session Act 1830
　s 33 .... 12.03
Court of Session Act 1850
　s 16 .... 12.03
Criminal Law (Consolidation) (Scotland)
　Act 1995
　s 5, 13 .... 2.10

Damages (Scotland) Act 1976
　Sch 1 .... 1.02
Data Protection Act 1998 .... 2.20, 2.23
　s 1 .... 2.21

PARA

s 2 .... 2.20, 2.22
　4 .... 2.21
　17(1) 2.23
　21 .... 2.23
　27(4) 2.21, 2.22
　　(5) 2.21
　35(2) 2.21
　Sch 1 .... 2.21
　Sch 2
　　para 1 .... 2.21
　Sch 3
　　para 1 .... 2.22
Debtors (Scotland) Act 1987
　s 54 .... 15.01, 15.03
　　(1) 15.01, 15.03, 15.05
　　(2) 15.03
　　73 .... **18.16**
　　(1) 15.01
　　87(1) 15.01
　　(2) 15.01, 15.13
　　(3) 15.01
　　90 .... 15.03
　　(1) 15.05
　　101 .... 15.10, 15.16
　　106 .... 5.09, 8.03, 15.03, 15.05,
　　　　　　　　　　　　　　　　18.17
Debts Arrangement and Attachment
　(Scotland) Act 2002 .... 15.01
　Sch 3
　　para 7 .... 15.05
　　　8 .... 15.01
　　　17(9) 15.01
Divorce (Scotland) Act 1976 .. 19.03, 19.04
　s 1 .... 1.08
　　(2) 1.08
　　2(1) 1.10
　　4 .... 1.07, 1.09
　　(1) 2.10
Domicile and Matrimonial Proceedings
　Act 1973
　s 7, 8 .... 1.09

Execution of Diligence (Scotland)
　Act 1926 .... 19.01

Family Law Act 1986
　s 26(1) 7.07

PARA

Family Law (Scotland) Act 1985 .... 4.02,
    4.03, 8.01, 8.04, 9.11, 12.09,
    19.01, 19.03, 19.04, 19.06
Pt I 19.06
s 1 .... 19.05
    (1) 1.02, 8.05, 11.04, 12.03
    (2) 19.06
    2 .... **18.14**
    (4) 7.02
    (6)-(9) 19.06
    3-6 .... 19.06
    7 ..... 5.08, 5.19, 8.02, **18.15**, 19.02
    (1) 5.12, 8.06
    (2) 5.12, 8.04, 8.05, 8.09
    (2A) 8.04
    (4) 8.05
    (5) 8.04
    8 .... 1.02
    (1) 19.03, 19.04, 19.06
    (2) 4.07, 19.06
    (6) 10.05
    9 .... 1.02, 4.07
    (1) 19.01, 19.03, 19.04, 19.06
    10 .... 1.02
    (1), (2) 19.06
    (3) 19.03, 19.04, 19.06
    (4) 19.06
    (6) 4.02, 19.06
    (7) 19.06
    11 .... 1.02
    (2)-(4), (7) 19.06
    12 .... 1.02
    12A 10.01, 19.01, 19.03
    (2) 10.01
    13 .... 1.02
    (1) 8.12
    (4) 8.11, 8.12
    14 .... 1.02
    (1) 4.07
    (2) 4.07, 19.06
    (4) 19.06
    (6) 4.07
    16 .... 5.12, 5.21, 8.02
    (1) 4.02, 5.12, 8.07, 8.12,
                12.03, 16.02, 16.04
    (2) 8.07, 16.02

PARA

    s 14(2A) 16.02
    (3) 8.08
    (4) 8.08, 16.02
    17 .... 1.02, 16.04
    18 .... 1.11, 6.03, 15.01, 19.05
    19 .... 1.11, 6.03, 19.05
    (1) 15.09
    20 .... 19.05
    24 .... 12.03
    (1) 4.02
    25 .... 4.03, 12.03, 19.01,
                19.02, 19.06
    26 .... 4.03, 12.03
    27(1) 12.03, 19.03, 19.04
    Sch 1
    para 1 .... 1.07
Finance Act 2003
    s 79(3) 5.14
    Sch 3
    para 3(d) 5.14
    Sch 11
    para 2 .... 5.14
Financial Services and Markets Act 2000
    s 19 .... 2.17
    23 .... 2.17
Foster Children (Scotland)
    Act 1984 .... 7.14, 7.15
    s 1 .... 7.14
    4, 5 .... 7.14
    14(1)-(3) 7.14

Gender Recognition Act 2004 .... 1.14
    s 26 .... 1.14

Housing (Scotland) Act 1988
    s 31(4) 1.20
Housing (Scotland) Act 2001
    s 22 .... 1.02, 1.20
    108(1) 1.02, 1.20
    Sch 3 .... 1.02, 1.20
Human Fertilisation and Embryology
    Act 1990 .... 7.03, 9.16
    s 27-29 .... 7.01
    30 .... 7.04, 7.05, 9.16
Human Rights Act 1998 .... 11.03

PARA

Income and Corporation Taxes Act 1988
  s 347B(1), (1A), (3), (5A), (7)... 5.13
Inheritance Tax Act 1984
  s 22, 43 .... 4.06
Interpretation Act 1978
  s 6(a), (b) 3.18
    (c) 3.24
  17 .... 19.01

Law Reform (Husband and Wife) (Scotland)
  Act 1984
  s 1(1) 4.01
  5 .... 4.02
Law Reform (Miscellaneous Provisions)
  (Scotland) Act 1966
  s 8 .... 8.09, 8.13
Law Reform (Parent and Child) (Scotland)
  Act 1986
  s 5(1), (3) 7.01
Legal Aid (Scotland) Act 1986
  s 12(3) 5.15
  17(2B) 5.15
Legitimation (Scotland) Act 1968
  s 1(1) 1.04

Maintenance Orders Act 1950 .... 14.03
Marriage (Scotland) Act 1977 .... 2.10
  s 1-4 .... 1.02
  5 .... 1.02
  s 5(4) 1.14, 1.16, 11.01
  6-20 .... 1.02
Married Women's Policies of Assurance
  (Scotland) Act 1880 .... 4.08, 12.10
  s 2 .... 4.07
Married Women's Property (Scotland)
  Act 1881 .... 4.02
Married Women's Property (Scotland)
  Act 1920 .... 4.02
Matrimonial Causes Act 1973
  s 18(2) 1.09
Matrimonial Homes (Family Protection)
  (Scotland) Act 1981
  s 4(6) 1.11
  13 .... 19.01
  14, 15 .... 1.11
  18 .... 1.02

PARA

Mental Health (Care and Treatment)
  (Scotland) Act 2003 .... 2.11
  s 328 .... 2.11

Proceeds of Crime Act 2002 .... 2.18
  s 327 .... 2.18
  328 .... 2.18
    (1) 2.18
  329 .... 2.18
  330(1)-(6), (10), (11) 2.18
  331, 332 .... 2.18
  333 .... 2.18
    (3), (4) 2.18
  335(2)-(7) 2.18
  340(2) 2.18
  Sch 9 .... 2.18
Protection from Abuse (Scotland) Act 2001
  s 1, 3 .... 1.11
Protestant Religion and Presbyterian
  Church Act 1707 .... 1.12, 11.01, 18.02
Public Records (Scotland) Act 1809
  s 1-8 .... 3.34
Public Records (Scotland) Act 1937
  s 9 .... 3.36
  15 .... 3.34
Public Registers and Records (Scotland)
  Act 1948
  s 1(2) 3.36

Registration Act 1698 .... 3.35
Registration of Births, Deaths and
  Marriages (Scotland) Act 1965
  s 42(5) 1.15
Requirements of Writing (Scotland)
  Act 1995 .... 19.01, 19.07
  s 1 .... 5.08, 5.09
    (2) 8.03
  3 .... 3.24, 3.34
    (1) 3.24
    (3) 3.26, 3.31
    (4) 3.24, 3.25, 3.26
    (5) 3.25
    (6) 3.24
    (7) 3.27
    (8) 3.31
    (9) 3.31

PARA

s 4 ....3.24, 3.30, 3.34

5 ....3.30

6 ....5.08

(1), (2) 3.24, 3.34

(4) 3.35, 5.08, 19.01

7(1), (3), (5) 3.28

8(1), (5) 3.29

9 ....3.30

10 ....3.31

12(1) 3.29

Sch 5 ....3.35

Scotland Act 1998 ....11.01

s 53(2) 3.31, 14.07

Sch 5

para 1 ....11.01

Sheriff Court and Legal Officers (Scotland)
Act 1927

s 16...3.34

Sheriff Court (Civil Jurisdiction and
Procedure (Scotland) Act 1963

s 3 ....17.09

Sheriff Courts (Scotland) Act 1907

s 5 ....12.03

(5) 17.24, 19.01

20 ....12.03

Sheriff Courts (Scotland) Extracts
Act 1892

s 7(1) 15.01, 15.13

Slave Trade Act 1824

s 9 ....7.13

Solicitors (Scotland) Act 1980

s 61 ....2.04

Stamp Act 1891

s 122(1) 3.14

Statute Law Revision (Scotland)
Act 1906.......................................3.34

Succession (Scotland) Act 1964

s 8, 9...1.02

10(2) 1.02

12 ....1.17, 4.05

Surrogacy Arrangements Act 1985

s 1A 7.15

2, 3 ....7.13

Titles to Land Consolidation (Scotland)
Act 1868

s 38 ....2.21

138 ....3.34, 3.35, **18.05**

PARA

s 159 ....15.15

Union with England Act 1707 .... 1.12,
11.01, 18.03

Welfare Reform and Pensions
Act 1999................. 10.08, 12.09, **18.20**

Pt III...........................19.03, 19.04

Pt IV 19.03, 19.04

s 26(1) 19.03

27(2) 19.03

28 ....12.09

(1) 10.02, 19.03

(3) 3.34, 5.08, 10.02, 19.03

(6) 19.03

(7) 10.03, 10.04, 19.03

(8) 19.03

(9) 10.03, 19.03

(10) 10.04, 19.03

34 ....19.03

47(2) 19.04

48 ....12.09, **18.21**

(1) 10.02, 19.04

(3) 3.34, 5.08, 10.02, 19.04

(6) 10.03, 10.04, 19.04

(7), (8) 19.04

(9) 10.04, 19.04

49 ....19.04

Sch 5 ....19.03, 19.04

para 1(3) 19.03

3(3) 19.03

4(2) 19.03

Wills Act 1837

s 18...1.17

18A 1.19

Writs Execution (Scotland)
Act 1877............................3.36, 14.01

s 1, 2 ....3.36, 5.08

3 . 15.01, 15.02, 15.13, **18.06**, 19.01

5, 7 ....3.36

Schedule 3.36

France
Civil Code

art 515-8 ....6.01

1317 ....14.01

United States of America
Defense of Marriage Act 1996 .... 11.10

Table of statutory instruments

Numbers on the right-hand side are to paragraph numbers. Those paragraph numbers in **bold** indicate where a Statutory Instrument is set out in part or in full.

PARA

Act of Sederunt (Child Care and
Maintenance) Rules 1997, SI 1997/291
  r 5.1 .... **18.32**
  5.2 .... **18.33**
  5.3 .... **18.34**
  5.4 .... 15.05, **18.35**
  5.5 .... **18.36**
  5.34 .... 15.15
  5.38 .... 14.13, 14.15, **18.37**
    (1) 14.13, 14.22
    (2) 14.14
    (3) 14.20
  5.39 .... **18.38**
  5.40 .... **18.39**
  5.41 .... **18.40**
  5.42 .... **18.41**
    (1) 14.23
  5.43 .... 15.05, **18.42**
  Sch 1 .... **18.43**
Act of Sederunt (Rules of the Court of
Session) 1994, SI 1994/1443
  r 7.6 .... 15.15
  13.6A 15.09
  14.1 .... 15.22
  14.2(g) 17.24
  16.12(1), (2), (4) 15.04
  38.10 .... 14.24
  49.8(1) 10.01
  49.43(1) 8.09
  49.46(1) 16.03

PARA

  49.49(1) 8.13
  59.1(1) ... 15.06, 15.07, 15.11, 15.14
    (3) 15.08
    (4) 15.08, 15.14
    (4A) 15.11
    (4B) 15.09, 15.11
    (5) 15.09
  62.1 .... 15.22
  62.27 .... 15.22
  62.40 .... **18.30**
    (4)-(6) 14.34
Act of Sederunt (Rules of the Court
of Session Amendment No 6)
(Diligence on the Dependence) 2003,
SI 2003/537 .... 15.08
  para 2(2) 15.09
    (9) 15.08
Act of Sederunt (Sheriff Court Ordinary
Cause Rules) 1993, SI 1993/1956
  r 5.4 .... 15.04
  33.7(1) 10.01
  33.48(1) 16.03
  33.51(1) 8.13
  33.51(3) 19.03, 19.04
  33.58(2) 8.09
  33.59(1), (2) 8.04
  33.84 .... 8.09, 8.13
Act of Sederunt (Summary Applications,
Statutory Applications and Appeals etc
Rules) 1999, SI 1999/929

PARA

r 2.6 .... 14.23
Act of Sederunt (Summary Case Rules)
2000, SI 200/132
    r 32.1 .... 17.09
    32.2 .... 17.09
Adoption (Designation of Overseas
Adoptions) Order 1973,
SI 1973/19 .... 7.06
Adoption of Children from Overseas
(Scotland) Regulations 2001, SI 2001/
236 .... 7.13
Advice and Assistance (Scotland)
Regulations 1996, SI 1996/2447 . 14.31
    reg 16(2) 5.15
        (3) 5.16

Child Maintenance (Written Agreements)
Order 1993, SI 1993/620 .... 9.04
Child Maintenance (Written Agreements)
(Scotland) Order 1997,
SI 1997/2943 .... 9.04
Child Support Act 1991 (Commencement
No 3 and Transitional Provisions) Order
1992, SI 1992/2644 .... 9.01
Child Support (Amendments to Primary
Legislation) (Scotland) Order 1993,
SI 1993/660
    art 2(5) 8.08
Child Support (Applications: Prescribed
Date) Regulations 2003,
SI 2003/194 .... 9.01
Child Support (Maintenance Assessment
Procedure) Regulations 1992,
SI 1992/1813
    reg 34 .... 9.08
Child Support (Maintenance Calculation
Procedure) Regulations 2000, SI 2001/
157 .... 9.01
    Sch 1 .... 9.01
Child Support (Maintenance Arrangements
and Jurisdiction) Regulations 1992,
1992/2645
    reg 4(1) 9.11
        (2), (3) 9.11, 9.18
        7A.. 9.16

PARA

Child Support (Written Agreements)
(Scotland) Order 1997, SI 1997/2943
    art 1 .... 9.06
Civil Jurisdiction and Judgments
Act 1982 (Interim Relief) Order 1997,
SI 1997/302 .... 15.21
Civil Jurisdiction and Judgments Act 1982
(Provisional and Protective Measures)
(Scotland) Order 1997, SI 1997/2780
    art 2 .... 15.19
        (a) 15.21
        3(a) 15.20, 15.21
Civil Jurisdiction and Judgments
Act 1982 (Gibraltar) Order 1997,
SI 1997/2602 .... 14.31, 14.36
    art 2, 3 .... 14.03
Civil Jurisdiction and Judgments (Authentic
Instruments and Court Settlements)
Order 1993, SI 1993/604
    art 3 .... 15.05
        (1) 14.24
        7 .... 14.03
        8 .... 14.01
Civil Jurisdiction and Judgments (Authentic
Instruments and Court Settlements)
Order 2001, SI 2001/3928 .. 14.15, 14.17
    art 1 .... **18.27**
        2 .... **18.28**
        3 .... 14.03
        4 .... 14.01
Civil Jurisdiction and Judgments Order
2001, SI 2001/3929 .... 14.07, 14.15,
                                        14.22, 15.21
    art 3 .... 14.15, 14.17
        (1) 14.10
        4(3) 14.24
        9 .... 14.07
        (7) 14.07
    Sch 1 .... **18.29**
    Sch 3
        para 26 .... 15.21
Civil Legal Aid (Scotland) Regulations
2002, SI 2002/494 .... 14.31
    reg 33(a), (b) 5.15
        40 .... 5.16
        46(1), (2) 14.31

PARA

Court of Session etc Fees Order 1997,
  SI 1997/688
    art 5(c) 14.31

Divorce etc (Notification and Treatment of
  Pensions) (Scotland) Regulations 2000,
  SI 2000/1050 .... 10.01

Financial Services and Markets Act 2000
  (Regulated Activities) Order 2001, SI
  2001/544
    art 33 .... 2.17
Foster Children (Private Fostering)
  (Scotland) Regulations 1985, SI 1985/
  1798 .... 7.14
    reg 3-5, 8 .... 7.14

Money Laundering Regulations 2003,
  SI 2003/3075 .... 2.19
    reg 4, 6 .... 2.19
         7 .... 2.18

Papers on Divorce etc (Pension Sharing)
  (Scotland) Regulations 2000,
  SI 2000/1051
    reg 2, 4 .... 3.01
Parental Orders (Human Fertilisation and
  Embryology) (Scotland) Regulations
  1994,
  SI 1994/2804
    reg 2.37-2.44 .... 7.03
    Sch 1
      para 3 .... 7.04
Parental Responsibilities and Parental
  Rights Agreement (Scotland)
  Regulations 1996,
  SI 1996/2549 .... 1.04, 7.03

PARA

Pensions on Divorce (etc) (Pensions
  Sharing) (Scotland) Regulations 2000,
  SI 2000/1051 .... 19.03
    reg 1 .... **18.22**
         2 .... 5.10, **18.23**, 19.03
         3 .... **18.24**, 19.03
         4 .... 5.10, **18.25**, 19.04
         5 .... **18.26**, 19.04
Pensions on Divorce etc (Provisions of
  Information) Regulations 2000, SI 2000/
  1048
    reg 5 .... 10.03, 19.03
Proceeds of Crime Act 2002 (Business in
  the Regulated Sector and Supervisory
  Authorities) Order 2003, SI 2003/3074
    art 2 .... 2.18
    Schedule
      para 1(1) 2.18

Registration of Births, Still-births, Deaths
  and Marriages (Prescription of Forms)
  (Scotland) Regulations 1965, SI 1965/
  1839
    reg 3 .... 1.15

Scotland Act 1998 (Consequential Modifica-
  tions) (No 2) Order 1999, SI 1999/1820
    art 2(2) 14.07
Sheriff Court Fees Order 1997, SI 1997/687
    art 2(1) 14.31
         7(1) 14.31
    Schedule
      para 17 .... 14.20
Stamp Duty Land Tax (Administration)
  Regulations 2003, SI 2003/2387
    reg 8 .... 5.14
    Sch 1 .... 5.14

Table of European legislation

Numbers on the right-hand side are to paragraph numbers. Those paragraph numbers in **bold** indicate where legislation is set out in part or in full.

PARA

Directives
2004/38/EC (*on the rights of citizens of the Union and their family members to move and reside freely within the territory if the Member States*) OJ L158, p 77

    art 2(2) 1.23
        3(2) 1.23
        13 .... 1.25

Regulations
Council Regulation (EEC) 1612/1968 (*on freedom of movement for workers within the Community*) OJ L257, p 2

    art 10(1) 1.22
Council Regulation (EC) 1347/2000 (*on jurisdiction and the recognition and enforcement of judgments in matrimonial matters and in matters of parental responsibilities for children of both spouses*) OJ L160, p 19

    art 2 .... 1.09, 7.22
Council Regulation (EC) 1348/2000 (*on the service in the Member States of judicial and extra-judicial documents in civil or commercial matters*) OJ L160, p 37 14.23, 14.36, 14.23

    art 19 .... 14.23
        (1) 14.23
Council Regulation (EC) 44/2001 (*on*

PARA

jurisdiction and the recognition and enforcement of judgments in civil and commercial matters) OJ L12, p 1 ..... 5.11, 14.02, 14.03, 14.04, 14.10, 14.15

    Preamble 14.03
        para 21-23 .... 14.03
    art 1 .... **18.44**
        (3) 14.03
        26(2)-(4) 14.23
        31 .... 15.19
        38 .... **18.45**
        (2) 14.07
        39 .... **18.46**
        (1), (2) 14.07
        40 .... **18.47**
        (1) 14.19
        (2) 14.18, 14.20
        (3) 14.20
        41 .... 14.21, **18.48**
        42 .... **18.49**
        (1) 14.21
        (2) 14.21, 14.27
    art 43 .... 14.23, **18.50**
        (1), (2), (4) 14.22
        (4) 14.23
        (5) 14.22
        44 .... 14.24, **18.51**
        45 .... **18.52**
        46 .... **18.53**
        (1)-(3) 14.28

PARA

47 .... 15.23, **18.54**
(2), (3) 14.22
48 .... 14.29, **18.55**
49 .... **18.56**
50 .... 14.30, **18.57**
51 .... 14.20, **18.58**
52 .... 14.20, **18.59**
53 .... 14.10, **18.60**
(1) 14.20
(2) 14.12
54 .... **18.61**
(4) 14.32
55 .... 14.25, **18.62**
(2) 14.20
56 .... 14.20, **18.63**
57 .... 14.35, 14.34, **18.64**
(1) ... 14.06, 14.25, 14.26, 14.08
(2) 14.25, 14.09
(3) 14.10
(4) 14.10, 14.11, 14.21,
14.25, 14.27
59 .... **18.65**
(1), (2) 14.07
68 .... **18.66**
(1) 14.03, 14.04
69 .... **18.67**
Annex II 14.03, 14.07, **18.68**
III 14.03, **18.69**
IV 14.24, **18.70**
VI 14.15, **18.71**

PARA

Council Regulation (EC) 2201/2003
(*concerning jurisdiction and the recognition
and enforcement of judgments in matrimonial matters and the matters of parental
responsibility*) OJ L338, p 1
art 2(7) 7.22
46 .... 7.22
Council Regulation (EC) 805/2004 (*creating
a European Enforcement Order for
uncontested claims*) OJ L143, p 15 . 14.37
art 5, 19 .... 14.37
21(1) 14.37
25 .... 14.37
(3) 14.37
27 .... 14.37

Table of conventions, treaties and other international instruments

Numbers on the right-hand side are to paragraph numbers. Those paragraph numbers in **bold** indicate where the material is set out in part or in full.

PARA

Conventions

Brussels Convention on the Jurisdiction and
the Enforcement of Judgments in Civil
and Commercial Matters (Brussels, 1968)
14.01, 14.02, 14.03, 14.04, 14.07, 14.10,
14.13

14.15, 14.20, 14.21, 14.22, 14.23, 14.26,
.... 14.31, 14.36, A2.01

art 1 .... **18.71**

20(2), (3) 14.23

24 .... 15.19

31 .... **18.73**

(2) 14.07

art 32 .... 14.31, **18.74**

(1), (2) 14.07

33 .... 14.19, 14.31, **18.75**

(1) 14.19

(2) 14.13, 14.20

(3) 14.20

34 .... 14.31, **18.76**

(1) 14.21

35 .... 14.21, 14.31, **18.77**

36 .... **18.78**

(1), (2) 14.22

37 .... **18.79**

(1) 14.22

(2) 14.24

38 .... **18.80**

PARA

art 38(1)-(3) 14.28

39 .... 15.23, **18.81**

(1), (2) 14.22

40 .... 14.23, **18.82**

(2) 14.23

41 .... 14.24, 14.31, **18.83**

42 .... 14.29, **18.84**

44 .... 14.30, **18.85**

45 .... 14.20, **18.86**

46 .... **18.87**

(1) 14.10, 14.20

47 .... **18.88**

(1) 14.20, 14.26

(2) 14.20

48 .... 14.25, **18.89**

(1), (2) 14.20

49 .... 14.20, **18.90**

50 ...... 14.06, 14.25, 14.26, 14.08,
18.91

(2), (3) 14.10

52(1), (2) 14.07

Annexed Protocol **18.92**

art IV 14.36

Hague Convention on the Recognition and
Enforcement of Decisions relating to
Aliment Obligations (Hague, 1973)14.02

art 1 .... 14.02

15 .... 14.23

PARA

Lugano Convention on Jurisdiction and
  the Enforcement of Judgments in
  Civil and Commercial Matters
  (Lugano, 1988) 14.01, 14.03, 14.05,
                14.07, 14.10, 14.13, 14.15,
                14.20, 14.21, 14.22, 14.23,
                14.26, 14.31, 14.36, A2.01
  art 1 .... **18.93**
    20(2), (3) 14.23
    24 .... 15.19
    31 .... **18.94**
      (2) 14.07
    32 .... 14.31, **18.95**
      (1), (2) 14.07
    33 .... 14.19, 14.31, **18.96**
      (1) 14.19
      (2) 14.13, 14.20
      (3) 14.20
    34 .... 14.31, **18.97**
      (1) 14.21
    35 .... 14.21, 14.31, **18.98**
    36 .... **18.99**
      (1), (2) 14.22
    37 .... **18.100**
      (1) 14.22
      (2) 14.24
    38 .... **18.101**
      (1)-(3) 14.28
    39 .... 15.23, **18.102**
      (1), (2) 14.22
    40 .... 14.23, **18.103**
      (2) 14.23
    41 .... 14.24, **18.104**
    42 .... 14.29, **18.105**
    44 .... 14.30, **18.106**
    45 .... 14.20, **18.107**
    46 .... **18.108**
      (1) 14.10, 14.20
    47 .... **18.109**
      (1) 14.20, 14.26
      (2) 14.20
    48 .... 14.25, **18.110**
      (1), (2) 14.20
    49 .... 14.20, **18.111**
    50 .... 14.06, 14.25, 14.26,
                14.08, **18.112**

PARA

    art 50(2), (3) 14.10
      52(1), (2) 14.07
    Protocol No 1 .... **18.113**
      art IV 14.36, **18.113**
        va **18.113**
    Protocol No 2 .... **18.114**
      art 3 .... A2.01

Treaties

Treaty of Amsterdam, 1997 .... 3.10
Treaty of Athens
  art 2 .... 14.05
Treaty establishing the European
  Community, 1957
    art 299 .... 14.03, 14.04
Treaty of European Union (Maastricht),
  1992 .... 3.10

Recommendations

88(3) of the Committee of Ministers to
    Member States on the Validity of
    Contracts between Persons Living
    Together as an Unmarried Couple and
    their Testamentary Disposition, adopted
    7 March 1988 .... 6.01, **18.115**

Table of cases

AB v CD (1853) 15 D 372 .... 5.18
AM or W v JW (24 February 2004, unreported), OH 2.13, 17.01
Advocate General for Scotland v Taylor 2004 SC 339, 2003 SLT 1340,
    2003 GWD 36-998, IH 15.09

Bank of East Asia Ltd v Scottish Enterprise 1997 SLT 1213, [1996] 5 Bank LR 93,
    [1996] CLC 351, Times, January 24, 1996, HL 17.03, 19.01
Bank of Scotland v Graham's Trustee 1992 SC 79, 1993 SLT 252, 1992 SCLR 306,
    IH affirming 1991 SLT 879, OH 3.14
Barbeau v British Columbia (2003) 1 May, BC, CA 11.02
*Bellinger v Bellinger [2003] UKHL 21, [2003] 2 AC 467, [2003] 2 WLR 1174,
    [2003] 2 All ER 593, [2003] 1 FLR 1043, [2003] 2 Campbell v Campbell* 1923
    SLT 670, OH 5.18

Campbell v Campbell (Husband and Wife: Separation Agreement) 1976 SLT
    (Sh Ct) 69, Sh Pr 5.18
Cassidy v Cassidy 2002 SCLR 576, Sh Ct 5.12
Commissioner's Case No CSCS/5/97 [1999] FLR 37 .... 3.35, 9.06, 9.07, 15.02
Cooper's Judicial Factor v Valentine 1976 SLT 83 .... 1.19
Couper's Judicial Factor v Valentine 1976 SC 63, 1976 SLT 83, 1976 SLT
    (Notes) 11, OH 1.19
Cramond v Allan (1757) Mor 6157 .... 5.01, 5.19
Crighton v Abercromby (1561) Mor 5877 .... 5.01
Cumming v Duncan (1717) Mor 9191 .... 5.19

D and Sweden v Council (31 May 2001, unreported) 1.22
Darke v Strout [2003] EWCA Civ 176, CA 5.12, 15.01
De Cavel v De Cavel (No 2) Case 120/79 [1980] ECR 731, [1980] 3 CMLR 1, ECJ 15.20
Diwell v Farnes [1959] 1 WLR 624, [1959] 2 All ER 379, 103 SJ 431, CA 6.01
Douglas v Douglas (1931) 47 Sh Ct Rep 303 .... 17.10

Drummond v Drummond 1995 SC 321, 1996 SLT 386, 1995 SCLR 428, IH 8.02, 8.05,
11.04, 19.01. 19.06
Drummond v Rollock (1634) Mor 6152 .... 5.01
Dunnett v Railtrack Plc [2002] UK HL 30 .... 6.08

Ghaidan v Godin-Mendoza, sub nom Ghaidan v Mendoza; Godin-Mendoza v Ghaidan;
   Mendoza v Ghaidan [2004] UKHL 30, [2004] 3 WLR 113, [2004] 3 All ER 411,
   [2004] 2 FLR 600, [2004] 2 FCR 481,16 BHRC 671, [2004] Fam Law 641,
   [2004] 27 EGCS 128, (2004) 101(27) LSG 30, (2004) 154 NLJ 1013,
   (2004) 148 SJLB 792, [2004] NPC 100, Times, June 24, 2004, HL 6.08, 17.15
Gib v Miller, 14 March 1634 .... 5.01, 5.21
Gillanders v Gillanders 1966 SC 54, 1966 SLT 120, OH 15.10
Gillon v Gillon (No 1) 1994 SLT 978, 1993 SCLR 768, OH 16.03
Gillon v Gillon (No 2) 1994 SLT 984, 1994 SCLR 278, IH 16.03
Gillon v Gillon (No 3) *1995 SLT 678, 1995 SCLR 405, OH* 16.02, 16.03
Gilmour v Finney (1831) 9 S 907 .... 5.12
Goodwin v United Kingdom (2002) 35 EHRR 447, (2003) 97 AJIL 659 .... 1.14
Goodridge v Dept of Public Health (2003) 18 November, Massachusetts Supreme
   Judicial Court 5.01

Hunter v Dickson (1831) 5 W&S 455 .... 5.21
Hyde v Hyde, sub nom Hyde v Hyde and Woodmansee (1865-69) LR 1 P & D 130,
   [1861-73] All ER Rep 175, Divorce Ct 11.01

Inglis v Inglis 1999 SLT (Sh Ct) 59, 1998 GWD 26-1335, Sh Ct 16.03

Jackson v Jackson 2003 GWD 33-941, Sh Ct 8.11

K v K (Ancillary Relief: Prenuptial Agreement) [2003] 1 FLR 120, [2002] Fam Law 877,
   Fam Div 4.02
KB v National Health Service Pensions Agency (C117/01) [2004] 1 CMLR 28,
   [2004] ICR 781, [2004] IRLR 240, [2004] 1 FLR 683, [2004] Pens LR 191,
   [2004] Fam Law 249, Times, January 15, 2004, ECJ 1.14
Kerrigan v Hall (1901) 4 F 10 .... 6.05, 7.04, 7.15, 7.17, 7.23, 17.04

L v L, sub nom Beattie v L 2000 SLT (Sh Ct) 12, 1999 GWD 38-1839, Sh Ct 8.05
Lady Buchannan v The Larid, 23 July 1629 .... 5.01, 15.01
Lady Foulis v Husband (1626) Mor 6158 .... 5.01
Lawrence v Texas (2003) 26 June, Supreme Court of the United States 11.03
Lawson v Macculloch (1797) Mor 6157 .... 5.12, 5.19, 5.20
Livingston v Begg (1666) Mor 6153 .... 5.01, 5.02, 5.19
Logan v Wood (1561) Mor 5877 .... 5.01

McAfee v McAfee 1990 SCLR 805, OH 16.01

P v P (Ancillary Relief: Proceeds of Crime), sub nom P v P (Divorce: Ancillary Relief)
  [2003] EWHC 2260, [2004] Fam 1, [2003] 3 WLR 1350, [2003] 4 All ER 843,
  [2004] 1 FLR 193, [2003] 3 FCR 459, [2003] WTLR 1449, [2004] Fam Law 9,
  (2003) 100(41) LSG 33, (2003) 153 NLJ 1550, (2003) 147 SJLB 1206, Times,
  October 14, 2003, Fam Div 2.18
Palmer v Bonar (1810) 15 FC 535 .... 5.02, 5.21
Pearce v Pearce (1898) 5 SLT 338 .... 5.18
Pope v Pope 1995 SCLR 963, Sh Pr 9.01
Pow (Jemima) v Pow (Alexander) 1987 SC 95, 1987 SLT 127, 1987 SCLR 290, OH ... 15.10
*Purdon v Purdon (*1884) II Guthrie's Select Cases 15.17

R v Secretary of State for Transport, ex p Factortame Ltd (No 2) [1991] 1 AC 603,
  [1990] 3 WLR 818, [1991] 1 All ER 70, [1991] 1 Lloyd's Rep 10, [1990]
  3 CMLR 375, (1991) 3 Admin LR 333, (1990) 140 NLJ 1457, (1990)
  134 SJ 1189, HL 14.32

Stuart-Gordon v Stuart-Gordon (1899) 1 F 1005 .... 1.20
Sutton v Mischon de Reya (a Firm) (2003) Times, 19 December 2003 .... 6.01, 6.04
Symington v Symington (1875) 3 R 205 .... 15.10

Taylor (William Smart), Petitioner 1931 SLT 260 .... 3.35, 15.02
Tonon v Office Cantonal de la Jeunesse de tuttlingen, Rev Crit DIP (1994) 557,
  Cour de Cassation, First Civil Chamber, 12 January 1994, [1995] ILPr 23 .... 14.08
Tweedie v Tweedie 1966 SLT (Notes) 89, OH 15.20

V v V (Child Maintenance; Periodical Payments) [2001] 2 FLR 799, [2001] Fam
  Law 649, Times, August 16, 2001, Fam Div 9.05
Vallance, Re, Vallance v Blagden (1884) LR 26 Ch D 353, Ch D 6.07
Vallance v Lady Touch 3 May 1707, Lothian's Consistorial Law 5.01, 5.02, 17.20
Van den Boogaard v Laumen (C220/95) [1997] QB 759, [1997] All ER (EC)
  517, [1997] ECR I-1147, [1997] ILPr 278, [1997] 2 FLR 399, [1997]
  3 FCR 493, [1997] Fam Law 599, Times, March 26, 1997, ECJ 14.01, 14.29
Ventisei v Ventisei's Executors 1966 SC 21, IH 1.17

W v W (Nullity: Gender), sub Nom W v W (Physical Inter-sex) [2001] Fam 111,
  [2001] 2 WLR 674, [2001] 1 FLR 324, (2001) 58 BMLR 15, [2001]
  Fam Law 104, Times, October 31, 2000, Fam Div 1.15
Walker v Maclean (1922) 38 Sh Ct Rep 152 .... 5.12
Walker v Roberts 1998 SLT 1133, 1998 GWD 14-721, OH 1.02
Webster v Webster's Trustee (1886) 14 R 90 .... 6.07
White v White 1908 SC 93 .... 6.03

Chapter 1

Giving advice

'And what's all this about the mysterious relationship between a man and a woman?'

Ivan Turgenev, *Fathers and Sons* (1862)

1. Women and men

Marriage versus cohabitation

1.01 Marriage, unregulated by any agreement[1], is often the best way in which to confer and regulate rights and obligations between men and women sharing their lives, and also the upbringing of any children, together.

1   See CHAPTER 4.

The woman's position

1.02 Cohabitation, while it may confer some rights on the parties to the arrangement[1], does not, in itself, give the woman the status of 'common law wife'. She needs to be regularly married to her man to become his wife[2]: if the man does not intend to be married to her she will not become his wife irregularly with cohabitation and repute as the necessary agreement as to marriage cannot be inferred[3]. It is only with marriage that she will obtain the status of her man's wife and the resulting rights to aliment, financial provision on divorce or annulment of marriage, and legal and prior rights in relation to succession to his estate[4].

1   For example: Damages (Scotland) Act 1976, Sch 1; Matrimonial Homes (Family Protection) (Scotland) Act 1981, s 18; Housing (Scotland) Act 2001, ss 22, 108(1), Sch 3.
2   Marriage (Scotland) Act 1977, ss 1–20.
3   *Walker v Roberts* 1998 SLT 1133.
4   Succession (Scotland) Act 1964, ss 8, 9, 10(2); Family Law (Scotland) Act 1985, ss 1(1)(a), (b), 8–14, 17.

1.03   These important implications should be explained to any woman seeking advice about cohabiting with her man, even though he may be unlikely to have a change of heart and do the honourable thing by marrying the woman he professes to love. Usually on the pretence that 'marriage is only a bit of paper', he neatly sidesteps all the financial obligations he would incur if the woman were his wife. The best protection that the woman can obtain in these circumstances is to have any house in which she and her man are to live together put into their common ownership, and she should be strongly advised to do this.

The man's position

1.04   If the man seeks advice prior to cohabitation, he must be told the advantages that such an arrangement confers on him in the event that he wishes to break off the relationship in the future. But if it is his woman's wish to be married to him, he should be asked to consider doing that. The law wisely recognises that a father can only expect parental rights and responsibilities in relation to his children's upbringing and property if he marries the child's mother and incurs the obligations and duties marriage confers on him towards her as well[1]; the mother may, but is not obliged, to confer parental responsibilities and rights on him outside of marriage by an agreement under the Children (Scotland) Act 1995[2]. In marriage, the woman acquires status as his wife; and the children the status of legitimacy[3]. The decision is his, but he should be told both the advantages[4] and disadvantages of marriage[5].

1   Children (Scotland) Act 1995, s 3(1)(b).
2   Section 4; Parental Responsibilities and Parental Rights Agreement (Scotland) Regulations 1996 (SI 1996/2549).
3   Erskine, *Institute* I, 6, 49; Legitimation (Scotland) Act 1968, s 1(1).
4   The financial advantages of marriage are summed up in an article in The Times, 'Why Marriage is Good for your Wealth' (2004) The Times, 3 January, p 46.
5   The disadvantages of marriage are summed up in an article by Tim Lott, 'Any Man Who Gets Married Now is Mad' (2003) Evening Standard, 20 November.

Marriage agreements

1.05   Where both man and woman wish to be married to each other, questions may occasionally arise as to whether they should regulate by agreement the property rights that would be conferred, or are conferred, on each other by their marriage. This is not an entirely unknown situation but usually it turns out not to be a good idea for them to have such an agreement for the reasons discussed in CHAPTER 4.

Cohabitation agreements

1.06 In practice it is unlikely that many men who refuse to marry their women will have a change of heart, or will consider it necessary in the first place, to propose a cohabitation agreement conferring property rights on the woman during and after the fact of their cohabitation. He will want as clean a break as possible if he moves on from the relationship. Many women, perhaps ignorant of the true legal situation, are willing to compromise and accept the inferior legal position as the man's cohabitant in exchange for a relationship as his 'partner', and the birth of their illegitimate children, though her deepest wish is often to be married to the man she loves. For these reasons cohabitation agreements are relatively rare in practice, but this book gives some guidance on how to conclude these agreements in those rare circumstances in which they may be required[1].

1   See CHAPTER 6; CHAPTER 19, style 6.

Separation

1.07 Clients frequently ask about a 'legal separation'. It then has to be explained that there is normally no *need* for any procedure whereby spouses are legally separated. They *could* seek to obtain a decree of separation[1] but that is not necessary in most cases. Rather their separation is something which has taken place and has certain consequences which can be handled practically and by agreement if necessary. Only where immediate problems have arisen, eg over children or aliment, or where there is a need to obtain an interim interdict or interim exclusion order on behalf of a client, should the client be advised to consider urgent court action. Even then the required remedies need not be sought in an action for separation[2]. Often the last thing the client wants to consider immediately after separating (though she may want it later) is an action of divorce, although some initial advice may have to be given about the grounds of divorce and the availability of those grounds for the client and perhaps also a general explanation of the underlying principles of financial provision on divorce and the concept of matrimonial property, including pensions.

1   The correct name of the action is an action of separation, and not judicial separation or (its former name in the Court of Session) an action of separation *a mensa et thoro*: see Divorce (Scotland) Act 1976, s 4.
2   This was necessary in the sheriff court in respect of aliment (but not the Court of Session – Bankton, *Institute* 1, 5, 37) until 1985: see Family Law (Scotland) Act 1985, Sch 1, para 1.

1.08 A solicitor must at all times show sympathy and understanding towards the client's predicament and needs in what is often a difficult emotional time for the client. This needs to be tempered with realism, for example as to the financial settlement a wife might expect, or what a husband is likely to have to pay. The reality check often extends as to the meaning of adultery. Few clients are willing to accept that being unfaithful to their wife or husband after separation is truly adultery and can found an action for divorce[1]. But it is[2] and it can[3] and there is no point in pretending otherwise. Being frank at the beginning is the best way of managing client expectations later.

1   Beza, *Life of Calvin* (Lyons, 1564), p 134 shows that even in the Geneva of his time adultery was often regarding by some as a 'harmless indulgence or [a] subject for entertainment'. While he regarded adultery as 'a crime worthy of death', 'yet you will not find in this city a single case of an adulterer being sentenced to capital punishment' (p 137). Perceptions of adultery, and its seriousness, have changed over time; yet, in law, adultery can be given no other meaning than its *Scriptural* meaning since that is the basis of the law of divorce for adultery (Bankton, *Institute* I, 5, 126). A person who is married but separated from his or her spouse and who cohabits with someone *to whom he is not married* commits adultery: Calvin, *Institutes of the Christian Religion* 2.8.41.
2   Ex 20:14; Deut. 5:18; Calvin, *Institutes of the Christian Religion* 2.8.41.
3   Divorce (Scotland) Act 1976, s 1(2)(a) refers to adultery *since the date of the marriage*; separated parties are still married and therefore they can commit adultery until the marriage bond is dissolved. The pursuer's own adultery might once have been a defence (Bankton, *Institute* I, 5, 128), but this is not provided for by the Divorce (Scotland) Act 1976, s 1.

Action of separation

1.09   A divorce decree dissolves a marriage whereas a decree of separation frees a spouse from the obligation to adhere to the other but otherwise the parties continue to remain married to each other. It may be a useful remedy for those whose religious persuasion does not permit them to seek a divorce. It is obtained on the same grounds as divorce, with the same defences available[1], and has the effect that property of the wife acquired after the decree of separation is distributed as though her husband has pre-deceased her if she dies intestate[2]. The husband obtains no similar benefits as a result of the decree being granted[3]. The grounds of jurisdiction in the action are the same as in a divorce action[4].

1   Divorce (Scotland) Act 1976, s 4.
2   Conjugal Rights (Scotland) Amendment Act 1861, s 6.
3   In English law, while a decree of separation is in force and the separation is continuing, the estate of either party devolves, in intestacy, as though the other spouse were dead: Matrimonial Causes Act 1973, s 18(2).
4   Domicile and Matrimonial Proceedings Act 1973, ss 7, 8; Council Regulation (EC) 1347/2000 on jurisdiction and the recognition and enforcement of judgments in matrimonial matters and in matters of parental responsibilities for children of both spouses, art 2 (OJ L160, 30.6.2000, p 19).

Reconciliation

1.10   While it is not the solicitor's job to encourage reconciliation of man and wife where their relationship has clearly ended, or the wife's personal safety is in danger through the risk of domestic abuse on the part of her husband, there may be cases in which the relationship has not yet come to an end, and may be capable of being saved. In an action of divorce or separation[1] the court has a duty to continue the proceedings to enable attempts to be made to effect a reconciliation. Similarly, a solicitor should in appropriate cases discuss with his client whether the relationship is over or whether there is a possibility of saving it. If necessary, he should advise his client to seek personal or marriage guidance before consideration is given to a separation agreement.

1   Divorce (Scotland) Act 1976, ss 2(1), 4(1).

1.11   The solicitor should equally bear in mind that it is not in all cases that a separation agreement should be preferred over litigation or that reconciliation should be attempted. A court action will be essential as the first step to protect the woman's safety, the welfare of her children, or to prevent the husband disposing of his property to defeat her claims for aliment, or financial provision on divorce. In these cases, it is appropriate to proceed immediately to court for interim interdict with power of arrest[1], interim exclusion order[2], interim residence order[3], and for inhibition and arrestment on dependence of the action or interdict in connection with a claim for aliment or financial provision[4]. A separation agreement can be used later to compromise the divorce action.

1   *Murdoch v Murdoch* 1973 SLT (Notes) 13; Matrimonial Homes (Family Protection) (Scotland) Act 1981, ss 14, 15; Protection from Abuse (Scotland) Act 2001 (asp 14), ss 1, 3.
2   Matrimonial Homes (Family Protection) (Scotland) Act 1981, s 4(6).
3   Children (Scotland) Act 1995, s 11(2)(c), (13).
4   Family Law (Scotland) Act 1985, ss 18, 19.

2. Sexual minorities

Persons of the same sex

1.12   Persons of the same sex cannot marry each other in Scotland, but can enter into a cohabitation contract, or (prospectively) register their relationship as a 'civil partnership' in the circumstances described in CHAPTER 12. A same sex cohabitation agreement which seeks to establish 'a marriage' between those persons will be void as it is contrary to the express terms of the Confession of Faith Ratification Act 1690, incorporated into the Act of Union 1707 by the Protestant Religion and Presbyterian Church Act 1707[1].

1   See CHAPTER 18, extracts 1–3.

1.13   The solicitor, if taking instructions, should inform his client of both the merits and de-merits of entering into a civil partnership as opposed to an unregulated cohabitation, or regulation by a cohabitation contract.

Transsexuals and hermaphrodites

1.14   At present, transsexuals legally retain the sex with which they were born and cannot marry a person of that same sex: they can marry a person of the opposite sex even after surgery to alter their sexual features[1]. This is considered incongruous and also contrary to both European Community law[2], and human rights law[3]. The Gender Recognition Act 2004, when in force, will allow transsexual persons legally to change sex (and to prohibit them marrying a person of their former sex)[4].

1   Marriage (Scotland) Act 1977, s 5(4)(e); *Bellinger v Bellinger* [2003] 2 AC 467, [2003] 2 WLR 1174, HL.
2   Case C–117/01 *KB v National Health Service Pensions Agency and Secretary of State for Health* (2004) Times, 15 January.
3   *Goodwin v United Kingdom* (2002) 35 EHRR 447, (2003) 97 AJIL 659.
4   This Act received Royal Assent on 1 July 2004 and will come into force on a date appointed by the Secretary of State after consulting the Scottish Ministers and the Department of Finance and Personnel in Northern Ireland (s 26).

1.15   Stair considered that hermaphrodites could not marry if they were not predominantly of one sex[1]. A sex will now be assigned to a child at birth, subject to subsequent correction of the entry in the Register of Births[2]. If a sex can be assigned to a person of doubtful sex irrespective of the sex he was registered as at birth, he can obtain declarator to that effect and marry a person of the opposite sex[3].

1   Stair, *Institutions* I, 4, 6.
2   Registration of Births, Still-births, Deaths and Marriages (Prescription of Forms) (Scotland) Regulations 1965 SI 1965/1839, reg 3; Registration of Births, Deaths and Marriages (Scotland) Act 1965, s 42(5); *X* 1957 SLT (Sh Ct) 61.
3   Campbell, 'Successful Sex in Succession: Sex in Dispute – The *Forbes-Semple* Case and Possible Implications' (1998) JR 257 and 325; *W v W (Physical Inter-sex)* [2001] 2 WLR 674.

1.16   Neither of these issues impinges significantly on the law of separation and cohabitation agreements[1]. If the persons cannot marry or enter into a civil partnership, there will be no separation agreement; if they can, there will always be that possibility. On the other hand, since persons of the same or opposite sex can cohabit and enter into a cohabitation agreement, a person's sex is obviously legally irrelevant as a factor in the conclusion of these agreements and transsexuals can thus enter into a cohabitation agreement with persons of their opposite sex or the same sex as them. An agreement in anticipation of a marriage or a civil partnership will depend on the parties to it being of opposite or the same sex respectively[2].

1   The numbers involved are very small: it is estimated there are only 5,000 transsexuals in Britain ('Shamed by Father's Sex Swap' (2004) The Times, 12 July, p 26). There were fewer than 80,000 persons declaring themselves living in a homosexual or lesbian relationship in England and Wales in the 2001 Census: ('Out and Proud but only in Tolerant South' (2004) The Times, 4 February, p 3; 'Where Have All the Gays Gone?' (2004) The Times, 5 February, T2, p 4). Belgian and Dutch statistics on same sex marriage, and in the Netherlands, registered partnerships, are available at www.statbel.fgov.be and www.cbs.nl, respectively.
2   Marriage (Scotland) Act 1977, s 5(4)(e); Civil Partnership Act 2004, s 84(1)(a).

3. Succession

1.17 Thought should be given to succession rights when drawing up a family law agreement.

It would be most unwise for a spouse to surrender his or her prior or legal rights in a marriage contract unless something better is obtained by means of a legally binding, and effectually enforceable contract, or a trust settlement in her favour.

On the other hand, it is usual practice in a separation agreement for the spouses to give up their entitlements on succession to other party's estate if death should intervene prior to the termination of the marriage by divorce. While it is not competent for parents to surrender their children's rights to legitim from their estates, they can discharge their own rights in respect of the other spouse's estate[1].

Married or cohabiting couples can make a contract, if so minded, for mutual wills in favour of the other, though preferably with the right to revoke such provision on separation, or termination of the cohabiting relationship[2].

Marriage does not revoke existing wills and, if necessary, a new will should be made, revoking the old, in contemplation of the marriage[3].

1   McLaren, *The Law of Wills and Succession* (3rd edn, 1894), ch VII, pp 135–147; Succession (Scotland) Act 1964, s 12.
2   *Cairney v Macgregor's Trustees* 1916 1 SLT 357; *Ventisei v Ventisei's Executors* 1966 SC 21.
3   In English law, marriage revokes the will *unless* made in contemplation of marriage: Wills Act 1837, s 18.

1.18 A separating spouse should be advised to make a will if he or she does not already have one: while the other spouse's legal rights cannot be excluded if not already discharged, she can prevent him acquiring prior rights in her intestate estate.

If the client already has a will, consideration should be given to its revision so as to adapt it to current circumstances, and a revocation of the earlier will: a *de facto* separation is not sufficient to revoke testamentary provisions made in respect of the other spouse or cohabitant[1].

The will can also usefully be used to appoint guardians to her children in the event of the mother's death[2].

The father can only appoint guardians in his will if he is entitled to act as the child's legal representative: usually by obtaining parental responsibilities and rights for the child through marriage to the mother, or by agreement with her under s 4 of the Children (Scotland) Act 1995[3].

1   See also para **1.09** for the effect of a decree of separation in both Scots and English law.
2   Children (Scotland) Act 1995, ss 7, 8.
3   See para **1.04**.

1.19   A decree of divorce or annulment does not automatically revoke testamentary provisions in a will in favour of a spouse[1]: it is all a matter of construction of the will whether a provision in it in favour of a spouse remains valid after divorce[2]. The client would therefore be best advised, in the interests of certainty and avoiding litigation, to revoke any existing will, and make a new one, well in advance of any decree affecting the conjugal relationship, or bringing the marriage to an end.

1   In English law, a divorce or annulment revokes testamentary provisions in a will in respect of a spouse, unless a contrary intention appears by the will: Wills Act 1837, s 18A.
2   *Burn's Trustees* 1961 SC 17; *Couper's Judicial Factor v Valentine* 1976 SC 63.

1.20   A child born subsequent to the date of an existing will can invoke the doctrine of presumed revocation of the will: *conditio si testator sine liberis decesserit*[1]. As this, if successfully invoked, results in intestacy, careful thought should be given to re-drafting existing wills in contemplation of marriage or cohabitation so as either to make provision for future children or to exclude them from the will. This is particularly important in cohabitation as revocation of the will leaves the surviving cohabitant no rights on succession to the other's estate[2].

1   *Stuart-Gordon v Stuart-Gordon* (1899) 1 F 1005; *Milligan's Judicial Factor v Milligan* 1910 SC 58.
2   Except in relation to tenancies of dwelling houses: Housing (Scotland) Act 1988, s 31(4); Housing (Scotland) Act 2001 (asp 10), ss 22, 108(1)(a), Sch 3.

4.   Taking title to heritable property

1.21   Clients contemplating marriage or cohabitation should be informed of the possibility of taking title subject to a survivorship destination[1].

Whether this is best for a particular client will depend on the circumstances of that client, although in marriage it is the usual way of taking title. Care should be taken as to whether this is best for a cohabiting couple: a particular client may wish to retain freedom to dispose of his share in the couple's home to someone other than his cohabitant.

1   This topic, including evacuation of special destinations, is dealt with further in Hiram, *The Scots Law of Succession* (Butterworths, 2002), pp 171–180, paras 6.46–6.57.

5.   Free movement of persons in the European Economic Area

1.22   Workers, self-employed persons, and students who are European Economic Area citizens, have, subject to certain limitations and restrictions, the right to freely move and reside within the European Economic Area (EEA) of the European Union, Iceland, Liechtenstein and Norway[1].

Spouses and cohabitants can enjoy these rights individually, where each is an EEA citizen. Where, however, one of the partners wishes to work or study in another EEA country and the other will not be working or studying, but will be economically dependent on him while abroad, or is not an EEA citizen, she can move with him only if a 'family member'.

Family members currently include spouses and dependant children under 21 years[2].

'Spouse' is restricted to the husband and wife of a married person. It does not include a registered partner, cohabitant, or the other party to a Belgian or Dutch *homohuwelijk*[3].

1   Lenaerts and Van Nuffel, *Constitutional Law of the European Union* (Sweet & Maxwell, 1999), pp 140–177, paras 4-104 to 4-146.
2   Council Regulation (EEC) 1612/68 of 15 October 1968 on freedom of movement for workers within the Community, art 10(1)(a) (OJ L257, 19.10.1968, p 2).
3   Joint cases C-122 and 125/99P *D and Sweden v Council* (31 May 2001, unreported).

1.23   From 30 April 2008, the definition of family member will be extended, however, to include (in addition to a person's spouse and dependant children under 21 years):

> 'the partner with whom the Union citizen has contracted a registered partnership, on the basis of the legislation of a Member State, if the legislation of the host Member State treats registered partnerships as equivalent to marriage and in accordance with the conditions laid down in the relevant legislation of the host Member State[1].'

Partners with whom an EEA citizen has a 'durable relationship, duly attested' will also benefit from the freedom of movement provisions[2].

No specific reference has been made to a same sex spouse in this definition; it is open to the European Court of Justice to extend the definition in this way or, pending such a decision, for other Member States to recognise such persons as 'spouses'[3].

What is of most interest for family law agreements is the concept of a 'durable relationship, duly attested'. It is recommended that if two cohabitants wish to move freely within the EEA they should include in their cohabitation agreement a reference to their date of cohabitation and narrate the main circumstances in their lives together by which it has become a durable relationship; it should also refer to their future joint intention to continue living together in this way.

The agreement will be 'duly attested' if subscribed with the necessary formalities for registration in the books of council and session, or sheriff court books; an extract should be sufficient proof of its attestation.

1   Directive 2004/38/EC of the European Parliament and of the Council of 29 April 2004 on the right of citizens of the Union and their family members to move and reside freely within the territory of the Member States, art 2(2) (OJ L158, 30.4.2004, p 77).

2   Directive 2004/38/EC, art 3(2)(b).

3   The European Parliament originally favoured including same sex spouses and cohabiting couples (same or opposite sex) within the definition of family member ('Report on the proposed Directive', 23 January 2003, COM(2001) 257, proposed amendments 14–17). The resulting definition is the result of political compromise. In its explanatory Memorandum on the proposed amendments, the Commission noted that:

'Parliament's amendments would recognise as family members the spouse of the same sex in the same way as the spouse of a different sex, the registered partner in accordance with the legislation of the Member State of origin, and non-married partners in accordance with the legislation or practice of the host or home Member State.

On this point the Commission feels that harmonisation of the conditions of residence for Union citizens in Member States of which they are not nationals must not result in the imposition on certain Member States of amendments to family law legislation, an area which does not fall within the Community's legislative jurisdiction.

The Commission feels that the amended proposal represents an equitable solution to these issues: firstly, it complies with the principle of non-discrimination in as much as it requires Member States to treat couples from other Member States in the same way as its own nationals; and, secondly, it allows for a possible change in interpretation in the light of developments in family law in the Member States.'

1.24   As spouses and children under 21 enjoy freedom of movement as family members, there is no need for any formal marriage contract to ensure such rights are accorded to them in the EEA.

1.25   Divorced spouses, and former registered partners where the partnership has been dissolved, have certain rights of continuing residence after separation, divorce, or termination of the registered relationship[1].

1   Directive 2004/38/EC, art 13.

Further research

1.26   Those interested in pursuing further the issue of free movement of persons in the EEA may wish to consult the following articles:

—   McGlynn, 'Families and the European Union Charter of Fundamental Rights: progressive change or entrenching the status quo?' (2001) 26 EL Rev 582;

—   Peers, 'Dazed and Confused: Family members' residence rights and the Court of Justice' (2001) 26 EL Rev 76;

—   Stychin, 'A Stranger to its Laws: Sovereign Bodies, Global Sexualities, and Transnational Citizens' (2000) 27 JLS 601;

—   di Torella and Reid, 'The changing shape of the 'European family and fundamental rights' (2002) 27 EL Rev 80.

1.27   See also:

— Boele-Woelki and Fuchs (eds), *Legal Recognition of Same-sex Couples in Europe* (Intersentia, Antwerpen, 2003), part 3, 'Homosexuality and European Law'.

Chapter 2

Acting for the client

1. Taking instructions

Identifying what the solicitor can do to help

2.01   In most separations, the solicitor will wish to discuss the following issues with the client, usually in detail and over more than one meeting:

(a)   with whom any children are primarily to live and the contact the other parent will have with the children;

(b)   where the spouses themselves are to live and whether the matrimonial home, if owned, is to be sold or, if tenanted, is to be transferred to one of the parties and for what price or compensation;

(c)   maintenance (aliment and child support);

(d)   property division (including bank accounts, motor vehicles, and pensions);

(e)   entitlement to State benefits following upon separation; and

(f)   pension sharing.

2.02   In some instances the client may be referred to other agencies for help with these problems eg the Benefit Agency regarding benefits, the local authority if seeking to be re-housed as a homeless person, or a bank if wishing to close down a joint account. The solicitor's role should be concentrated on taking any necessary court action for the client or negotiating and drafting a separation agreement if court proceedings are not immediately to be raised. At an early stage, detailed information should be obtained about the spouses' financial positions and property, including pensions, and recorded in a schedule to be retained in the file.

Terms of engagement letter

2.03   A terms of engagement letter should be sent to the client, recording her instructions, who will carry out her work, what fees are to be paid, and to whom in the firm any complaints are made[1]. Such a letter will be necessary in connection with any conveyancing of the matrimonial home to be carried out in relation to the implementation of the agreement[2].

1   Code of Conduct for Scottish Solicitors 2002, para 5(e).
2   Solicitors (Scotland) (Client Communication) (Residential Conveyancing) Practice Rules 2003 r 3; Law Society of Scotland, 'Guidance Notes on Terms of Business Letters in Residential Conveyancing' (2003).

Fees

2.04   The client's eligibility for Legal Advice and Assistance and Legal Aid should be checked and explained, together with the regulations for recovery of fees out of property recovered or preserved. Where the client does not qualify for either of these, fees and their payment have to be agreed privately. Terms of business should be confirmed by issuing the firm's terms of business letter to the client. Care should be taken not to act for both husband and wife or in any potential conflict of interest situation[1]. A written fee charging agreement with a client under s 61A (1) of the Solicitors (Scotland) Act 1980 must not contain a consent to registration for preservation and execution[2].

1   Law Society of Scotland, 'Guidelines on Acting for Separated Spouses' (July 1998).
2   Solicitors (Scotland) (Written Fee Charging Agreements) Practice Rules 1993, r 4.

Negotiating agreements

2.05   Once terms of business, including payment of fees, have been agreed with the client, the solicitor's main function thereafter, if he or she is not to raise court proceedings at this stage, is to reach agreement with the other party or his solicitors as to the contents of the separation agreement, and which solicitor is to draft it. If the solicitors are involved in negotiation, the solicitor will proceed to carry out those negotiations and to draft (or revise) a separation agreement in accordance with the client's instructions.

2.06   It can be difficult to deal with a spouse who will not engage a solicitor; this may be a case in which it is better to sue that spouse. Otherwise, the solicitor can draft the agreement and put it to the other party for his comments. He should not send the engrossment to the other party for signature without informing him as to the legally binding nature of the agreement when signed, and reminding him he should obtain independent legal advice before doing so[1].

1   Solicitor (Scotland) Practice Rules, r 7; Law Society of Scotland 'Guidelines on Conflict of Interest' (May 1999).

Mediation and arbitration as alternatives to negotiation

2.07   Agreement can be reached through negotiation, mediation, and (for aliment) arbitration. More is said about mediation, and arbitration for aliment in CHAPTER 17; but solicitors must always identify those cases which are suitable for mediation or arbitration and refer the client for mediation or arbitration in those cases if that is her wish.

2.08   Mediation will not be appropriate in cases of domestic or child abuse, or where emergency applications need to be made to the court. It is often appropriate in cases not involving these considerations and in which agreement might be reached more speedily with the intervention of a mediator at significantly less cost to both parties than engaging their solicitors to carry out negotiations. The solicitor's task is then to draft the legal separation agreement reflecting the common accord drawn up by the mediator and signed by both parties.

What to do where the 'agreement' has already been reached

2.09   The 'agreement' may have been dictated by the husband, often using subtle psychological pressure including threats to deprive the woman of her children. The solicitor's job is to act in his or her client's interests, and to strongly advise her against signing an agreement that is not in her best interests. He should also explain her true legal position to her and the potential outcome of any court proceedings if she does not reach agreement with her husband. If she has been threatened with violence in an attempt to extort her into signing a particular agreement, he should advise her to consider reporting these threats to the police. He should not take instructions to act for the woman if she is acting under duress; in less extreme cases, he must judge what realistically the wife can expect from litigation, and whether she can afford it. There is nothing to prevent him advising his client that the 'agreement' should be re-negotiated with solicitors acting on both sides and taking instructions on that basis.

He can decline to accept instructions if he does not think the wife is acting in her best interests; if he takes instructions in these circumstances he should always confirm his advice in writing and have her sign his letter, acknowledging she has declined his advice and he is acting on her specific instructions though he has advised her that those instructions are not in her best interests[1].

1   Family Law Protocol, Law Society (England and Wales), 2002, Main Protocol, chapter 5.1(7).

Capacity to contract

2.10 Instructions to enter into a family law agreement should only be taken from a person aged 16 years or over[1]; any contract for cohabitation or marriage before that age would be unlawful as contrary to the prohibitions on marriage, sexual intercourse, and homosexual conduct, under that age[2].

1 Age of Legal Capacity (Scotland) Act 1991, s 1(1).
2 Marriage (Scotland) Act 1977, s 1; Criminal Law (Consolidation) (Scotland) Act 1995, ss 5, 13.

2.11 The client, even if an adult, may not have the capacity to enter into the contract, although in all but the most obvious cases, it will be possible to rely on the presumption of adult capacity[1]. 'Adult' for these purposes means a person aged 16 years or over[2]. 'Mental disorder' is (prospectively) defined in the Mental Health (Care and Treatment) (Scotland) Act 2003[3] as comprising mental illness, personality disorder, or a learning disability[4].

The following are not, however, regarded as mental disorders:
(a) sexual orientation;
(b) sexual deviancy;
(c) transsexualism;
(d) transvestism;
(e) dependence on, or use of alcohol or drugs;
(f) behaviour that causes, or is likely to cause, harassment, alarm or distress to any other person; and
(g) acting as no prudent person would act[5].

1 *HMA v Mitchell* 1951 JC 53 at 53, per LJC Thomson.
2 Adults with Incapacity (Scotland) Act 2000 (asp 4), s 1(6).
3 (Asp 13).
4 s 329(1).
5 s 328(2).

Drafting the agreement

2.12 The techniques of legal drafting are discussed in detail in CHAPTER 3.

However, as a preliminary matter, the solicitor must take instructions upon, and decide if there is to be, a separate agreement for the children's aliment, and/or a separate parenting agreement for the children's upbringing. The reasons why separate agreements for these matters may be necessary are:
(a) the yearly renewal of a child's aliment agreement to oust Child Support Agency jurisdiction[1];
(b) the avoidance of the parenting agreement as an enforceable authentic instrument in Europe[2].

1   See CHAPTER 9.
2   See CHAPTER 7.

2. Professional responsibility

Duty to give objective advice

2.13   It has been emphasised that solicitors acting for separated spouses must:

'[D]o so in an objective manner, consistent…with their professional obligations to their clients…

[T]hey [should] seek to reach agreements and compromises which reduce hostilities between the parties and the expense to them both in emotional and financial terms. A realistic approach to what the parties' entitlements are should also…be applied in assisting them to reach decisions as to how best they might best resolve their disputes[1].'

1   Opinion of Lord Clarke, *AM or W v JW* (24 February 2004, unreported), OH, at [58].

Conflict of interest

2.14   A solicitor must not act for two or more parties whose interests conflict[1]; accordingly, the same firm of solicitors should not act for both husband and wife in negotiating a separation agreement – or even in preparing a document that reflects the parties' own agreement[2]. If one of the spouses refuses to get independent advice, he cannot be forced to do so, but the solicitor should ensure he only acts for one of them; he is then entitled to deal with the other spouse as an unrepresented party[3].

There are circumstances in which a solicitor should not act. He should not act if this involves placing himself in an acute dilemma arising from conflicting interests of his client on the one hand and the interests of a third party to whom the solicitor may have some obligation[4]. In *Bolton v Jameson & Mackay*[5], the Lord Ordinary considered as relevant averments in a negligence action against the solicitors that they ought not to have acted for Mrs Bolton's husband in the sale of the matrimonial home in circumstances where they ought reasonably to have known that, in doing so, they were helping him put the free proceeds of sale out of the wife's reach.

1   Solicitors (Scotland) Practice Rules 1986, r 3.
2   Law Society of Scotland, 'Guidelines on Conflict of Interest' (May 1999).
3   See para **2.06**.
4   *Moody v Cox and Hatt* [1917] 2 Ch 71 at 81, per Lord Cozens-Hardy, MR.
5   1987 SLT 291.

Sale of the matrimonial home

2.15 Solicitors must be aware of the Law Society of Scotland's guidance on acting for separated spouses in relation to the sale of the matrimonial home[1]. The basic rule is that a firm of solicitors can act in the conveyancing, and for one of the spouses in relation to the separation, only if there is a written agreement, which need not be a full separation agreement, providing for the free proceeds of sale. The agreement must be signed by both spouses.

The free proceeds must be distributed in accordance with the agreement; a solicitor must not accept unilateral instructions from one of the spouses to alter that agreement.

If there is no agreement, then a separate firm of solicitors must be instructed to carry out the conveyancing. Conversely a firm which is acting in the sale of a matrimonial home for spouses which it discovers are separated must advise each spouse to seek independent legal advice about their matrimonial situation. The solicitors acting in the sale where there is no agreement as to disposal of the free proceeds must account to each spouse in accordance with the title.

Where solicitors are not acting for both parties in the sale, they are able to accept instructions from their own client to do diligence on the dependence of an action or in execution of an agreement.

1   Contained in (a) Law Society of Scotland, 'Guidelines on Conflict of Interest' (May 1999); and (b) Law Society of Scotland, 'Guidelines on Acting for Separated Spouses' (July 1998).

2.16   If the title is in the name of only one of the spouses, the same firm should not act for both of them. The firm acting for the entitled spouse may accept instructions in the sale of the property, but must not act for the non-entitled spouse[1].

1   The Law Society of Scotland, 'Guidelines on Acting for Separated Spouses' (July 1998), para 2.

Investment advice

2.17   A firm of solicitors should not give advice about pensions and other investments in clients' changed financial circumstances as a result of marriage, cohabitation or separation, unless authorised to do so by the Financial Services Authority[1]. They should, however, consider the appropriateness of referring the client for any necessary advice on these matters to an independent advisor[2]. If licensed by the Law Society of Scotland to carry on 'incidental investment business', they can discuss with the client the advice obtained from another authorised person and obtain his advice regarding the matrimonial investment assets. They may also seek the independent advisor's valuation of those assets and his advice on the best way of dealing with them. They can comment on such advice in negotiating a financial settlement in a matrimonial dispute on the client's instructions[3].

1   Financial Services and Markets Act 2000, ss 19, 23.

2   Law Society of Scotland, 'Guidelines on Pension Sharing on Divorce' (2001), final paragraph; this is a permitted activity by virtue of the Financial Services and Markets Act 2000 (Regulated Activities) Order 2001 (SI 2001/544), art 33.

3   Law Society of Scotland, 'Guidance to the new system of investment business under the Financial Services Authority and the Solicitors (Scotland) (Incidental Investment Business) Practice Rules' (2001), s 3, example (4) of what they may constitute incidental investment business (see CHAPTER 10 for more detailed guidance concerning pensions). The Solicitors (Scotland) (Incidental Financial business) Practice Rules 2004 have now replaced the Solicitors (Scotland) (Incidental Investment Business) Practice Rules 2001, but that does not prejudice the Society's earlier guidance.

3. Money laundering

Proceeds of Crime Act 2002

2.18   Solicitors must report suspected money laundering by their clients to the National Criminal Intelligence Service ('NCIS') in one of two circumstances.

First, if by acting in the negotiation, drawing up or implementation of a family law agreement a solicitor facilitates the acquisition, retention, use or control of 'criminal property' by or on behalf of another person including his or the other solicitor's client[1].

'Criminal property' is defined as a benefit from the conduct of an offence, or which would constitute an offence in any part of the United Kingdom[2]. Legal privilege does not apply in this context; the information must be divulged to NCIS via the firm's Money Laundering Reporting Officer (MLRO[3]) *and* in order to continue acting for the client the firm must obtain NCIS's consent[4]. Such consent will be treated as having been given if refusal is not given within 7 days[5]. Refusal within that period places a moratorium on the solicitor acting for the client for a period of 31 days from the receipt of the refusal notice[6].

Secondly, if the solicitor knows or suspects his client has committed a money laundering offence[7], and he is acting in respect of estate agency, conveyancing, financial transaction, or trust matters, he must report his knowledge or suspicion to the firm's MLRO or NCIS[8]. So long as the solicitor is not complicit in the money laundering offence, he is not obliged to disclose information protected by legal privilege[9].

Failure to disclose in either of these circumstances is a criminal offence[10]. The solicitor also commits an offence if he 'tips off' his client that he has made the disclosure[11]. But a solicitor may continue to give advice to a client unless it is with the intention of furthering a criminal purpose[12].

Detailed guidance is provided by the Law Society of Scotland in relation to these matters[13].

The Act applies no matter how big or small the sum involved[14].

1 Proceeds of Crime Act 2002, s 328(1); *P v P* [2003] 4 All ER 843.
2 Proceeds of Crime Act 2002, s 340(2).
3 The expression 'MLRO' is not used in the Act; it refers instead to the 'nominated officer'; the Money Laundering Regulations 2003 (SI 2003/3075), reg 7, makes further provision in connection with the 'nominated officer'. In practice the 'nominated officer' is frequently called the MLRO.
4 *P v P* [2003] 4 All ER 843.
5 Proceeds of Crime Act 2002, s 335(2), (3), (5), (7).
6 Proceeds of Crime Act 2002, s 335(2), (4), (6), (7).
7 Proceeds of Crime Act 2002, ss 327–329.
8 Proceeds of Crime Act 2002, s 330(1)–(5) and Sch 9 (as substituted by the Proceeds of Crime Act 2002 (Business in the Regulated Sector and Supervisory Authorities) Order 2003 (SI 2003/3074), art 2, Schedule, para 1(1)(f), (l), (m)).
9 Proceeds of Crime Act 2002, s 330(6)(b), (10), (11).
10 Proceeds of Crime Act 2002, ss 331, 332.
11 Proceeds of Crime Act 2002, s 333.
12 Proceeds of Crime Act 2002, s 333(3)(b), (4); for guidance on these obscure provisions, see *P v P* [2003] 4 All ER 843 at 863, paragraph [57].
13 'Simple Guide to Anti-Money Laundering Regulations and Associated Legislation' available online at www.lawscot.org.uk. See also Deutsch, 'Dirty Money in Litigation' 2004 Civ PB 57-1.
14 *P v P* [2003] 4 All ER 843 at paragraph [56]; Solicitors (Scotland) Accounts etc Rules 2001, r 24(3).

Money Laundering Regulations 2003

2.19 Solicitors must take appropriate steps to identify their clients, and keep appropriate records of these steps, in relation to all matters of business involving the transfer of funds of or exceeding 15,000 euros (£9,000) or in respect of which they know or suspect involves money laundering[1].

The Law Society of Scotland notes that the placing of funds in the name of a spouse or children is commonplace and it gives detailed guidance to solicitors in relation to compliance with the Money Laundering Regulations 2003[2].

1 Money Laundering Regulations 2003 (SI 2003/3075), regs 4, 6; Solicitors (Scotland) Accounts etc Rules 2001, r 24.
2 'Simple Guide to Anti-Money Laundering Regulations and Associated Legislation', available online at www.lawscot.org.uk.

4. Data protection

Data protection principles

2.20 Consideration needs to be given to the data protection principles provided in the Data Protection Act 1998 as to the recording of personal information relating to a client in a family law agreement in the books of council and session or sheriff court books. Once registered in this way, the agreement becomes a public record.

The contents of the agreement will usually include the client's address, and financial information about that client. It may also include 'sensitive personal data' in relation to his or her sexual life: for example, a confession of adultery, or an agreement between civil partners as to whether sexual relationships are permissible to either or both partners outside the relationship[1].

It is sensible, whatever the strict data protection requirements, to explain to the client the consequence of registering the agreement in relation to the individual's privacy; at the same time, the advantages should be emphasised in relation to the carrying out of diligence by registering the agreement for execution[2]. The latter consideration will usually outweigh the former.

1   Data Protection Act 1998, s 2 defines 'sensitive personal data' including, in s 2(f), a person's 'sexual life'.
2   See CHAPTER 15.

2.21   A solicitor is probably 'processing data' when registering a family law agreement in the court books[1]. He must therefore comply with the relevant data protection principles[2]. However, personal data may be disclosed where this is necessary 'for the purposes of establishing, exercising or defending legal rights'[3] and where the data subject has given his consent to the processing. It is suggested that consent to the processing of information, by registration in the court books, follows from the clause whereby both parties consent to its registration, whether for preservation or execution, or both[5].

The solicitor should therefore be protected from an unauthorised disclosure to the extent the agreement 'establishes' legal rights: arguably that is the whole purpose of the family law agreement.

1   Data Protection Act 1998, s 1.
2   Data Protection Act 1998, s 4, Sch 1.
3   Data Protection Act 1998, s 35(2).
4   Data Protection Act 1998, s 27(4), (5), Sch 2, para 1.
5   Titles to Land Consolidation (Scotland) Act 1868, s 138.

2.22   Special care should be taken, though, with regard to 'sensitive personal data' as this may be disclosed only with the 'explicit consent' of the data subject[1]. The amount of such information should therefore be kept to the essential minimum necessary to establish legal rights.

The solicitor responsible for registering the agreement should either have his client sign an agreement to the disclosure of this information, or if the information relates to the other client, he should write to that client's solicitor and obtain written consent to him disclosing the information.

'Sensitive personal data' in relation to a family law agreement could include:
(a)   the racial or ethnic origin of the data subject;

(b)   his political opinion;

(c)   his religious beliefs or other beliefs of a similar nature;

(d)   whether he is a member of a trade union;

(e)   his physical or mental health or condition;

(f)   his sexual life;

(g)   commission or alleged commission by him of any offence; or

(h)   any proceedings for any offence committed or alleged to have been committed by him, the disposal of such proceedings or the sentence of any court in such proceedings[2].

1   Data Protection Act 1998, s 2(c), s 4, and Sch 3, para 1.
2   Data Protection Act 1998, s 2.

Registration with Information Commissioner

2.23   Firms must be registered if disclosing information held on computer[1]. This means that, if not registered for their general business in any event, most firms will be registered with the Information Commissioner for data protection purposes.

It is an offence to process data and not to be registered when this is required by the Data Protection Act 1998[2].

1   Data Protection Act 1998, s 17(1).
2   Data Protection Act 1998, s 21.

Further research

2.24   Generally:

—   Brown, *Proceeds of Crime* (W Green, 2004);

—   Carey, *Data Protection: A Practical Guide to UK and EU Law* (OUP, 2nd edn, 2003);

—   Dick and Ballatine, *The Art of Family Law* (W Green, 2001);

—   Jones, 'Divorce Lawyers and Proceeds of Crime Disclosure' (2003) 48 JLSS, November, p 34;

—   Law Society of England and Wales, 'Family Law Protocol', (2002);

—   Webster, *Professional Ethics and Practice for Scottish Solicitors* (Avizandum, 4th edn, 2004).

Chapter 3

Drafting, executing and registering family law agreements

1. Drafting the agreement

Style

3.01 Except for pension sharing provisions in separation agreements[1], there are no regulations as to the form family law agreements should take. This is left to individual choice and will often follow a lawyer's own preference, or reliance on office styles. The content and the formalities of execution are what are most important. However, meaning has to be conveyed in words and so far as possible it is desirable to make the agreement as easy to understand for the client and others as may possibly be done. There is an increasing trend in legal drafting towards clarity of layout and expression and the use of plain language where that is possible[2]. It has even been suggested the word 'shall' is ambiguous and superfluous and should be avoided in legal drafting[3]. Good drafting techniques include:

(a) Dividing the agreement into different numbered sections or parts dealing with discrete parts of the agreement, such as the matrimonial home, financial provision, aliment, the children, and so on.

(b) The use of headings to introduce the different parts of the agreement, and, if needed, sub-headings within each part.

(c) The breaking up of long paragraphs into a series of shorter numbered paragraphs or numbered sentences.

(d) Clear sentences conveying one idea or concept at a time.

(e) The elimination where possible of archaic or superfluous words such as 'hereinbefore', 'said' and 'same'. 'Hereinbefore' can always be substituted with a precise reference to a precise clause or paragraph of the agreement. 'Said' can nearly, but not always, be avoided: a single child can be referred to by his or her name instead of 'the said child'. What other child is there? 'Same' should never be used and can normally be replaced by the simple pronoun 'it'. Examples of archaic and superfluous words can readily be multiplied: for more information, the reader is referred elsewhere[4].

1 Pensions on Divorce etc (Pension Sharing) (Scotland) Regulations 2000 (SI 2000/1051), regs 2, 4.
2 Adler, *Clarity for Lawyers* (Law Society of England and Wales, 1990).
3 Clive, *Law-making in Scotland from APS to ASP* (1999) 3 ELR 131 at 142, 143; Asprey, *Plain Language for Lawyers* (Sydney, 2nd edn, 1996) at 175–181.
4 *Adler*, above; *Asprey*, above; and Sinclair, *Legal Drafting in Scotland* (2001).

3.02 An attempt has been made to incorporate the above drafting techniques into the styles contained in this book, without making any claim to perfection for those styles[1].

1 See CHAPTER 19.

3.03 The agreement should always take the form of:
(a) recital of parties to the agreement;
(b) recitals, or preamble, setting out the circumstances of the agreement;
(c) the substantive provisions of the agreement;
(d) final provisions;
(e) testing clause; and
(f) any schedules or annexes to the agreement.

3.04 'Final provisions' include:
(a) costs of registering the agreement;
(b) costs associated with the drafting of the agreement;
(c) the legal effects of the agreement in relation to entitlement to financial provision on divorce, statutory entitlement to aliment, and other matters designed to make the agreement as unalterable and binding on the parties to it as possible;
(d) set off of obligations;
(e) continuing effect of agreement after divorce[1];
(f) interpretation of agreement: definition of terms used in it;
(g) governing law; and
(h) consent to registration for execution.

1 *Mackenzie v Mackenzie* 1987 SCHR 671 at 673, per SP O'Brien, makes it plain that an agreement between husband and wife may cease with divorce unless there is provision extending it after the divorce.

3.05 The recitals set out the parties to the agreement, and explain its purposes. It is sufficient to refer to the agreement as an 'Agreement between' the named parties to it. There is no need to call the agreement a 'separation agreement' or 'cohabitation agreement', or a 'minute of agreement' expressed in the past tense: obligations should be expressed in the present or future tense of the verb 'to be'. There is no need to use expressions such as 'the parties hereby undertake' or 'hereby agree' when it is sufficient to say, for example,

'The wife *is* to occupy the matrimonial home to the exclusion of the husband...'; or

'The husband *will* aliment the wife...';

instead of:

'The husband *hereby undertakes that he shall* allow the wife to occupy the matrimonial home...'; or

'The husband *hereby agrees* to aliment the wife...[1].'

1   See articles entitled 'Plain Speaking' by Ellis Simpson at (2002) 47 JLSS, June, p 52; July, p 47; August, p 53; September, p 48; October, p 44; and November, p 44 and letter by sheriff Andrew Lothian at (2002) 47 JLSS, August, p 14 in response as to modern drafting techniques, and a defence of the traditional way of doing things. With respect to sheriff Lothian, this author nevertheless considers that lawyers must make an effort to clarify, and make precise, the legal documents that they draft. Retaining the word 'hereby' makes some sense as it relates to the instrument constituting the obligation, but it really may not be necessary.

Structure

3.06   The usual practice is to run together in one big paragraph a number of provisions relating to a particular topic, such as the sale of the matrimonial home[1]. This is not, however, the best way of doing things: potentially it is a recipe for disaster as it invites omissions, contradictions and unnecessary superfluage of language. It is also very difficult to read and to identify what obligations have been constituted and in whose favour. It is always better to take one idea or concept at the time, and deal with it in a separate sentence or short paragraph.

1   See, for example, *Green's Practice Styles*, Vol II, Division G: 'Family Law'.

3.07   Indented lists should be used to identify contingencies upon which a right or situation is dependant, and for all the different things a party is obliged to pay for or reimburse, for example, in connection with the upkeep of the matrimonial home during one party's exclusive residence of it for a period after separation.

3.08   Examples of lists are as follows:
(a)   The matrimonial home will continue in the common ownership of the parties until the earlier of:
    (i)   Catherine attaining the age of 16 years[1]; or
    (ii)   Mrs Allan ceasing to have the parental right to have both children reside with her as recognised in this agreement[2].
    Mrs Allan's parental right of having both children reside with her as recognised in this agreement can only be terminated by an order of a competent court[3].
(b)   Mrs Allan will occupy the matrimonial home to the exclusion of Mr Allan during the time it remains in their common ownership and until its sale in accordance with paragraphs [X] and [Y] of this agreement. During that time Mr Allan will immediately pay when falling due:
    (i)   all the loan instalments secured over the matrimonial home;

(ii)   all the premiums due for the mortgage protection policy;

(iii) all the council tax payments due for the matrimonial home; and

(iv)   all the insurance premiums for the buildings and contents of the matrimonial home.

1   There are two children to this marriage. As Catherine is the youngest, only she need be named.

2   'Both' means Mrs Allan keeps residing in the house even if she only has one child residing with her.

3   This acts as a disincentive against Mr Allan abducting or enticing the children away from Mrs Allan and forcing a sale of the matrimonial home merely on a factual charge of circumstances (which he has created) concerning with which parent the children are to reside.

Paragraphs, clauses or sections

3.09   It does not matter whether the agreement is split into 'paragraphs' or 'clauses'. It may be better to avoid 'section', which should be an alternative name for a 'part' of the agreement. However, it is necessary to be consistent for the purposes of cross-reference. Use 'paragraphs' to refer to 'paragraphs' and 'clauses' to refer to 'clauses', being each separately numbered provision of the agreement.

Numbering

3.10   Each paragraph should be assigned a number corresponding to the part of the agreement in which it appears. For example, para 7.5 should be the fifth paragraph in part seven of the agreement. If, in the drafting of the agreement, new paragraphs have to be added, this system will avoid the re-numbering of the whole agreement. Do not use letters as there are only 26 of these in the English alphabet, and more numbers than that may be needed[1]. Make sure that all cross-references are correct in the final draft. Be consistent in numbering: 'having chosen a [numbering] system, the drafter should apply it remorselessly[2]'.

1.   Again a not-so-obvious point. The Treaty of European Union (Maastricht) originally adopted a numbering system using letters; this was later abandoned and numerals were introduced in place of the original system by the Treaty of Amsterdam.

2.   Peter Butt and Richard Castle, *Modern Legal Drafting* (Cambridge University Press, 2001), p 137.

The language of obligations and accessory obligations

3.11   Remember in constituting obligations to correctly specify who is the obligant and who is the creditor in the obligation[1]. For example, is the wife obliged to aliment the husband, or the husband the wife? There is a particular danger in parties being designated 'first' and 'second' party rather than 'Mr' and 'Mrs' or 'husband' and 'wife' because it is easier to forget who is the first or second party. If a mistake is made the wrong party will be obliged to aliment the other, so this is a crucial drafting point.

1   Bankton, *Institute* I, 4, 1.

3.12   All obligations need to be performed within a certain time. Consideration must also be given to the place and manner of performance of obligations, and any provisions for interest for late payment[1]. For example, having decided the husband is to aliment the wife, the following questions need to be asked:

(a)   how much and how often (manner);
(b)   where payments are to be made (place);
(c)   how payments are to be made (manner);
(d)   when the payments are to commence and when they are to end (time); and
(e)   whether, and how much, interest is to be due on late payments (interest).

1   Stair, *Institutions* I, 17, 16–20.

3.13   When considering the time of performance, avoid the ablative 'by' as this also word means the method through which something is achieved, as well as 'besides'. A person travels by car or plane, for example. It is of course common enough for people to say that something must be done 'by' a particular date: but does this include or exclude that date? Use instead precise expressions such as:

'The husband must vacate the matrimonial home on [date]'; or

'The husband must return his wife's wedding ring to her[1] no later than' [date].

1   Which, in this example, he stole from her.

3.14   Further, in computing time, remember there must be a starting point. Usually the date of execution of the agreement is a useful choice. But make sure that this is defined as *signature* of the agreement; otherwise it may be argued that it means *implementation* of the agreement. While 'execution' in the context of the date of an agreement usually does mean signature[1], it is best to avoid any doubt about this. It has been described as a 'slippery word. Its use is to be avoided except when accompanied by explanation[2]'.

1   *Earl of Dalhousie v Crokat* (1868) 6 M 659 at 655, per Lord Deas; *Earl of Moray v Petr* 1950 SLT 188;
Stamp Act 1891, s 122(1); *Bank of Scotland v Graham's Trustee* 1993 SLT 252.
2   *Black's Law Dictionary* (7th edn), vol 1, p 589, entry 'executed'.

The rules of grammar

3.15   The overriding concern is to achieve clarity and precision of meaning. There is no need to worry about the more refined rules of grammar, such as not splitting infinitives, the 'correct' use of shall (which in any event is not the same in Scottish English, as opposed to Standard English)[1], or avoiding starting sentences with 'And'. Fowler[2] (despite its vintage) will always be a good guide in relation to these quite unnecessary rules, but it is recommended that a drafter does acquire a good understanding of the rules of English grammar and that he or she applies these creatively in the construction of clear and precise sentences[3].

1   Amis, *The King's English* (Harper Collins, 3rd edn, 1998), pp 204–207.
2   Fowler, *A Dictionary of Modern English Usage* (1926).
3   Gowers, *The Complete Plain Words* (HMSO, 3rd edn, 1986) is a good starting point. *The Oxford Companion to the English Language*, edited by Tom McArthur (1992), is an excellent reference book in relation to many aspects of English language and usage.

3.16   As an example of good English, but one that breaks the rule against starting sentences with 'And', consider the closing paragraph of Edgar Allan Poe's *Masque of the Red Death*:

'And now was acknowledged the presence of the Red Death. He had come like a thief in the night[1]. And one by one dropped the revellers in the blood-bedewed halls of their revel, and died each in the despairing posture of his fall. And the life of the ebony clock went out with that of the last of the gay. And the flames of the tripods expired. And Darkness and Decay and the Red Death held illimitable dominion over all[2].'

'And' is used effectively in this example to start most sentences in the paragraph. Clearly it can become monotonous in other contexts. Used sparingly, or poetically, it can have a useful effect.

1   This appears to be a reference to 2 Thessalonians 5:2.
2   The Collected Tales and Poems of Edgar Allan Poe, 1992 Modern Library Edition, New York, p 273.

3.17   The passage from Poe's *Masque of the Red Death* also introduces an important topic: that of gender and language. Consider these sentences from the Poe extract:

'…one by one dropped the revellers in the blood bedewed halls of *their* revel.'

'…and died each in the despairing posture of *his* fall.'

3.18   It is made clear in the story that the revellers are both male and female. Poe correctly uses the plural 'their' in the first of these sentences to correspond to 'the revellers'. In the next sentence, 'each' of the revellers (the singular) dies in 'the despairing posture of *his* fall'. The effect would have been lost with 'his or her' fall, or even worse, 'their' fall. Fowler is undoubtedly correct, that the best solution is to follow convention (as did Poe) and use the masculine pronoun synecdochically to stand for both sexes[1]. The politically correct use of 'she' for this purpose, or using 'she' and 'he' in alternating paragraphs, jars and is best avoided. 'She' should be used as the collective pronoun in any context in which it refers exclusively or predominantly to women, such as mothers, wives, or parents with care of children[2].

1   Fowler, 'Number (11)', *Wordsworth Reference Edition* (1994), pp 391, 392; Interpretation Act 1978, s 6(a).
2   See the Interpretation Act 1978, s 6(b).

3.19   If the drafter cannot accept this advice, then these are the options:

'their' to refer to a single person;

's/he';

'he or she'; or

'she or he'.

3.20   'Their' lacks logic and is an example of consistently badly written English. 'S/he' is awkward and is not even a word. 'He or she' or 'she or he' has contained within it the issue of whether the masculine or feminine should come first. Inevitably, there must be some convention and it is suggested that 'he or she' will usually be the best alternative to 'he', and should be particularly used to refer to children of both sexes. But if possible, construct sentences so as to avoid singular gender pronouns standing for both sexes. And always make sure that the correct pronoun is employed when referring to individuals, especially children. For example:

'She [ie the wife] is entitled to…'

'She [ie Jenny, the child] will attend Paisley Grammar School…'

3.21   And remember to use the neutral pronoun often. For example:

'The matrimonial home and its repair'; not

'The matrimonial home and the repair of the matrimonial home'.

3.22   Never use 'the same' for 'it' or 'them'. Fowler thought 'the same' should be avoided 'by all who have any skill in writing[1]'.

1   *Wordsworth Reference Edition* (1994), pp 511, 512.

Punctuation

3.23   Punctuation is a rational part of English composition, and there is no reason to deprive legal documents of it[1]. Punctuate correctly as it is an effective aid in achieving clarity and precision of meaning. Remember that the colon (:) introduces a list, or an elaboration of a previous point; the semi-colon (;) divides parts of a sentence, or a list introduced by colon[2]. Separate sentences are marked by a full stop, not a comma. The apostrophe indicates possession and should always be used in legal documents; it comes before the 's' in singular nouns, and after it in plural nouns. It is not used for plurals without possession. Exceptions are:

(a)   its (possessive, no apostrophe);
(b)   it's (means it is); and

(c) children's (children is a plural form)[3].

1 *Houston v Burns* [1918] AC 337 at 348, HL, per Lord Shaw (this was a Scottish appeal; it does not, however, appear to be reported in the Scottish law reports).
2 *Oxford Companion to the English Language* (1992), pp 232, 916.
3 While all of this may sound obvious, it has been found to be a problem in England: Adler, *Clarity for Lawyers* (Law Society of England and Wales, 1990), ch 5, pp 65–70.

2. Execution of the agreement

Requirements

3.24 The agreement cannot be registered for preservation or execution in the books of council and session, or sheriff court books[1], unless it is presumed under ss 3 or 4 of the Requirements of Writing (Scotland) Act 1995 to have been subscribed by the granters[2]. It will be presumed to have been subscribed by the parties to the agreement ('the granters') if it:
(a) bears to have been subscribed by both of them[3];
(b) each of their signatures bears to have been signed by a witness[4] and the agreement, or its testing clause, bears to state the name and address of the witnesses; and
(c) there is nothing in the document or testing clause to indicate that it was not subscribed as it bears to have been subscribed or was not validly witnessed for any of the reasons in s 3(4)(a)–(e) of the Act[5].

1 See paras **3.34–3.36**.
2 Requirements of Writing (Scotland) Act 1995, s 6(1)(b), (2)(a); Interpretation Act 1978, s 6(c).
3 It appears that a document can be registered in the books of council and session, or sheriff court books, if it is presumed under the Requirements of Writing (Scotland) Act 1995, ss 3 or 4, 'or partly under the one section and partly under the other', to have been subscribed by only one of the granters (s 6(2)(b)), but this is not recommended. Always make sure both parties properly subscribe the agreement, and both their signatures are properly witnessed.
4 It is recommended there be a separate witness for each signature: see the Requirements of Writing (Scotland) Act 1995, s 3(6) for the position if a single witness witnesses the two signatures.
5 Requirements of Writing (Scotland) Act 1995, s 3(1).

3.25 A signature will not be validly witnessed for any of the following reasons[1]:
(a) the witness's signature is not the signature of the person whose signature it bears to be, whether by reason of forgery or otherwise;
(b) the witness is a person named in the document;
(c) the witness did not know the granter at the time of signature[2];
(d) the witness was under the age of 16 years at the time of signature;
(e) the witness was mentally incapable of acting as a witness at the time of signature;
(f) the person did not witness the granter's signature.

1 Requirements of Writing (Scotland) Act 1995, s 3(4)(a)–(e).

2   'Knowledge' means credible information as to the granter's identity at the time of the agreement: Requirements of Writing (Scotland) Act 1995, s 3(5).

3.26   The witnesses' names must be added to the agreement (not necessarily by themselves) prior to its registration for preservation in the books of council and session, or sheriff court books[1]. If it is established, after registration, that the name or address of the witnesses, or either of them, is erroneous in any material respect, then the agreement loses the presumption it was validly subscribed by the granter[2]. Especial care should therefore be taken over the witnessing of the agreement, and preferably this should be done by a person known to the solicitor, such as his secretary.

1   Requirements of Writing (Scotland) Act 1995, s 3(3)(a)(ii).
2   Requirements of Writing (Scotland) Act 1995, s 3(4)(f).

3.27   A person witnesses a signature if:
(a)   he sees the granter signing it; or
(b)   the granter acknowledges his signature to the witness[1].

1   Requirements of Writing (Scotland) Act 1995, s 3(7).

3.28   It is sufficient that the parties to the family law agreement sign it at the end of the last page; or one of them signs there, and the other on an additional page[1]. They, and the witnesses, should sign with the full name by which they are identified in the agreement, or the testing clause, or with at least one initial of their forenames preceding their surname[2].

1   Requirements of Writing (Scotland) Act 1995, s 7(1), (3).
2   Requirements of Writing (Scotland) Act 1995, s 7(1)(a), (b), (5).

3.29   Annexations (schedules, annexes, inventories, and other writings[1]) to a family law agreement do not need to be signed or subscribed if they are:
(a)   referred to in the agreement; and
(b)   identified on their face as being the annexations referred to in the agreement[2]
but may be signed at any time before the agreement is registered for preservation in the books of council and session or sheriff court books[3].

1   Requirements of Writing (Scotland) Act 1995, s 12(1).
2   Requirements of Writing (Scotland) Act 1995, s 8(1).
3   Requirements of Writing (Scotland) Act 1995, s 8(5).

3.30   For special cases, such as subscription on behalf of a blind granter or a granter unable to write[1], alterations to the agreement[2], and applications to the sheriff under s 4 of the Requirements of Writing (Scotland) Act 1995 to find that an agreement was subscribed by a party to the agreement where there is no presumption of subscription by the granter under s 3 of the Act, reference should be made elsewhere[3].

1   Requirements of Writing (Scotland) Act 1995, s 9.
2   Requirements of Writing (Scotland) Act 1995, s 5.
3   Rennie and Cusine, *The Requirements of Writing* (Butterworths, 1995).

Testing clause

3.31   The agreement is concluded with a testing clause recording the details of subscription and attestation. It is commonly added after execution of the agreement and prior to its registration for preservation in the books of council and session, or sheriff court books[1]. The Scottish Ministers have power to prescribe forms of testing clause by regulation[2]. In practice, the testing clause sets out the names and addresses of the witnesses, and the date and place of signature of the agreement. If the agreement is presumed to have been signed by its granters and there is nothing in the agreement or testing clause indicating that the statement as to date and place of signature is incorrect, the agreement is presumed to have been subscribed on the date and at the place stated in the testing clause[3].

1   Requirements of Writing (Scotland) Act 1995, s 3(3)(a)(ii).
2   Requirements of Writing (Scotland) Act 1995, s 10; functions of Secretary of State transferred to the Scottish Ministers by the Scotland Act 1998, s 53(2).
3   Requirements of Writing (Scotland) Act 1995, s 3(8), (9).

3.32   An example of a testing clause follows:

'IN WITNESS WHEREOF this agreement[1] on this and the preceding [number of] pages[2] is subscribed by the husband signing his usual signature E Allan[3] at Paisley on [date] before [name and address of witness][4] signing her usual signature S Thomson[5] and by the wife signing her usual signature A Lee[6] at Elderslie on [date] before [name and address of witness][7] signing her usual signature K Thompson[8].'

1   'This agreement' rather than the conventional 'these presents'.
2   Always specify the number of pages.
3   This is necessary if the husband signs with an initial of one or more of his forenames, and surname. It is not necessary if he signs all his names in full.
4   In practice, the designation (occupation) of the witness is usually added. This is not necessary.
5   See fn 3.
6   See fn 3.
7   See fn 4.
8   See fn 3.

3.33   The usual order of signing is:

S Thomson, witness	E Allan
K Thompson, witness	A Lee

Note the practice that the witness signs with the word 'witness' after her name.

3. Registration

3.34   Registration is either in the books of council and session or sheriff court books[1]. In practice, the books of council and session are mostly used. It is essential to make use of these books if it is intended to give effect to pension sharing provisions in a separation agreement[2]. The agreement must be presumed to have been subscribed by the granters (or one of them) under ss 3 or 4 of the Requirements of Writing (Scotland) Act 1995 in order to be registered for preservation or execution in either the books of council and session, or sheriff court books[3]. The clause consenting to registration does not need to specify in which court books the agreement is to be registered[4], but it is wise to do so, especially if a pension sharing agreement is involved. Between 1685 and 1906 the parties to an agreement registered in sheriff court books had both to reside in the court's jurisdiction but that is no longer necessary[5]. The Keeper of the Registers of Scotland has long ceased to be responsible for issuing the registers to sheriff clerks in which to register self-proving agreements[6]. This is now a matter for regulation by the Court of Session by Act of Sederunt[7]. Agreements registered in the books of council and session have the advantage that diligence can, if necessary, be served edictally[8].

1   Public Records (Scotland) Act 1809, ss 1–7 (now repealed) restricted registration for preservation and execution to the books of council and session and sheriff court only.
2   Welfare Reform and Pensions Act 1999, ss 28(3)(b), 48(3)(b).
3   Requirements of Writing (Scotland) Act 1995, s 6(1)(b), (2)(b); see paras **3.24–3.30**.
4   Titles to Land Consolidation (Scotland) Act 1868, s 138.
5   (Aps 1685), c 47; repealed Statute Law Revision (Scotland) Act 1906.
6   Public Records (Scotland) Act 1809, s 8 (repealed by the Public Records (Scotland) Act 1937, s 15).
7   Sheriff Court and Legal Officers (Scotland) Act 1927, s 16; none, however, has been made.
8   See para **15.04**.

3.35   Registration is either for preservation of the agreement[1], for execution, or both. The necessary effect of registering the agreement is its preservation and no clause of consent to registration for this purpose has been necessary since 1698[2]. It remains essential to insert a clause for consent to registration for execution[3]. This must be inserted prior to execution of the agreement; it is professional misconduct for a solicitor to insert it afterwards, without authorisation of both parties[4]. Registration for execution permits certain diligences to be done on an extract of the agreement[5]: the extract is equivalent to a decree of the court in whose books the agreement is registered[6]. This is a very useful provision for the creditor in money obligations constituted by the agreement, and her solicitor should always insist on the agreement containing a clause consenting to registration for execution when these obligations (as they usually are) are constituted by the agreement. The agreement thus registered will have the added advantage of being an authentic instrument for the purposes of enforcement of aliment in other European countries[7].

1   See paras **2.20–2.23**, regarding data protection.
2   Presently Requirements of Writing (Scotland) Act 1995, s 6(4) (the Registration Act 1698 originally authorised registration for preservation in the absence of a clause of consent for that purpose; it was replaced by the Requirements of Writing (Scotland) Act 1995, s 6(4), and Sch 5 of which Act repealed the 1698 Act).
3   Titles to Land Consolidation (Scotland) Act 1868, s 138.
4   Case 798/90 *Scottish Solicitors' Discipline Tribunal*, reported in Smith and Barton, *Procedures and Decisions of the Scottish Solicitors' Discipline Tribunal* (Law Society of Scotland/T&T Clark, 1995), para 12.02, pp 119, 120.
5   See CHAPTER 15.

6   *Taylor v Petr* 1931 SLT 260; *Commissioner's Case No CSCS/5/97* 1999 Fam L R 37.
7   See CHAPTER 14.

3.36 Forms of warrant of execution for agreements registered in the books of council and session, or sheriff court books, are provided by the Writs Execution (Scotland) Act 1877[1]; extracts of agreements from the books of council and session are equivalent to the original document[2], and are issued by the Keeper of the Registers of Scotland[3]. The sheriff clerk is responsible for issuing extracts of agreements in the sheriff court books[4].

1   By ss 1, 2, Schedule.
2   Writs Execution (Scotland) Act 1877, s 5.
3   Writs Execution (Scotland) Act 1877, ss 1, 7; Public Records (Scotland) Act 1937, s 9; Public Registers and Records (Scotland) Act 1948, s 1(2).
4   Writs Execution (Scotland) Act 1877, s 2.

Further research

3.37 Generally:
—   Adler, *Clarity for Lawyers* (Law Society of England and Wales, 1990);
—   Asprey, *Plain Language for Lawyers* (Federation Press, Sydney, 2nd edn, 1996);
—   Butt and Castle, *Modern Legal Drafting* (Cambridge University Press, 2001);
—   Quail, 'Separation: The Beginning of the End' (2003) 48 JLSS, November, p 27.

3.38 Clarity, the organisation for the promotion of clear legal language, has its website at:
—   www.clarity-international.net.

See also:
—   www.plainenglish.co.uk.

Chapter 4

Agreements in contemplation of, or during, marriage

'[T]he conjunction of bodies as well as of minds, as the general end of the institution of marriage, is the solace and satisfaction of [humankind].'

Stair *Institutions* I, 4, 6

1. Terminology

4.01   Marriage contracts are either antenuptial or postnuptial: they are, in other words, entered into before and in contemplation, or consideration, of marriage, or after the marriage has taken place.

An antenuptial marriage contract will only have effect after the marriage has taken place; no promise to marry is enforceable in Scots law, and no action lies in respect of breach of that promise[1].

1   Law Reform (Husband and Wife) (Scotland) Act 1984, s 1(1).

2. Purpose

4.02   Marriage contracts were important when married woman did not have the right to administer their own property: they were a device whereby the parties could create their own property regime during marriage, protect dispositions to the wife from being gratuitous dispositions in connection with the husband's insolvency, and permit the wife to settle an alimentary right on her from her own funds.

All vestiges of this former regime have been swept away[1], and husband and wife now enjoy their own property rights unaffected by the marriage[2] It is only on divorce or annulment that one or both of the parties to the marriage will have the right to financial provision from the other in accordance with the provisions of the Family Law (Scotland) Act 1985. In deciding what orders for financial provision to make the court can have regard to 'the terms of any agreement between the parties on the ownership or division of any of the matrimonial property'[3]. It can vary any agreement or any term of an agreement as to financial provision on divorce or annulment where it 'was not fair and reasonable at the time it was entered in to'[4].

In view of these provisions, contemporary marriage contracts might wish to address the division of matrimonial property on divorce or annulment, or create some form of community of property during marriage.

1   Married Women's Property (Scotland) Act 1881; Married Women's Property (Scotland) Act 1920; Law Reform (Husband and Wife) (Scotland) Act 1984, s 5.
2   Family Law (Scotland) Act 1985, s 24(1).
3   Family Law (Scotland) Act 1985, s 10(6)(a); *K v K (Ancillary Relief: Prenuptial Agreement)* [2003] 1 FLR 120.
4   Family Law (Scotland) Act 1985, s 16(1)(b); see CHAPTER 16 for a discussion of this power.

4.03   In most cases, though, a marriage contract is inadvisable because:
(a)   The Family Law (Scotland) Act 1985 creates a fair and sensible system for financial provision on the breakdown of a marriage. There is generally no need to depart from it. Any departure may, in due course, become outdated and inappropriate, especially with the passage of time, changed circumstances, and the birth of children. It is not possible to anticipate everything in advance. It may prove just to be a waste of time and money.
(b)   The spouses will provide for each other during marriage 'by means such as titles in joint names, occupational pension schemes, equalisation of savings, insurance policies and wills'[1].
(c)   There are presumptions of equal shares in household goods[2], and in money and property derived from a housekeeping allowance[3].
(d)   It is generally inadvisable to discuss the arrangements for the breakdown of a marriage before it has begun or at regular intervals during the marriage: this may damage or destroy the trust between the parties to the contemplated marriage, or become a recurring source of trouble after marriage[4].

1   Clive, *The Law of the Husband and Wife in Scotland* (5th edn, 1997), p 313, para 17.007.
2   Family Law (Scotland) Act 1985, s 25.
3   Family Law (Scotland) Act 1985, s 26.
4   Clive, above, p 315, para 17.013.

4.04   Conversely, a marriage contract might be of some use where:
(a)   One of the parties is very wealthy, and giving his spouse a generous, but less than 50 per cent split, of matrimonial property on divorce would be more than ample for her and the children's needs.
(b)   One of the parties brings to the marriage an item of non-matrimonial property, such as a house acquired prior to the marriage, or a gift or inheritance from a third party acquired during the marriage. An antenuptial or postnuptial marriage contract could identify the item as non-matrimonial property, put a value on it, and allow for the deduction of that value, or part of it, from matrimonial property if the item is subsequently sold or used for the purpose of acquiring matrimonial property.

(c)   There is some particular item of matrimonial property which it is desirable to exclude from a property split on divorce, for example book, coin or stamp collections or pets.

(d)   There is a possibility of the parties moving abroad to a country with a community of property regime, and they wish to opt out of it there.

3. Exclusion of child's right to legitim

4.05   An antenuptial marriage contract cannot now exclude a child's right to legitim from his parent's estate unless the child accepts whatever provision is made in the contract in lieu of legitim[1]. Legitim could not, and cannot, be discharged by a postnuptial contract[2].

1   Succession (Scotland) Act 1964, s 12.
2   McLaren, *The Law of Wills and Succession* (3rd edn, 1894), pp 135, 136, paras 263, 265.

4. Gifts and inheritance tax

4.06   An antenuptial marriage contract could in theory be employed to enable spouses to gift money to each other, or settle money on each other by setting up a trust or liferent.

Such arrangements would be very unusual in contemporary circumstances and, if contemplated, would presumably be part of a wider agreement as to community of property during marriage, and its division on divorce or annulment.

Up to £2,500 gifted or settled in this way in consideration of marriage (ie in an antenuptial contract) is exempt for the purposes of inheritance tax[1], but entering into a marriage contract solely for this purpose seems something of a waste of time and money.

1   Inheritance Tax Act 1984, ss 22, 43.

5. Assurance policies

4.07   A marriage contract might more usefully be used as a vehicle for one or both of the spouses effecting a policy of assurance on his or her own life, but expressly for the benefit of his or her spouse or children. The policy subsequently taken out operates as a trust in favour of the spouse or children without the necessity for delivery or intimation[1]. The marriage contract should address whether the spouse's right to assign her benefit under the trust is restricted, and whether it terminates on divorce. The court has power to make an incidental order before, on or after marriage or annulment setting aside or varying any term of the trust[2], on such conditions it considers expedient (if any) to give effect to the principles in s 9 of the Family Law (Scotland) Act 1985 or an order made under s 8(2) of that Act[3].

1   Married Women's Policies of Assurance (Scotland) Act 1880, s 2.
2   Family Law (Scotland) Act 1985, s 14(1), (2)(h), (6).
3   Family Law (Scotland) Act 1985, s 14(2)(k).

Further research

4.08   Generally:
—   Clive, *The Law of Husband and Wife in Scotland* (5th edn, 1997), ch 17, 'Marriage Contracts'; ch 14, paras 14.109–14.123, 'Married Women's Policies of Assurance (Scotland) Act 1880'.

Chapter 5

Separation agreements

1. Marriage and separation agreements

5.01 It is a principle of the law of Scotland to favour and maintain the obligations of marriage in all possible cases[1].

In an early case, *Drummond v Rollock*, it was considered that a voluntary separation agreement should not be upheld since the separation had not been 'lawfully authorised by a legal and judicial sentence'[2]. However, this was not a typical decision, and from the early seventeenth century[3] the prevailing view (despite *Drummond v Rollock*) was that a voluntary contract of separation was valid[4], but revocable at any time during the subsistence of the marriage by either of the parties who was willing to cohabit[5], provided at the date of the purported revocation the other party did not have reasonable cause (such as the husband's violence) to refuse the offer of resumed cohabitation[6].

Separation agreements were always considered valid in cases of de facto separation caused by the husband's ill-treatment, or desertion of his wife. In both these cases, the wife had a right to aliment and there could be no objection to the amount of aliment being fixed by agreement rather than by the court in an action for aliment at the wife's instance[7]. It was even possible to refer to arbitration the question whether the husband had ill-treated his wife and, if so, for the arbiters to determine the amount of aliment to be paid by the husband to his wife[8]. Where a husband required to live abroad for a period and entered into an agreement for his wife's aliment during his absence, the wife was entitled to raise an action for modification of a suitable amount of aliment if he defaulted in his agreement[9].

Separation agreements have always been revoked by the genuine resumption of cohabitation between the spouses[10].

1   McGlashan, *The Law and Practice in Actions of Aliment* (1837), p 6.

2   (1634) Mor 6152; Auchinleck's *Reports of Decisions of the Lords of Council and Session*, p 18 (Mor 1 Supp 349); *Gib v Miller*, 14 March 1634, Durie's Decisions, p 712; According to McGlashan, *The Law and Practice in Actions of Aliment* (1837), p 7 this case was overruled in *Cramond v Allan* (1757) Mor 6157, FC, vol 2, p 7, but neither of these reports makes this clear. For an earlier case between the same parties on 25 Jan 1756, see Mor 5886.
3   *Hattonhall v Crantons* (1631) Mor 6151;
4   *Livingston v Begg* (1666) Mor 6153; *Earl of Argyle v His Lady* (1695) Mor 6054.
5   *Hattonhall v Cranstons* (1631) Mor 6151.
6   *Home v Lady Eccles* (1734) Mor 6159.
7   *Crighton v Abercromby* (1561) Mor 5877; *Logan v Wood* (1561) Mor 5877; *Howieson v Rae* (1594) Mor 5902; *Lady Foulis v Husband* (1626) Mor 6158; *Home v Lady Eccles* (1734) Mor 6159; *Shand v Shand* (1832) 10 S 384.
8   *Vallance v Lady Touch* 3 May 1707, Lothian's Consistorial Law, p 100.
9   *Lady Buchannan v The Laird*, 23 July 1629, Durie's Decisions, p 466.
10 *Forbes v Abernethy* (1713) Mor 6154.

5.02   Separation agreements have thus been regarded as in accordance with public policy though revocable by a genuine and reasonable offer of resumption of cohabitation, or the genuine reconciliation of the spouses. Public policy prevents the parties from contracting out of an option to revoke their agreement in the event of a genuine offer to resume cohabitation, or their reconciliation[1], but it is thought that the spouses could agree to suspend their separation agreement during a period of a trial reconciliation[2].

1   *Livingston v Begg* (1666) Mor 6153; *Vallance v Lady Touch* 3 May 1707, Lothian's Consistorial Law, p 100; *Forbes v Abernethy* (1713) Mor 6154; *Palmer v Bonar* (1810) 15 FC 535 at 541.
2   Clive, *The Law of Husband and Wife in Scotland* (5th edn, 1997), p 356, para 19.019.

5.03   A separation agreement nowadays would typically seek to regulate the position both during separation and on divorce; one which deals only with separation, while competent, is less attractive and not common in modern practice[1].

1   Clive, *The Law of Husband and Wife in Scotland* (5th edn, 1997), p 350, para 19.003.

5.04   A separation agreement may accordingly be defined as:

'A contract made between husband and wife, revocable by either while their marriage subsists, on one of the spouses making a genuine offer to resume cohabitation with the other spouse (except where the other spouse has reasonable cause to refuse to resume cohabitation), which defines their property rights either during their separation only or both during their separation and on and after any subsequent divorce[1].'

1   See paras **5.18–5.21** for further information on revocation of separation agreements.

5.05   'Property rights' in this definition should be taken to refer to all rights of property, corporeal, incorporeal, heritable and moveable, and all obligations, including obligations to pay money, refrain from doing an act, to relieve another person of his obligations, to pay aliment, or to administer children's property[1]. The separation agreement will usually include some form of parenting agreement in respect of the upbringing of the parties' children, and the exercise of their parental responsibilities and rights for the children[2].

1   *Institutes of Gaius* 2.14; *Institutes of Justinian* 2.2.2; see further: Robin Evan-Jones and Geoffery MacCormack, 'Obligations', in Metzger (ed), *A Companion to Justinian's Institutes*, (Duckworth, 1998), pp 127, 128 for the classification of obligations as part of the law of property.
2   See CHAPTER 7.

5.06   It is not necessary in this definition of a separation agreement for the spouses to have actually separated from each other; they may intend to separate soon or, more commonly, they may be living together in the same house as separated spouses and wish to proceed with a sale of the matrimonial home.

2.   Scope and form of the agreement

5.07   The separating or separated spouses will most commonly enter into an agreement with each other setting out what they want to do about their property and the children during their separation and after their divorce from each other.

5.08   The agreement can be as complicated or as simple as required for these purposes. It can be limited to a single issue if necessary, eg aliment or pension sharing. It can be constituted orally[1] except for obligations[2] or provisions[3] which must be constituted in writing. However, the various issues to be covered by a separation agreement are such that writing, desirable in any event for evidential reasons, is essential legally to provide for all of them. Moreover, if properly executed, the agreement can be made self-proving and registered with express provision in the agreement[4] in the books of council and session[5] or the sheriff court books[6] for execution. It is not necessary to have a clause providing merely for registration for prevention of a self-proving agreement[7]. For all these reasons, references in this chapter to a separation agreement mean a *written* separation agreement between spouses.

1   See Family Law (Scotland) Act 1985, s 7 regarding agreements as to aliment: there is no requirement that the agreement be in writing, though in practice it commonly is.
2   Requirements of Writing (Scotland) Act 1995, s 1.
3   Those relating to pension sharing must be in writing since they must be registered in the books of council and session: Welfare Reform and Pensions Act 1999, ss 28(3), 48(3).
4   Requirements of Writing (Scotland) Act 1995, s 6.
5   Writs Execution (Scotland) Act 1877, s 1.
6   Writs Execution (Scotland) Act 1877, s 2. Pension sharing agreements must, however, be registered in the books of council and session: Welfare Reform and Pensions Act 1999, ss 28(3)(b), 48(3)(b).
7   Requirements of Writing (Scotland) Act 1995, s 6(4).

5.09   If the sole area of agreement is in relation to aliment to be paid to a spouse, or for the children, during the parties' separation, then this might be constituted in writing as a unilateral obligation undertaken towards the other spouse, or the children (an 'alimentary bond')[1]. Such an obligation must be in writing to be valid[2].

1   Debtors (Scotland) Act 1987, s 106 (part (h) of the definition of 'maintenance order').
2   Requirements of Writing (Scotland) Act 1995, s 1.

5.10   Except for pension sharing provisions[1], there are no regulations as to the form a separation agreement should take. The advice given in CHAPTER 3 of this book as to the drafting and execution of family law agreements generally should be followed in respect of the preparation and execution of separation agreements.

1   Pensions on Divorce (etc) (Pension Sharing) (Scotland) Regulations 2000 (SI 2000/1051), regs 2, 4.

3.   Practical and legal considerations

5.11   These are considered in the context of the separation styles themselves, to which detailed notes are appended[1]. Seven topics are, however, considered in some detail in individual chapters, as follows:

(a)   aliment and financial provision – see CHAPTER 8.
(b)   child support and its effect on separation agreements – see CHAPTER 9.
(c)   pension sharing and earmarking – see CHAPTER 10.
(d)   separation agreements as 'authentic instruments' for the purposes of the Civil Jurisdiction and Judgments Act 1982 and Council Regulation (EC) 44/2001 – see CHAPTER 14.
(e)   diligence and enforcement – see CHAPTER 15.
(f)   challenging family law agreements – see CHAPTER 16.
(g)   resolving disputes – see CHAPTER 17.

1   See CHAPTER 19, styles 1–4.

4.   Contract and property law considerations

5.12   A separation agreement is a contract and, with some specialities, the normal rules of contract and property law apply when drawing up the agreement. The exceptions are that the court, in appropriate circumstances, may vary aliment or periodical allowance provided for in a separation agreement[1], or set aside an agreement which was not fair or reasonable when it was entered into[2]. A provision in the agreement which purports to restrict the right of any person to apply for a maintenance calculation under the Child Support Act 1991[3], prevents a spouse obtaining a decree of divorce or separation[4], or from suspending a charge for payment of aliment due under the agreement[5], is void. Provisions concerning the children are ultimately not enforceable since if difficulties arise the court's paramount consideration is the welfare of the children and not the parties' agreement[6]. Similarly, while it may be useful so to provide, agreement to consent to divorce after two years non-cohabitation as husband and wife is probably not enforceable since either party has an absolute discretion to grant or withhold consent at any time[7]. Finally, when entering into the contract parents should be mindful of their obligations to consult their children over issues affecting the children where they are of sufficient age and maturity to express a view on these issues[8]. Cases involving breach of family law agreements require the application of common law principles relating to breach of contract[9].

1   Family Law (Scotland) Act 1985, ss 7(2), 16.
2   Family Law (Scotland) Act 1985, ss 7(1), 16(1)(b)
3   Child Support Act 1991, s 9(4).
4   *Lawson v Macculloch* (1797) Mor 6157; *Walker v Maclean* (1922) 38 Sh Ct Rep 152.
5   Bankton, *Institute* IV, 38, 19; *Forrester v Walker & Hunt*, June 27, 1815 FC; *Gilmour v Finney* (1831) 9 S 907.
6   Children (Scotland) Act 1995, s 11(7).
7   *Boyle v Boyle* 1977 SLT (Notes) 69.
8   Children (Scotland) Act 1995, s 6(1).
9   *Redfern's Executors v Redfern* 1996 SLT 900; *Cassidy v Cassidy* 2002 SCLR 576; *Darke v Strout* [2003] EWCA 176.

5.   Taxation: maintenance

5.13   There is tax relief available in respect of maintenance payments where the parties are separated or divorced and either spouse was born before 6 April 1935[1]. To qualify for relief the maintenance payment must be made under a court order or 'a written agreement'[2] for the benefit and maintenance of the other party and for the maintenance of any child of the family aged under 21[3]. The relief is given in the form of a reduction in income tax equivalent to 10 per cent of the married couples' allowance[4]. In the unlikely (but not impossible) event of payments for children aged under 21 being made to separated spouses where one of the spouses is born before 6 April 1935, the provisions in style 1 in CHAPTER 19 for aliment should be amended to reflect payments being made in accordance with the tax relief provision, if it is desired to take advantage of this relief.

1   Income and Corporation Taxes Act 1988, s 347B(1A).
2   Income and Corporation Taxes Act 1988, s 347B(1)(a).
3   Income and Corporation Taxes Act 1988, s 347B(1)(b), (7).
4   Income and Corporation Taxes Act 1988, s 347B(3), (5A).

6.   Stamp duty land tax

5.14   A transaction between husband and wife is exempt from stamp duty land tax if it is effected at any time in pursuance of an agreement of the parties made in contemplation or otherwise in connection with the dissolution or annulment of the marriage, or their judicial separation. The spouse in whose favour heritable property is transferred in consequence of the separation agreement should present a 'self-certificate' to the Keeper of the Registers of Scotland on registering the transfer to the effect that no land transaction return is required in respect of the transaction[2].

1   Finance Act 2003, Sch 3, para 3(d).

2   Finance Act 2003, s 79(3)(b), Sch 11, para 2; Stamp Duty Land Tax (Administration) Regulations 2003 (SI 2003/2387), reg 8, Sch 1.

7. Legal Aid: recovery or preservation of property

5.15   Where the client is in receipt of Legal Advice and Assistance or Civil Legal Aid, and a settlement is achieved by way of a separation agreement, the solicitor's fees and outlays are paid in the following order of priority:

(a)   from the client's contribution(s) (if any);
(b)   from any expenses recovered;
(c)   out of any property 'recovered or preserved' for the client; and finally
(d)   from the Legal Aid Fund[1].

The first £4,395 of any money or property recovered or preserved as a capital payment or transfer of property is exempt from these provisions; and further, the provisions do not apply in respect of payments of aliment of periodical allowance due under a separation agreement[2].

1   Legal Aid (Scotland) Act 1986, ss 12(3), 17(2B).
2   Advice and Assistance (Scotland) Regulations 1996 (SI 1996/2447), reg 16(2)(a)(vi), (2)(b); Civil Legal Aid (Scotland) Regulations 2002 (SSI 2002/494), reg 33(a)(vi), (b).

5.16   It is accordingly important to consider whether property in excess of £4,395 will be 'recovered or preserved' in respect of a legally assisted client in drawing up a separation agreement[1]: the client should be advised of the consequences in terms of the Scottish Legal Aid Board ('SLAB') seeking to recover fees and outlays from the excess, and SLAB's powers in relation to recovery of any sums due[2]. SLAB will insist on a transfer of property being valued at the date of transfer, *not* the date of separation[3]. It has, in relation to grants of Advice and Assistance only, but not Civil Legal Aid, the power to waive the payment of fees and outlays out of property recovered or preserved in cases of hardship[4].

1   There is no statutory definition of 'property recovered or preserved', but see SLAB, 'Guidance on Property Recovered or Preserved', available at www.slab.org.uk.
2   Civil Legal Aid (Scotland) Regulations 2002 (SSI 2002/494), reg 40.
3   See SLAB guidance, above, para 9.6.
4   Advice and Assistance (Scotland) Regulations 1996 (SI 1996/2447), reg 16(3).

5.17   The separation agreement should be drafted to show in detail any exchange of property and benefits (duly valued) at the date of transfer if it is to be argued with SLAB that a *net* transfer represents the property 'recovered or preserved'. An example of this would be the transfer of £10,000 of the husband's net share of the matrimonial home to the wife but in exchange, for example, the family car owned by the wife, worth £5,000. Instead of the wife recovering £10,000, she would recover £5,000, and be liable to pay to SLAB only £605 for her fees and outlays as an assisted person. If she were considered as having received the full value of the husband's share in the house it is arguable that all her legal fees and expenses would be recoverable by SLAB.

Assumption of both secured and unsecured debts in exchange for matrimonial property can be taken into account in calculating the net recovery or preservation of property but the agreement (or supporting correspondence) should clearly demonstrate if the acquisition of debt is clearly and unambiguously directly referable to the transfer of property to the opponent[1].

1   SLAB, 'Guidance on Property Recovered or Preserved', para 9.7, available at www.slab.org.uk.

8.   Revocation of the agreement

5.18   A separation agreement may be revoked by either party under certain circumstances. While it is open to one of the spouses to offer to reconcile, this offer may be refused if it is a sham[1], or not made in good faith[2], or where the other spouse has reasonable cause (such as her husband's violence) to refuse to resume cohabitation[3]. Reasonable cause to refuse to resume cohabitation will be demonstrated if the spouse refusing to resume cohabitation has an interdict in her favour preventing violence by her husband (or lawburrows against him[4]), or if the separation agreement proceeds on an acknowledgement of his ill-treatment towards her[5]. In the latter of these two cases, the husband must establish judicially that, contrary to his admission, he did not in fact ill treat his wife, before he can revoke the separation agreement[6].

A separation agreement will also be revoked where the parties resume cohabitation with each other[7]. There must be a genuine resumption of cohabitation to effect revocation of the agreement. It was not sufficient to revoke a separation agreement in a case where the wife returned to her husband, but he threw her out two days later[8].

1   *Earl of Argyle v His Lady* (1695) Mor 6054.
2   *Hood v Hood* (1871) 9 M 449.
3   *Home v Lady Eccles* (1734) Mor 6159; *Shand v Shand* (1832) 10 S 384.
4   *AB v CD* (1853) 15 D 372.
5   *Home v Lady Eccles* (1734) Mor 6159; *McKeddie v McKeddie* (1902) 9 SLT 381.
6   *Campbell v Campbell* 1923 SLT 670.
7   *Forbes v Abernethy* (1713) Mor 6154; *Campbell v Campbell* 1976 SLT (Sh Ct) 69; *Bennett v Rennie* 1988 GWD 12-525; *Methven v Methven* 1999 SLT (Sh Ct) 117.
8   *Pearce v Pearce* (1898) 5 SLT 338.

5.19   Where an agreement is revocable, and is revoked, this does not excuse the person obliged to pay money under the agreement from payment of arrears due up until the date of the revocation[1]. A wife formerly had the privilege of revoking an agreement for aliment and suing for a greater amount of aliment where this was required[2]. Nowadays, application should be made for variation of the agreement[3].

1 *Livingston v Begg* (1666) Mor 6153; *Gordon v Gordon* (1715) Mor 6155; *Cumming v Duncan* (1717) Mor 9191.
2 *Cramond v Allan* (1757) Mor 6157; *Lawson v Macculloch* (1797) Mor 6157; *McKeddie v McKeddie* (1902) 9 SLT 381.
3 Family Law (Scotland) Act 1985, s 7.

5.20 Where there is a reconciliation and a second separation, it is open to the parties to make a new separation agreement or ratify the terms of the old one[1].

1 *Lawson v Macculloch* (1797) Mor 6157.

5.21 Neither the surviving spouse nor the deceased spouse's executor can revoke a separation agreement after the death of one of the spouses. In general, the effects of separation agreements will cease with the termination of the marriage by death, but provisions in the agreement affecting rights to aliment, or succession to the other spouse's estate, remain binding on the surviving spouse if the agreement has not been validly revoked during the subsistence of the marriage[1].

A wife could previously revoke the agreement at common law if it was shown to have been grossly unequal[2], but nowadays separation agreements would be challenged as unfair and unreasonable under s 16 of the Family Law (Scotland) Act 1985[3].

1 *Gib v Miller*, 14 March 1634, Durie's Decisions, p 712; *Palmer v Bonar* (1810) 15 FC 535.
2 *Hunter v Dickson* (1831) 5 W&S 455.
3 See CHAPTER 16.

Further research

5.22 Generally:
— Cubie, 'Agreements and Divorcing Clients' 2003 Fam LB 62-2;
— Junor, 'Rescinding Separation Agreements – the Continuing Story' 2000 Fam LB 43-2;
— Junor, 'Separation Agreements and Common Law Remedies' 1998 Fam LB 36-1.

Chapter 6

Cohabitation agreements

'[B]yzitten hier te lande gheen voordeel en hebben boven andere byslaepsters.'

Hugo de Groot, *Inleidinge tot de Hollandsche rechtsgeleerdheid* I, 12, 5

1. Present or contemplated cohabitation

6.01 In the passage above, Grotius sums up a basic principle of law: cohabitants have no financial rights in relation to the other cohabitant by mere fact[1] of their cohabitation. 'They have, in our country, no greater benefits above those women who have sex with men[2]'; or, as Voet more colourfully put it 'concubines have no rights greater than those of other strumpets and harlots[3]'.

Attitudes have moved on: agreements involving present or contemplated cohabitation, once regarded as contrary to public policy[4], are no longer so regarded[5]. But the basic principle remains. If cohabitants want rights and obligations from each other, they must contract for those rights and obligations. If they want to grant rights on succession to their estate to their fellow cohabitant, they must make wills, or mutual wills, to that effect. Alternatively they can marry each other or, in the case of a same sex couple, enter into a civil partnership when the Civil Partnership Act 2004 comes into force.

1 'Le concubinage est une union de fait, caractérisée par une vie commune présentant un caractère de stabilité et de continuité, entre deux personnes, de sexe différent ou de même sexe, qui vivent en couple': Le Code civil francais, art 515-8.
2 'Byslaepsters' has also been translated as 'wenches' by Lees, and as 'abandoned women' by Maasdorp in their translations of Grotius' *Inleiding*.
3 Voet, *Commentary on the Pandects* (The Hague, 1701), 24, 7, 3.
4 *Diwell v Farnes* [1959] 2 All ER 379; *Gloag on Contract* (2nd edn, 1929), p 562.
5 Recommendation No R 88(3) of the Committee of Ministers of the Council of Europe, adopted 7 March 1988; Scottish Law Commission Discussion Paper No 86 on the Effects of Cohabitation in Private Law, May 1990, pp 77, 78; *Sutton v Mischon de Reya (a Firm)* (2003) Times, 19 December.

6.02 It may, however, be the case that the law will render unenforceable cohabitation contracts as being contrary to public policy where:

(a)   the parties to the agreement are within the prohibited degrees of relationship in relation to marriage or civil partnership; or

(b)   one of the parties remains married to, or in civil partnership with, his existing spouse or civil partner.

6.03   Yet, even in these cases the law does not render unlawful the disposal of property between a married person, or civil partner, and his or her paramour, or between persons in the prohibited degrees of relationship[1]. An aggrieved spouse, or (prospectively) civil partner, can, however, in relation to a disposal to a paramour, or other person, apply to the court for interdict, inhibition or an order setting aside or varying a transfer in any case where his claim to aliment or financial provision on divorce, dissolution, or annulment would be defeated by the disposal of the property in question[2].

1   *Young v Johnson and Wright* (1870) 7 R 760; *White v White* 1908 SC 93.
2   Family Law (Scotland) Act 1985, ss 18, 19.

6.04   The following two categories of cohabitation agreement are unenforceable – one for lack of capacity, and the other on public policy grounds:
(a)   where either party is under the age of 16 years[1]; and
(b)   where the purpose of the agreement is for prostitution or is purely meretricious[2].

1   Age of Legal Capacity (Scotland) Act 1991, ss 1(1), 2(5).
2   *Sutton v Mischon de Reya (a Firm)* (2003) Times, 19 December; 'Prostitute loses fight for slave's £500,000' (2003) The Times, 20 December.

6.05   It is not competent to enforce a cohabitation contract so as to compel cohabitation, as:

'a contract will not be enforced to compel residence in a house after that residence has become distasteful to the person concerned[1].'

1   *Kerrigan v Hall* (1901) 4 F 10 at 16, per Lord McLaren.

6.06   More information is given in relation to cohabitation agreements in connection with style 6 in CHAPTER 19.

2.   Past cohabitation

6.07   It is possible to contract so as to provide aliment for a former cohabitant, after cohabitation has ceased[1].

1   *Re Vallance* (1884) 26 ChD 353; *Webster v Webster's Trustee* (1886) 14 R 90.

3. Same sex couples

6.08   Cohabitation contracts are also possible in respect of same sex couples[1].

1   See *Fitzpatrick v Sterling Housing Associate Ltd* [2001] 1 AC 27; *Ghaidan v Godin-Mendoza* [2004] UKHL 30.

Further research

6.09   Generally:
— Barlow, *Cohabitants and the Law* (Butterworths, 3rd edn, 2001);
— Barton, *Cohabitation Contracts* (Gower, 1985);
— *Butterworth's Scottish Family Law Service*, Division B, 'Cohabiting Couples';
— Dempsey, 'Same-Sex Couples in Scots Law' (2002) SCOLAG 181, 201.

Chapter 7

Parenting and surrogacy agreements

'It would, in my opinion, be very dangerous to allow a proof of such an agreement as this, as it would come very near to sanctioning the sale of a child by its parent.'

Lord President Balfour, *Kerrigan v Hall* (1901) 4 F 10 at 13

1. Parents and their children

Parents

7.01 Parents have both legal responsibilities for their children and rights in relation to them. This necessitates definitions of 'parent' and 'child'. A 'parent' means a person's genetic father or mother[1]. There is usually no difficulty in determining who a child's mother is; paternity of children is less assured. The presumption *pater est quem nuptiae demonstrant* decrees that: 'A man shall be presumed to be the father of a child if he was married to the mother of the child at any time in the period beginning with the conception and ending with the birth of the child'[2]. Where this presumption does not apply, a presumption of paternity arises only where both the man and the mother of the child have acknowledged that the man is the father and the man is registered as such in the statutory register in which the child's birth appears; or a decree of declarator is granted to that effect[3].

1 Children (Scotland) Act 1995, s 15(1); but subject to the Human Fertilisation and Embryology Act 1990, ss 27–29.
2 Law Reform (Parent and Child) (Scotland) Act 1986, s 5(1)(a).
3 Law Reform (Parent and Child) (Scotland) Act 1986, s 5(1)(b), (3).

Children

7.02 A 'child' is a person under the age of 18 years, where the expression is not otherwise defined[1]. Parent and child law defines what responsibilities parents have for their children, and what rights they have in relation to their persons and property. In practice, most issues relating to the child's person (upbringing) or property apply until the child is 16; when the child obtains that age, he has legal capacity to enter into transactions on his own behalf, and his parents cease to have the right to determine his place of residence[2]. However, an important exception is in relation to aliment payable for the child's benefit: that may be claimed by his parent, guardian, or other persons caring for him, on the child's behalf, until the child is 18[3].

1   Children (Scotland) Act 1995, s 15(1).
2   Age of Legal Capacity (Scotland) Act 1991, s 1(1)(b); Children (Scotland) Act 1995, ss 1(2)(a), 2(7).
3   Family Law (Scotland) Act 1985, s 2(4)(c).

Acquisition of parental responsibilities

7.03   Men and women acquire parental responsibilities and parental rights in different ways. Women always have parental responsibilities and rights in respect of their children, whether they are married to the child's father or not. Historically, men have acquired parental responsibilities and rights in one of three ways: marriage, legitimation and adoption[1]. To this list may also be added parental orders under s 30 of the Human Fertilisation and Embryology Act 1990 (orders granted by a court in respect of a child who is born in respect of a surrogacy arrangement and who is genetically related to at least one of the applicants for the order, who must be husband and wife, and who must also apply within six months of the birth of a child[2]). Unmarried fathers can acquire parental responsibilities and rights (or any of them) only by virtue of a court order or, in relation to the whole parental responsibilities and rights in respect of a child, by virtue of an agreement between the father and mother in the prescribed form registered in the books of council and session, such agreement being irrevocable, except by subsequent court order[3]. Step-parents can acquire parental responsibilities and rights only by order of the court; there is currently in Scotland no provision allowing step-parents to acquire parental responsibilities and rights by agreement with the child's parents[4].

1   Voet, *Commentary on the Pandects* (The Hague, 1701), 1, 6, 4.
2   Parental Orders (Human Fertilisation and Embryology) (Scotland) Regulations 1994 (SI 1994/2804); CCMR 1997, rr 2.37–2.44.
3   This addresses the legal position with regard to the Children (Scotland) Act 1995, ss 4, 11(2)(b), (11). As to the prescribed form of agreement, see the Parental Responsibilities and Rights Agreement (Scotland) Regulations 1996 (SI 1996/2549).
4   See the position in England and Wales under the Adoption and Children Act 2002, s 112 which, however, remains to be brought into force.

Exercise of parental responsibilities and rights

7.04   Parental responsibilities and rights have to be exercised with due regard to the welfare and wishes of the child concerned, taking into account the child's age and maturity, it being presumed that a child of 12 years of age or more is of sufficient age and maturity to form a view[1]. If more than one person has parental responsibilities and rights, either person may exercise them without the concurrence of the other[2]. If, however, there is a dispute between them, the court will ultimately have to resolve that dispute, having regard to the welfare of the child as the paramount consideration[3]. Parental responsibilities and rights cannot be waived or abandoned[4]. They can be transferred only by adoption order or a parental order under s 30 of the Human Fertilisation and Embryology Act 1990[5].

1   Children (Scotland) Act 1995, s 6(1).
2   Children (Scotland) Act 1995, s 2(2).
3   Children (Scotland) Act 1995, s 11(1), (2), (7)(a).
4   *Kerrigan v Hall* (1901) 4 F 10; Children (Scotland) Act 1995, s 3(5).
5   Adoption (Scotland) Act 1978, s 12(1)–(4); applied to parental orders under the Human Fertilisation and Embryology Act 1990, s 30 by the Parental Orders (Human Fertilisation and Embryology) (Scotland) Regulations 1994 (SI 1994/2804), Sch 1, para 3.

7.05   The court can make an order depriving a person of some or all of his parental responsibilities or parental rights in relation to a child[1]. Parental rights vested in parents can be lost by adoption orders, parental orders made under s 30 of the Human Fertilisation and Embryology Act 1990, or parental orders made under s 86 of the Children (Scotland) Act 1995 in favour of a local authority[2]. Parental responsibilities and rights are also lost with the death of the parent, or child; and when the duration of these responsibilities and rights ends. The insanity, insolvency or absence (including imprisonment) of the parent does not terminate that person's parental responsibilities and rights in relation to the child in the absence of a specific court order to that effect. Divorce or remarriage does not deprive a father of his parental responsibilities and rights[3].

1   Children (Scotland) Act 1995, s 11(2)(a).
2   Adoption (Scotland) Act 1978, s 12; Children (Scotland) Act 1995, s 86(1); see para 7.04, fn 5, regarding parental orders under the Human Fertilisation and Embryology Act 1990, s 30.
3   Spiro, *Law of Parent and Child* (Juta & Co, South Africa, 4th edn, 1985), pp 245–247.

Recognition of parental responsibilities and rights of persons not habitually resident in Scotland

7.06   An adoption order recognised in Scotland by virtue of s 38 of the Adoption (Scotland) Act 1978 has the effect that the child subject to the adoption order is treated as the legitimate child of the adopters[1]. Such persons will therefore have parental responsibilities and rights in respect of the child for the purposes of Scottish Law. This includes (prospectively) adoptions granted in favour of same or opposite sex cohabitants, and civil partners in England and Wales[2]. References to such persons having parental responsibilities under English law will, in Scotland, be taken to mean parental responsibilities and rights[3].

In addition to adoption orders made in England and Wales, Northern Ireland, the Isle of Man and the Channel Islands, adoption orders made in a great many countries are recognised in accordance with the Adoption (Designation of Overseas Adoptions) Order 1973[4]. Such adoptions can be annulled on certain grounds by the Court of Session, under s 47 of the Adoption (Scotland) Act 1978.

Adoption orders can also be recognised at common law[5].

1   Adoption (Scotland) Act 1978, s 39(1).
2   Adoption and Children Act 2002, ss 50, 144(4).
3   Adoption (Scotland) Act 1978; s 53A(1), as prospectively inserted by the Adoption and Children Act 2002, Sch 3, para 30.
4   SI 1973/19; Adoption (Scotland) Act 1978, s 38(1)(c).
5   Adoption (Scotland) Act 1978, s 38(1)(e); Anton and Beaumont, *Private International Law* (2nd edn, 1990), pp 505–507.

7.07   Persons on whom parental responsibilities and rights are conferred by the court of the child's habitual residence, will be recognised as having parental responsibilities and rights in relation to the child[1].

Where there is no such court order, persons will be recognised as having parental responsibilities and rights in relation to a child if parental responsibilities and rights have been granted to that person under the law of the place of the child's habitual residence at the time the person claiming such rights seeks to exercise them[2]. This does not prevent a Scottish court acting in any situation concerning the immediate protection of the child[3].

1   Family Law Act 1986, s 26(1).
2   Children (Scotland) Act 1995, s 14(3)(a).
3   Children (Scotland) Act 1995, s 14(3)(b).

7.08   Unmarried fathers in England and Wales now have parental responsibility for their children if registered in the birth register (including a Scottish birth register) as the child's father[1]. Accordingly, such fathers can exercise parental responsibilities and rights in Scotland if a child is habitually resident in England and Wales at the time the father seeks to exercise his parental responsibility.

1   Adoption and Children Act 2002, s 111.

2. Guardians, legal representatives and children's property

7.09   A child's parents may, by testamentary writing, appoint a person to act as the child's guardian in the event of their death[1]. The guardian, upon taking office, obtains the full extent of parental responsibilities and rights in relation to the child, provided that on the death of the parent appointing the guardian, the parent was entitled to act as the child's legal representative[2]. The appointment may be revoked by the parent prior to his or her death[3]. It terminates on the child attaining the age of 18 years, on the death of the child or guardian, or by court order[4]. If the guardian takes up office, he may himself in writing appoint a guardian to act after his death[5].

1   Children (Scotland) Act 1995, s 7(1).
2   Children (Scotland) Act 1995, s 7(1)(a)(ii), (5).
3   Children (Scotland) Act 1995, s 8(1)–(4).
4   Children (Scotland) Act 1995, s 8(5).

5   Children (Scotland) Act 1995, s 7(2).

7.10   The court also has power to appoint a guardian to a child[1]. But in this case it is not clear whether the appointment confers full parental responsibilities and rights on the guardian, or limits him in acting only as the child's legal representative. In practice, the court is likely to specify exactly what powers the guardian has been granted[2].

1   Children (Scotland) Act 1995, s 11(2)(h).
2   Wilkinson and Norrie, *Parent and Child* (2nd edn, 1999 by Kenneth Norrie), p 217, para 7.22.

7.11   Persons with parental responsibilities and rights, and guardians, have the right to act as a child's legal representative. This means that the person or guardian so acting may, in the interests of the child, administer any property belonging to the child and act in, or give consent to, any transaction in respect of which the child is incapable of so acting or consenting on his own behalf[1]. In administering the child's property, he must act as a reasonable and prudent person would act on his own behalf[2]. Subject to any restriction or direction imposed by court order, he is entitled to do anything which the child, if of full age and capacity, could do in relation to the property[3].

1   Children (Scotland) Act 1995, s 15(5).
2   Children (Scotland) Act 1995, s 10(1)(a).
3   Children (Scotland) Act 1995, s 10(1)(b).

7.12   A person validly appointed guardian to a child furth of Scotland in accordance with the law of the place of the child's habitual residence will be recognised as the child's guardian in Scotland[1], and will have the powers accorded to guardians in accordance with the law of the place of the child's habitual residence at the date of the exercise of the power concerned[2].

1   Children (Scotland) Act 1995, s 14(3)(c).
2   Children (Scotland) Act 1995, s 14(3)(a).

3. Adoption and surrogacy arrangements

7.13   Parental rights do not confer any sort of ownership of children on their parents. Parents cannot, therefore, lawfully sell, or enter into any sort of commercial transaction for the sale of their children[1]. It is an offence in particular circumstances:
(a)   to bring a child into the United Kingdom for the purposes of adoption, or to remove a child from the United Kingdom for that purpose[2];
(b)   to make any payment for the adoption, or arranging the adoption of a child[3];
(c)   to advertise for the adoption of a child[4];
(d)   to negotiate a surrogacy arrangement on a commercial basis[5]; and
(e)   to advertise about surrogacy arrangements[6].

1   *Reid v Scot* Fountainhall's Decisions of the Court of Session (1678–1712) 13 January 1687; Slave Trade Act 1824, s 9.

2   Adoption (Scotland) Act 1978, ss 50, 50A (prospectively amended and, in the case of s 50A substituted, by the Adoption and Children Act 2002, s 133); Adoption of Children from Overseas (Scotland) Regulations 2001 (SSI 2001/236).
3   Adoption (Scotland) Act 1978, s 51.
4   Adoption (Scotland) Act 1978, s 52 (prospectively repealed and replaced by the Adoption and Children Act 2002, s 123).
5   Surrogacy Arrangements Act 1985, s 2.
6   Surrogacy Arrangements Act 1985, s 3.

4. Private fostering of children

7.14   A foster child is a child being cared for by a person other than his parents, relatives or guardian[1].

Private fostering arrangements are subject to the provisions of the Foster Children (Scotland) Act 1984 and the Foster Children (Private Fostering) (Scotland) Regulations 1985[2]. In particular, these prohibit certain persons from keeping foster children without the local authority's written consent, and prohibit those certain persons from advertising their wish to foster children[3]. A parent must notify the local authority of his intention to foster his children[4], and a foster parent his intention to foster the child[5]. The local authority then undertakes an enquiry into the suitability of these arrangements[6].

A person who is not disqualified from doing so may advertise his willingness to foster children provided he truly states his name and address[7].

The Scottish Ministers have power to make regulations prohibiting a parent or guardian from advertising his child for fostering[8].

1   Foster Children (Scotland) Act 1984, s 1.
2   SI 1985/1798.
3   Foster Children (Scotland) Act 1984, s 14(3); SI 1985/1798, reg 8.
4   Foster Children (Scotland) Act 1984, s 4; SI 1985/1798, reg 3.
5   Foster Children (Scotland) Act 1984, s 5; SI 1985/1798, reg 5.
6   SI 1985/1798, regs 4, 5.
7   Foster Children (Scotland) Act 1984; s 14(1).
8   Foster Children (Scotland) Act 1984, s 14(2).

5. Enforceability and effect of surrogacy and other arrangements for care by persons other than child's parents

7.15   Surrogacy[1] and other arrangements whereby a person other than the child's parent or guardian assumes responsibility for the child's care and upbringing are competent[2], but unenforceable[3]; but this does not prejudice the court from determining adoption and parental responsibilities and rights applications by those persons, and making appropriate orders in the best interests of the children concerned[4]. Any private surrogacy or other arrangements for a child, resulting in the child being looked after by persons not his parents, relatives or guardian, is subject to the provisions of the Foster Children (Scotland) Act 1984[5]. Persons without parental responsibility and rights looking after a child can do what is reasonable in all the circumstances to safeguard the child's health, development and welfare, despite lacking parental responsibilities and rights in relation to the child[6].

1   Surrogacy Arrangements Act 1985, s 1A.
2   Children (Scotland) Act 1985, s 3(5).
3   *Kerrigan v Hall* (1901) 4 F 10.
4   *C v S* 1996 SLT 1387.
5   Children (Scotland) Act 1985, s 3(6).
6   Children (Scotland) Act 1985, s 5.

6. Parenting agreements

7.16   Persons having joint parental responsibilities and rights in relation to a child may wish to enter into a parenting agreement (otherwise known as a 'parenting plan') concerning such matters as:
(a)   the child's living arrangements;
(b)   the child's religious and cultural upbringing;
(c)   the child's school and out-of-school activities;
(d)   holidays; and
(e)   the child's health.

Such an agreement should be signed by the child's parents, and any other interested person involved with the child's upbringing, such as a step-parent or a grandparent. Each parent, and other signatory, should have a copy of the agreement, and they should agree on a timescale for reviewing the arrangements made under the agreement. The child's wishes should be taken into account when drawing up the agreement, where the child is of an age and degree of maturity to understand the implications of the decision in question[1].

1   Children (Scotland) Act 1995, s 6(1).

7.17   Parenting agreements are not ultimately enforceable as the court must regard the child's interests as paramount in any question relating to the child's welfare or administration of his property that comes before the court[1].

However, the parents can agree by formal deed, to restrict (but not to abdicate) their right to exercise a particular parental responsibility or right in relation to the child by not exercising it unless the parent obtains the other's consent[2].

This would be a recipe for endless interference and conflict unless applied only to the most important decisions concerning the child. Only the parents can define what these are, but in many cases they are likely to include: the child's name; the school which the child is to attend; the child's religious, or non-religious upbringing; and major health decisions, particularly where the child is ill or has a disability.

The parenting agreement (CHAPTER 19, style 9) thus confers on Mrs Allan, as the parent with whom Annabel and Catherine are living, the right to take day-to-day decisions for the children and their property, but to consult Mr Allan on major decisions relating to the children's upbringing.

1   *Kerrigan v Hall* (1901) 4 F 10; Children (Scotland) Act 1995, s 11(7).
2   Children (Scotland) Act 1995, ss 2(2), 3(5).

7.18   Style 7 in CHAPTER 19 combines a formal agreement on certain major issues, with the option for the parties to enter into an informal, but written, parenting agreement. To facilitate the parties entering into that between themselves, it seems unnecessary for an informal type of agreement to be registered in the court books for preservation. Nevertheless, the parties should each keep a copy of it.

7.19   There are many examples of parenting agreements available on the internet, usually from the USA[1]. Although drafted for England and Wales, it would be possible in Scotland to make use of the Department of Constitutional Affairs' form of parenting plan, copies of which are available in booklet form from the Department, or on its website[2].

1   Search under 'parenting agreement' and/or 'parenting plan'.
2   www.dca.gov.uk.

7.20   Child abduction issues are always suitable for a formal agreement. First, all persons having parental responsibilities and rights in relation to a child, or a residence or contact order in relation to the child, must consent to a child being removed or retained from the United Kingdom[1]. Secondly, it is a criminal offence for one parent to take or send a child out of the United Kingdom if the other parent has been granted a residence order in respect of the child, without the consent of that other parent, or leave of the court[2].

1   Children (Scotland) Act 1995, s 2(3), (6).
2   Child Abduction Act 1984, s 6.

7.21   The effect of these provisions is that the consent of the other parent, or leave of the court, is required if a child is to be taken out of the United Kingdom by one of the parents, even for a short holiday abroad[1]. A formal agreement is a useful way of recording such consent.

1   Scottish Law Commission, 'Consultative Memorandum No 67 on Child Abduction', para 3.17.

7. Parenting agreements as authentic instruments and enforceable agreements in the European Union

7.22   From 1 March 2005 two categories of agreement on parental responsibility will be recognised and can be enforced as though a court judgment of the European Union ('EU') Member State (except Denmark) in which it was made.

These categories are:

(a)   agreements formally drawn up or registered as authentic instruments and enforceable in one Member State; and

(b)   agreements between the parties that are enforceable in the Member State in which they were concluded.

'Parental responsibilities' means all rights and duties relating to the person or property of a child, given by judgment, operation of law or by an agreement having legal effect[2].

1   Council Regulation (EC) 2201/2003 of 27 November 2003 concerning jurisdiction and the recognition and enforcement of judgments in matrimonial matters and the matters of parental responsibility, art 46 (OJ L338, 23.12.2003, p 1, repealing Regulation (EC) 1347/2000); Jamieson 'The New Law on Parental Responsibility' 2004 SLT (News) 51.
2   Council Regulation (EC) 2201/2003, art 2(7).

7.23   The key word, in relation to both categories of agreement, is 'enforceable'.

Scottish agreements conferring or relating to the exercise of the parental responsibilities and rights are not enforceable in Scotland[1]. Thus they should not be exportable for enforcement in the other EU Member States.

1   *Kerrigan v Hall* (1901) 4 F 10.

7.24   However, it may be safer, if concluding a family law agreement to be registered in the books of council and session for execution, which has an EU dimension, to exclude parental responsibilities and rights from the main body of the agreement, and have a separate parental responsibilities and rights agreement, perhaps registered in court books for preservation, but not for execution[1]. This will then put the matter beyond doubt: it will not be an authentic instrument, enforceable in another Member State[2].

1   See CHAPTER **19**, style 8.
2   If there is no warrant for execution in an extract of the agreement, it cannot qualify as an authentic instrument as it lacks an essential element of the definition of authentic instrument. Registration is not enough: see para **14.08**.

7.25   Agreements enforceable in another Member State will be enforceable in Scotland as authentic instruments or enforceable agreements in the State in which they were concluded. Scottish clients should therefore be wary about entering into enforceable parental responsibility agreements in other EU Member States.

Further research

7.26   Generally:
— Cleland and Dick, *Child Centred Family Law Practice* (W Green, 2001).

7.27   On same sex parenting, see:
— Lehmann, *The Gay and Lesbian Family and Marriage Reader* (Gordion Knot Books, University of Nebraska Press, 2001);
— Morgan, 'Adoption Law: Sidelining stability and security' (Christian Institute, 2002);
— Morgan, 'Children as trophies? Examining the Evidence on same-sex parenting' (Christian Institute, 2002).

7.28   On how to become the legal parents of a surrogate child in the Netherlands, see:
— www.notaris.nl.

Chapter 8

Aliment and financial provision

Introduction

8.01 This chapter concentrates solely on the role of agreements for aliment, or periodical allowance.

The style separation agreements – styles 1 and 2 – in CHAPTER 19, and the notes to those styles, consider other aspects of financial provision on divorce, particularly in relation to the matrimonial home, and payment of a capital sum.

It is assumed that solicitors will agree separation agreements for their clients on the basis of the principles contained in the Family Law (Scotland) Act 1985 and will be familiar with those principles; hence this book does not go into these in any detail[1].

1   The most up-to-date commentary on them is by Anne H Dick, Solicitor, in her annotations to the Family Law (Scotland) Act 1985 in *Greens Scottish Family Law Legislation* (1997, and regularly updated, ed George Jamieson).

1. Creating maintenance obligations

A fundamental distinction

8.02 In drawing up separation agreements, a fundamental point that solicitors must keep in mind is the difference between aliment between spouses (marriage only) and periodical allowance (on and after divorce).

Agreements on aliment between spouses are regulated by the Family Law (Scotland) Act 1985, s 7; and on periodical allowance by s 16 of the Act.

There is no right to statutory aliment between divorced spouses. If the separation agreement refers to aliment in these circumstances, it will be binding on the parties, but there will be no statutory mechanism for varying the amount payable on a material change of circumstances[1]. This situation is highly undesirable, and always to be avoided.

1   *Drummond v Drummond* 1995 SC 321.

Unilateral obligations

8.03   If the sole area of agreement is in relation to aliment to be paid to a spouse, or for the children, during the parties' separation, then this might be constituted in writing as a unilateral obligation undertaken towards the other spouse, or the children (an 'alimentary bond')[1]. Such an obligation must be in writing to be valid[2].

1   Debtors (Scotland) Act 1987, s 106 (part (h) of definition of 'maintenance order').
2   Requirements of Writing (Scotland) Act 1995, s 1(2)(a)(ii).

2.   Variation of aliment and periodical allowance

Aliment

8.04   An application may be made under s 7(2) of the Family Law (Scotland) Act 1985 to vary or terminate an agreement on aliment on a material change of circumstances. The application in the sheriff court is made by summary application where no family action has been raised[1] or by crave in the initial writ or defences of a family action which has been raised[2]. 'Agreement' means an agreement entered into before or after the Family Law (Scotland) Act 1985 came into force and includes a unilateral voluntary obligation[3]. 'Material change' includes the making of a maintenance assessment under the Child Support Act 1991[4]. The aliment payable in respect of a child cannot be increased under s 7(2) of the Family Law (Scotland) Act 1985 if the court would not in certain circumstances have jurisdiction to make a maintenance order by virtue of s 8 of the Child Support Act 1991[5]; and a parent cannot apply for variation in respect of a child aged over 18[6]. Interim variation is not competent in respect of any obligation of aliment constituted by an agreement[7].

1   OCR 1993, r 33.59(1); *Young v Young* 1995 GWD 32-1635 (for the former rule, see *Mackenzie v Mackenzie* 1987 SCLR 671).
2   OCR 1993, r 33.59(2).
3   Family Law (Scotland) Act 1985, s 7(5).
4   Family Law (Scotland) Act 1985, s 7(2A).
5   Child Support Act 1991, s 9(5)(b); see para **9.13**.
6   *Hay v Hay* 2000 SLT (Sh Ct) 95.
7   *Woolley v Strachen* 1997 SLT (Sh Ct) 88.

8.05 The Family Law (Scotland) Act 1985, s 7(2) does not apply to obligations of aliment which are not owed by virtue of s 1(1) of the Act, eg aliment agreed between cohabiting or divorced couples who choose to create obligations akin to the statutory obligations[1]. The court having jurisdiction to vary or terminate the agreement is the court which would have jurisdiction and competence to entertain an application for aliment between the parties to the agreement[2]. Therefore, either the maintenance creditor or debtor must be domiciled or habitually resident in the sheriffdom, or the parties must have prorogated the jurisdiction of the court[3]. The sheriff may decline jurisdiction on account of *forum non conveniens*[4].

1   *Drummond v Drummond* 1995 SC 321.
2   Family Law (Scotland) Act 1985, s 7(4).
3   Civil Jurisdiction and Judgments Act 1982, ss 2(5), 5, Sch 8.
4   *L v L* 2000 SLT (Sh Ct) 12.

8.06 An agreement which purports to exclude future liability for aliment or to restrict any right to bring an action for aliment is of no effect unless fair and reasonable in all the circumstances of the agreement at the time it was entered into[1].

1   Family Law (Scotland) Act 1985, s 7(1).

Periodical allowance

8.07 The court has jurisdiction to vary or set aside an agreement relating to periodical allowance but only where this power has been specifically conferred on the court in the agreement[1]; if this is not done, the court does not have the power to set aside or vary the agreement as to periodical allowance[2]. The power to vary the agreement may be exercised at any time after granting decree of divorce[3].

1   Family Law (Scotland) Act 1985, s 16(1)(a).
2   *Ellerby v Ellerby* 1991 SCLR 608.
3   Family Law (Scotland) Act 1985, s 16(2)(a).

8.08 The agreement may also be varied or set aside by the court in relation to periodical allowance on the debtor's insolvency[1], or where child support maintenance has become payable by either party to the agreement with respect to a child to whom or for whose benefit periodical allowance is paid under the agreement[2]. Any term of the agreement which purports to restrict the right to apply for variation or setting aside of the periodical allowance in any of these circumstances is void[3].

1   Family Law (Scotland) Act 1985, s 16(3)(a)–(c).
2   Family Law (Scotland) Act 1985, s 16(d) (as inserted by the Child Support (Amendments to Primary Legislation) (Scotland) Order 1993 (SI 1993/660), art 2(5)(b)). This subsection does not make grammatical sense: periodical allowance is not paid to a child. What it probably means is that there is a material change of circumstances if the parent receiving periodical allowance under the agreement becomes entitled to child support maintenance.
3   Family Law (Scotland) Act 1985, s 16(4).

3. Agreement post-decree to vary aliment or periodical allowance

Aliment

8.09   In principle, the same considerations apply to variation of an aliment decree by agreement as apply to variation of a decree for periodical allowance[1]. Applications to the court for variation of an aliment decree are made by minute in the original process of a sheriff court action for aliment[2], and by motion in the original process of a Court of Session action for aliment[3]. It is possible to apply by family action in the sheriff court for variation of a Court of Session aliment decree[4].

1   See paras **8.10–8.13**. However, an informal agreement to a new aliment might be variable under the Family Law (Scotland) Act 1985, s 7(2).
2   OCR 1993, r 33.58(2).
3   RCS 1994, r 49.43(1).
4   OCR 1993, r 33.84; Law Reform (Miscellaneous Provisions) (Scotland) Act 1966, s 8.

Periodical allowance

8.10   An agreement to vary a periodical allowance awarded by the court is not in itself effectual, but may form the basis for applying to the court for variation of the decree[1].

1   *MacDonnell v MacDonnell* 2001 SC 77.

8.11   Any agreement which purports to grant additional periodical allowance, or to reduce the amount due under the decree, must be framed with the greatest of care, and preferably with reference to the decree itself.

Although it is usually best for parties to arrange their affairs amicably by means of agreement, an unopposed application to the court for variation of the decree to the agreed sum may often be the most expedient way of proceeding.

This could be achieved by formal letters between the parties' solicitors, whereby the parties agree to pay the increased amount until formal variation takes place by the court[1]. The creditor, if agreeing to accept less, could grant an undertaking not to enforce the arrears beyond the agreed amount and period of reduction; such period could be extended by subsequent letter, or made conditional on a change in circumstances which would have to be communicated to the creditor by the debtor upon it taking place.

The parties could also agree to the recall of a decree for periodical allowance and its substitution by an agreement on periodical allowance[2].

1   It is doubtful whether the court may vary an informal agreement of this nature. For this reason, any obligations so constituted should be limited in time, say to three months, or earlier variation: *Jackson v Jackson* 2003 GWD 33-941.
2   Family Law (Scotland) Act 1985, s 13(4)(a).

8.12   There is a further risk in trying to vary a degree by agreement: any additional sum to be paid by way of the agreement may not be a periodical allowance capable of variation by the court as the court may only vary or set aside an agreement made for periodical allowance 'on' (ie not after) divorce[1].

For this reason as well, it may be best just to agree to the court making a post-decree periodical allowance, when none has existed before[2], or to agree variation of an existing order[3]. Subsequent variation can be made by unopposed application to the court where the parties agree on the new amount to be paid[4].

1   Family Law (Scotland) Act 1985, s 16(1)(a).
2   Family Law (Scotland) Act 1985, s 13(1)(c).
3   Family Law (Scotland) Act 1985, s 13(4).
4   Family Law (Scotland) Act 1985, s 13(4).

8.13   Applications post-decree for variation of periodical allowance are made by minute in the original process in the sheriff court[1], and by motion in the original process in the Court of Session[2]. Variation of a Court of Session decree may also be sought by family action in the sheriff court[3].

1   OCR 1993, r 33.51(1).
2   RCS 1994, r 49.49(1).
3   OCR 1993, r 33.84; Law Reform (Miscellaneous Provisions) (Scotland) Act 1966, s 8.

Chapter 9

Child support and its effects on separation agreements

Introduction

9.01   The Child Support Agency ('CSA') began its phased takeover of child maintenance cases from the courts on 5 April 1993[1]. Since then, there have been a number of significant changes to the child support regime[2]. The current regime dates from 3 March 2003[3]. The operation of that regime is outside the remit of this book[4]; this chapter deals only with the effects the Child Support Act 1991 (as amended)[5] has on separation agreements registered in the books of council and session or sheriff court books, prior to 3 March 2003, and those made on or after that date, so far as children under the age of 16 are concerned[6].

1   Child Support Act 1991 (Commencement No 3 and Transitional Provisions) Order 1992 (SI 1992/2644, substituted and later repealed in part by SI 1993/996 and the Child Support Act 1995, s 18(8)); *Pope v Pope* 1995 SCLR 963; *McGilchrist v McGilchrist* 1997 SCLR 800.
2   Principally as a result of amendments made by the Child Support Act 1995 and the Child Support, Pensions and Social Security Act 2000.
3   Child Support (Applications: Prescribed Date) Regulations 2003 (SI 2003/194).
4   But see Bird, 'Child Maintenance: the New Law' *Family Law*, 2000.
5   See fn 2.
6   Child Support Act 1991, s 55(1)(a). See Bird, above, paras 2.5–2.9; and the Child Support (Maintenance Calculation Procedure) Regulations 2000 (SI 2000/157), Sch 1, for the position in relation to children over that age.

1. Jurisdiction: non-benefit cases

9.02   In most cases, the CSA will have jurisdiction to make and enforce a maintenance calculation against a non-resident parent[1].

Either that person, or the person with whom the child has his home (which will usually, but not necessarily, be his other parent)[2] may make application to the CSA for a maintenance calculation in respect of the child under s 4 of the Child Support Act 1991[3].

Such application is likely to be made, in practice, only if the parties concerned cannot reach agreement as to the amount of maintenance to be paid for the child or, having registered a written aliment agreement in the books of council and session or sheriff court books on or after 3 March 2003, one of the parties considers it more advantageous to have a maintenance calculation in the following year[4].

1   Child Support Act 1991, ss 1, 3, 29. The courts retain jurisdiction to make a maintenance order against a person with care of the child: Child Support Act 1991, s 8(10).
2   Child Support Act 1991, s 3(3).
3   Child Support Act 1991, s 4(1).
4   CSA jurisdiction in these cases is excluded only for a period of one year: see para **9.06**.

9.03   Where the CSA has jurisdiction to make a maintenance calculation under s 4 of the Child Support Act 1991, the jurisdiction of the court to award aliment for the child is ousted[1], except in relation to additional awards of aliment where:
(a)   a maintenance calculation has been made and the non-resident parent's net earnings exceed £2,000 a week[2];
(b)   the award is for the child's educational needs[3]; or
(c)   the child has a disability, and the award is to meet some or all of the expenses attributable to that disability[4].
In the latter two categories[5], the existence of a maintenance order does not preclude the parent with care, or child, applying for a maintenance calculation[6].

1   Child Support Act 1991, ss 8(1)–(3), 11(d).
2   Child Support Act 1991, s 8(6), Sch 1, para 10(3).
3   Child Support Act 1991, s 8(7).
4   Child Support Act 1991, s 8(8), (9).
5   Child Support Act 1995, s 18(7) allows the Secretary of State to prescribe additional categories.
6   Child Support Act 1995, s 18(6).

9.04   The court may also exercise its jurisdiction to make a maintenance order against the non-resident parent in the circumstances prescribed under s 8(5) of the Child Support Act 1991[1]. These are that there exists in relation to the child:
(a)   a written agreement (whether or not enforceable) providing for the making, or securing, by the non-resident parent of periodical payments to or for the benefit of the child; and
(b)   the maintenance order which the court makes is, in all material respects, in the same terms as that agreement[2].

1   Child Maintenance (Written Agreements) Order 1993 (SI 1993/620, in force 5 April 1993, England and Wales only); Child Support (Written Agreements) (Scotland) Order 1997 (SI 1997/2943, in force 2 January 1998).
2   Child Support Act 1991, s 8(5).

9.05   An order under s 8(5) of the Child Support Act 1991 is, in effect, a consent order of the court[1]. Until 3 March 2003, it was the principal means of eliding CSA jurisdiction in England and Wales[2]. The current position is that consent orders oust CSA jurisdiction for only one year beginning with the date of the court order[3]. Practitioners in England and Wales have been advised to renew their consent orders each year, in order to achieve the continued ousting of CSA jurisdiction[4].

1   Bird, 'Child Maintenance; the New Law' *Family Law* (2000), para 10.29, p 107; Neilson, 'Simple Support?' (2003) LS Gaz 100/10, pp 18, 19.
2   *V v V (Child Maintenance; Periodical Payments)* [2001] 2 FLR 799.
3   Child Support Act 1991, s 4(10)(aa); Bird, 'The Murky Waters of Child Support' (2002) LS Gaz 99/15, p 37.
4   Pirrie, 'Time for the Courts to Stand up to Child Support Act?' – an address to district judges', [2002] Fam Law 114.

9.06   Consent orders as a means of eliding CSA jurisdiction have only been possible in Scotland since 2 January 1998[1]. However, in practice they are neither necessary nor used very often (if at all) since an agreement for child maintenance registered in the books of council and session or sheriff court books is in itself a 'maintenance order' for the purposes of the Child Support Act 1991[2]. In the unusual case of an agreement not so registered, because there is no consent in it to its registration for execution, it would be possible to obtain a court order by applying under s 8(5) of the Child Support Act 1991[3]. A registered agreement, or Scottish consent order, for payment of aliment by the non-resident parent to the person having care of the child, elides CSA jurisdiction entirely, if registered before 3 March 2003, or for one year if registered on or after that date[4]. The CSA will, however, obtain jurisdiction if the person caring for the child subsequently obtains benefits[5].

1   Child Support (Written Agreements) (Scotland) Order 1997 (SI 1997/2943), art 1.
2   *Commissioners Case No CSCS/5/97* (1999) Fam L R 37.
3   Bird, 'Child Support: the New Law' *Family Law* (2000), para 10.29, p 107.
4   Child Support Act 1991, s 4(10)(a), (aa).
5   See para **9.08**.

2. Jurisdiction: non-benefit cases – children

9.07   A child aged 12 or over who is habitually resident in Scotland can apply to the CSA under s 7 of the Child Support Act 1991 for a maintenance calculation to be made against his non-resident parent if no such application has been made by the person caring for him[1]. The jurisdiction of the court to award aliment against his non-resident parent is ousted to the same extent as an application for aliment on the child's behalf by the person caring for him[2]. The child has capacity to instruct a solicitor to draw up an aliment agreement with his non-resident parent if he has a general understanding of what this means[3]. Any such agreement duly registered in court books ousts CSA jurisdiction for one year, or entirely, if made before 3 March 2003[4]. The CSA will, however, retain jurisdiction if the person caring for the child is treated as having applied for a maintenance calculation in any case where that person is receiving benefits[5].

1 Child Support Act 1991, s 7(1).
2 See paras **9.03–9.06**.
3 Age of Legal Capacity (Scotland) Act 1991, s 2(4A).
4 See para **9.06**.
5 See para **9.08**.

3. Jurisdiction: benefit cases

9.08 The person caring for the child cannot apply for a maintenance calculation under s 4 of the Child Support Act 1991 if benefit is being paid to that person in respect of caring for the child[1]. In these cases, the claimant may be treated by the Secretary of State as having applied for a maintenance calculation under s 6 of the Act [2]. Where that happens, the child is also precluded from applying for a maintenance calculation under s 7 of the Child Support Act 1991[3]. 'Benefit' for these purposes means income support and income-based jobseekers' allowance[4] and certain prescribed benefits[5]. The prescribed benefits include disability working allowance[6].

1 Child Support Act 1991, s 4(10)(b).
2 Child Support Act 1991, s 6(3).
3 Child Support Act 1991, s 7(1)(b).
4 Child Support Act 1991, ss 4(11), 6(1).
5 Child Support Act 1991, s 6(1);
6 Child Support (Maintenance Assessment Procedure) Regulations 1992 (SI 1992/1813), reg 34.

9.09 An application under s 6 of the Child Support Act 1991 differs from applications under ss 4 or 7 of the Act with respect to registered agreements, or consent orders under s 8(5), for payment of aliment for the benefit of children of non-resident parents in that the agreement does not have any effect so as to elide CSA jurisdiction. In benefit cases, CSA jurisdiction will therefore take precedence over the agreement, or over any order made by the court under s 8(5) of the Child Support Act 1991, whatever the date of the agreement or order[1].

1 Section 6 contains no exclusion of jurisdiction of the CSA as found in the Child Support Act 1991, s 4(10)(a) and (aa) in relation to section 4 applications, or Child Support Act 1991, ss 7(10)(a) and (b) in relation to section 7 applications. Other important sections, determining the relationship of court maintenance orders and maintenance agreements, on the one hand, and maintenance calculations, on the other, refer to Child Support Act 1991, ss 4(10) and 7(10), but not to equivalent provisions of s 6 for the obvious reason that there are no such provisions; see also Child Support Act 1991, ss 8(3A) and 9(3).

4. Jurisdiction: written maintenance agreements made before 5 April 1993

9.10   No application may be made under either ss 4 or 7 of the Child Support Act 1991 if there is in force a written maintenance agreement made before 5 April 1993[1].

This provision is of limited significance in Scotland, owing to the prevalence of registering written aliment agreements, by consent in the agreement, in the books of council and session or sheriff court books. From the date of such registration, the agreement becomes equivalent to a maintenance order for the purposes of CSA jurisdiction[2].

However, if the agreement has not been so registered, and is in writing, then it will exclude CSA jurisdiction if made before 5 April 1993.

'Made' in this context means the same as date of execution, which will normally be the later of the two dates on which the parties signed the agreement[3].

1   Child Support Act 1991, ss 4(10)(a), 7(10)(a).
2   *Commissioners Case No CSCS/5/97* (1999) Fam L R 37; see para **9.15**.
3   See para **3.14** for the meaning of the word 'execution'.

5. Variation of agreements for aliment payable by non-resident parent

9.11   The practice, even in relation to agreements registered in the books of council and session or sheriff court books for execution, is to apply for variation of the agreement under s 7 of the Family Law (Scotland) Act 1985[1]. There is, however, no point in applying for such a variation if a maintenance calculation is made under s 6 of the Child Support Act 1991, or under ss 4 or 7 of the Child Support Act 1991 in relation to an agreement registered on or after 3 March 2003 at any time after one year beginning with the date of registration[2]. In these cases the agreement is unenforceable for the period the maintenance calculation is in force[3]. It becomes enforceable again whenever a child support officer no longer has jurisdiction to make a maintenance calculation with respect to the child[4].

1   See para **8.04**; *Woolley v Strachan* 1997 SLT (Sh Ct) 88.
2   Child Support Act 1991, ss 4(10)(aa), 7(10)(b).
3   Child Support Act 1991, s 10(2); Child Support (Maintenance Arrangements and Jurisdiction) Regulations 1992 (SI 1992/2645), reg 4(1), (2).
4   SI 1992/2645, reg 4(3).

9.12   Where no maintenance calculation is in force, the court, if prevented from making a maintenance order because its jurisdiction has been ousted in favour of the CSA, is also prevented from varying an aliment agreement by inserting a provision in it that the non-resident parent makes or secures the making of periodical payments by way of aliment to or for the child's benefit[1].

1   Child Support Act 1991, s 9(5)(a).

9.13   The court is also precluded from *increasing* the amount of aliment payable for the child under the agreement if its jurisdiction to make a maintenance order in respect of the child will be excluded under s 6 of Child Support Act 1991[1]. This restriction applies from the date the person receiving benefits for the child is treated is having applied for a maintenance calculation under s 6(3) of the Act, not from the date of any calculation subsequently made[2]. It does not apply where the court retains jurisdiction under ss 4 or 7 of the Act (non-benefit cases)[3] to vary an agreement registered before 3 March 2003 or, within one year of registration of an agreement registered after that date[4].

1   Child Support Act 1991, s 9(5)(b), (6).
2   Child Support Act 1991, s 9(6)(a), (b).
3   Child Support Act 1991, s 9(6).
4   Child Support Act 1991, s 9(6), read with ss 4(10) and 7(10).

6. Child Support Act 1991 and agreements about maintenance

9.14   The Child Support Act 1991 does not prevent two or more persons entering into an agreement for the making, or for the securing of the making, of periodical payments by way of aliment for the benefit of any child[1].

Except in relation to agreements executed before 5 April 1993, the existence of the agreement does not prevent any party to the agreement, or any other person, applying for a maintenance calculation with respect to the child[2]. The reference to 'any other person' must be taken to mean a person with care of the child[3], or the child himself, if able to apply under s 7 of the Child Support Act 1991[4]. In addition, the restrictions on applying for a maintenance calculation referred to above[5] must also be considered as applicable in this context[6].

Any provision in a family law agreement which purports to restrict the right of any person to apply for a maintenance calculation is void[7].

1   Child Support Act 1991, s 9(1)(2).
2   Child Support Act 1991, s 9(3).
3   Child Support Act 1991, s 4(1).
4   Child Support Act 1991, s 7(1); see para **9.07**.
5   See paras **9.06** and **9.07**.
6   Child Support Act 1991, s 9(3) is in terms subject only to Child Support Act 1991, ss 4(10)(a) and 7(10). Since s 7(10) is referred to without any limitation, s 9(3) must have in mind here both s 7(10)(a) and (b). These correspond to s 4(10)(a) and (aa). No reference is made to s 4(10)(aa) in s 9(3). The explanation is probably that only ss 4(10)(a) *and* 7(10)(a) matter in the context of maintenance agreements, English law not having any equivalent to registration for execution in the court books. Section 9(3) is

about agreements, so it need only mention, by reference, agreements in other parts of the Child Support Act 1991. Once a written agreement is registered by consent in Scotland, it is equivalent to a court decree, ie a maintenance order: see paras **9.05** and **9.06**.

7   Child Support Act 1991, s 9(4).

7. Significance of date of registration of agreement for aliment payable by non-resident parent

9.15   An agreement for aliment payable by the non-resident parent qualifies as a maintenance order from the date of its registration in the books of council and session or sheriff court books[1]. Accordingly, it is the date of registration of the agreement that determines whether it is a maintenance order made before, or on or after, 3 March 2003 for the purposes of ss 4 and 7 of the Child Support Act 1991.

1   Maxwell, *The Practice of the Court of Session* (Scottish Courts Administration, Edinburgh, 1979), p 60.

8. Exclusion of CSA jurisdiction

9.16   The two principal cases in which the CSA does not have jurisdiction are:

(a) In relation to step-children. CSA jurisdiction applies only in respect of parents[1] and their own children. Adopted children and children subject to a parental order under s 30 of the Human Fertilisation and Embryology Act 1990 are included as a person's children for the purposes of the Child Support Act 1991[2].

(b) In relation to cases where any of the parent with care, non-resident parent, or the child is not habitually resident in the United Kingdom[3].

1   See para **7.01** for the meaning of 'parent'.
2   See para **7.04**, fn 5, para **7.05**, fn 2.
3   Child Support Act 1991, s 44(1); s 44(2A) contains some exceptions in relation to certain non-UK habitual residences of a non-resident parent. See also the Child Support (Maintenance Arrangements and Jurisdiction) Regulations 1992 (SI 1992/2645), reg 7A.

9. Practical considerations

9.17   The most important practical consideration applies in respect of non-benefit cases. Since, in these cases, a registered agreement will exclude CSA jurisdiction for only one year after registration where the date of registration is on or after 3 March 2003, it will be necessary to enter into new registered agreements for aliment each year. The styles in CHAPTER 19 (numbers 11 and 12) deal with this in more detail, taking into account the fact that the agreement would remain in force if no new aliment agreement, or application to the CSA, is made after that one year.

9.18 All aliment agreements for more than one child should constitute obligations separately for each child. That is because an application may be under ss 4 or 7 of the Child Support Act 1991 in respect of only one of a number of children. Any maintenance calculation made in respect of that child supersedes the agreement for the period it is in force but not in respect of the other children. If the agreement does not distinguish between the children in this way – eg £100 for the two children instead of £50 for each child – then it seems that the whole aliment provision becomes unenforceable[1].

1   Child Support Act 1991, s 10(2); Child Support (Maintenance Arrangements and Jurisdiction) Regulations 1992 (SI 1992/2645), reg 4(2), (3).

Further research

9.19   Generally:
— Bird, 'Child Maintenance: The New Law' Family Law, 2000;
— McDowell, *Child Support Handbook 2004/2005* (CPAG, 2004, updated annually).

Chapter 10

Pension sharing and earmarking

1. Earmarking orders

10.01 A separation agreement is not effective in itself to allow for payment of a capital sum from the other spouse's pension when its payment becomes due. An 'earmarking' order is needed from the court for this purpose[1], but there is no reason why the separation agreement cannot provide for the making of an earmarking order on divorce and the other party's consent to the making of that order. The court will require, however, to interpose its authority to the agreement by the making of the appropriate order if it is to take effect in relation to the pension trustees or managers[2]. Notice must be given in the court action to the pension trustees or managers of the application for an earmarking order[3].

1 Family Law (Scotland) Act 1985, s 12A; Divorce etc (Notification and Treatment of Pensions) (Scotland) Regulations 2000 (SI 2000/1050).
2 Family Law (Scotland) Act 1985, s 12A(2).
3 OCR 1993, r 33.7(1)(1); RCS 1994, 49.8(1)(1).

2. Pension sharing

10.02 It is possible for a pension sharing provision to be made in a separation agreement, albeit it takes effect only on the granting of divorce or an annulment of the marriage[1]. If the pension sharing provision is to be legally effective, the separation agreement must:
(a) be entered into in prescribed circumstances;
(b) be in the prescribed form; and
(c) be registered in the books of council and session[2].

The 'prescribed circumstances' and 'prescribed form' are dealt with in relation to styles 3 and 4 in CHAPTER 19, and the notes accompanying those styles.

1   Welfare Reform and Pensions Act 1999, ss 28(1)(f), 48(1)(f).
2   Welfare Reform and Pensions Act 1999, ss 28(1)(f)(i), (ii), (3), 48(1)(f)(i), (ii), (3).

10.03   Within two months of the granting of divorce or decree of nullity of marriage, the pursuer must send copies of the following to the pension trustees or managers or, in relation to State scheme rights, the Secretary of State[1]:
(a)   the pension sharing provision;
(b)   the decree;
(c)   documentary evidence confirming:
   (i)   the agreement containing that provision was entered into in the prescribed circumstances; and
   (ii)   was registered in the books of council and session; and
(d)   certain other prescribed information[2].

1   Welfare Reform and Pensions Act 1999, ss 28(7), (9), 48(6), (8).
2   See Pensions on Divorce etc (Provision of Information) Regulations 2000 (SI 2000/1048), reg 5.

10.04   The pension sharing provision is deemed never to have taken effect if these documents are not sent in time[1]. However, application can be made to the sheriff (presumably on good cause) for extension of the time in which the documents should have been sent, or may be sent[2].

1   Welfare Reform and Pensions Act 1999, ss 28(7), 48(6).
2   Welfare Reform and Pensions Act 1999, ss 28(10), 48(9).

10.05   Pension sharing is not competent where an earmarking order has already been made[1].

1   Family Law (Scotland) Act 1985, s 8(6).

3.   Actuarial and practical advice

10.06   Pension sharing in virtually all cases is to be preferred over earmarking orders[1].

The complexities involved in pension sharing are such that actuarial advice should always be obtained. The undernoted articles should be considered essential reading in this regard[2].

1   Smith, 'The Reality of Pension Sharing' (2003) 48 JLSS, April, p 24 and 'Pension Sharing' (2003) 48 JLSS, June, p 30.
2   See articles referred to above at (2003) 48 JLLS, April, p 21, and June, p 30.

10.07   Other practical issues in connection with pension sharing are dealt with elsewhere[1]. Practitioners should note, in particular, that pensions are items of matrimonial property and should therefore be identified as such, and valued appropriately[2]. These valuations must be offset against the values of other matrimonial property to determine whether one of the spouses will have an entitlement to capital from the other. If so, consideration should be given to whether the spouse entitled to capital from the other can obtain this from transfer of an asset of the other, or in some other reliable way, such as a cash payment (or instalments) by the other party.

In other words, it is not in every case that a pension sharing provision will be appropriate, or necessary, to give effect to the principle of fair sharing of the net value of the matrimonial property at the relevant date (usually separation).

As a general guide, where the sum cannot be obtained in any other way, or is considerable, pension sharing is likely to be more worthwhile. At the lower end of the scale, it may not be worth it, particularly as the costs involved can be considerable. However, what is appropriate in a given case will depend on the circumstances of that case, and the actuarial advice given to the client.

1   Bissett-Johnston, 'Changes in Pension Division on Divorce', 2000 SLT (News) 297.
2   Smith and Eden, 'Valuation of Pension Rights Revisited' (1999) Fam LB 42-3.

4. Investment advice

10.08   A firm of solicitors which is not authorised by the Financial Services Authority to undertake investment business must *not*, as incidental investment business under a licence issued by the Law Society of Scotland[1], 'provide or make arrangements in relation to a pension transfer or pension opt-out'[2]. The following guidance has been issued to solicitors by the Law Society of Scotland in connection with investment advice in the context of pension sharing:

'GUIDELINES ON PENSION SHARING ON DIVORCE 2001

Under the Welfare Reform and Pensions Act 1999 the following guidance in relation to the requirements of the financial services legislation has been given to the Judicial Procedure Committee of the Society. There are three stages to be considered separately in this area.

The first stage is the gathering of information about the value of the assets including the pension. This stage is not of itself Investment Business and can be done by a solicitor. Valuation methods used should be in accordance with the pension regulations, such as the cash equivalent method.

The second stage is the important decision on whether to opt for ear marking, sharing, or offsetting the pension entitlement. This stage is Investment Business under the Society's current Investment Business Rules. After the new legislation on Investment Business comes into force [in] November 2001 this will probably be an incidental activity which firms which do not need FSA authorisation can undertake under Law Society rules where it is connected with legal work. Until the new regime is brought into force, which is expected later this year, such financial advice can only be given by a firm authorised to conduct investment business or an independent financial adviser.

The third stage only applies if the client wishes to opt to share the pension. Advice on how to deal with that, and in particular whether [to] leave it in the existing pension scheme or take it out to put into a separate scheme, is specialist pension advice and would only be available from those with that particular authorisation. Currently there are only about six solicitors firms in Scotland with that authorisation but other Independent Financial Advisers with specialist pension authorisation could also provide this advice.

It should be borne in mind in all cases that, even where pension sharing is not used, clients may require pensions and other investment advice in their changed marital and financial status.'

1   See para 2.17.
2   The Law Society of Scotland, 'Guidance to the New System of Investment Regulation under the Financial Services Authority and the Solicitors (Scotland) (Incidental Investment Business) Practice Rules 2001', para 3, item 4, list of activities which are not to be incidental investment business.

Further research

10.09   There is no comprehensive textbook dealing with pensions on divorce in Scots law. English law is not identical to Scots law in these matters and accordingly English textbooks, while they may be of some assistance, must be treated with caution. Subject to that caveat recommended reading would be:

— Bird, 'Pension Sharing: the New Law' Family Law, 1999; and
— Ellison and Rae, *Family Breakdown and Pensions* (Butterworths, 2001).

Chapter 11

Same sex marriage

1. Existing position

11.01   The civil law (including Scots Law) has traditionally recognised marriage as a meeting point of divine and human law[1]. Throughout the history of western society marriage has provided the legal framework for the creation of families, and the transmission of property to legitimate heirs. It has always been understood as involving the union of one man and one woman 'till death [or divorce] shall separate them'[2]. The fundamentally heterosexual and monogamous nature of marriage is enshrined in constitutional law. The Union with England Act 1707, which incorporates the Protestant Religion and Presbyterian Church Act 1707 as a 'fundamental and essential condition' of the Union with England, made the Christian understanding of marriage as contained in Article 1 of chapter 24 of the Westminster Confession of Faith part of the law of the land. This provides that:

> 'marriage is between one man and one woman; neither is it lawful for any man to have more than one wife, nor for any woman to have more than one husband, at the same time[3].'

Any change to this constitutional provision must be made by the United Kingdom Parliament as constitutional matters are reserved to that Parliament under the Scotland Act 1998[4].

1   Modestinus, D23.2.1 *Politieke Ordonnantie van Hollandt*, (Vanden, 1 April 1580), art IV ('eene ordeninge Godts'); Erskine, *Institute* I, 6, 1; Levy et Castaldo, *Histoire du Droit Civil* (Dalloz, 2002), ch 3, pp 46, 47, ch 4, pp 83–85.
2   Justinian, *Institute* I, 9, 1; Voet, *Commentary on the Pandects* (The Hague, 1701), 23.2.1; de Groot, *Inleidinge tot de Hollandsche Rechtsgeleerdheid* I.5.1; Erskine, *Institute* I.6.1 and 44; Erskine, *Principles* I, 6, 1; *Hyde v Hyde* (1866) 1 P&D 130.
3   See CHAPTER 18, extracts 1–3; Marriage (Scotland) Act 1977, s 5(4)(e).
4   Scotland Act 1998, Sch 5, para 1(b).

11.02   The idea of same sex marriage (if not an oxymoron) appears first to have been mooted by Karl Heinrich Ulrichs in 1864[1] and revived more recently by Kees Waaldijk of Universiteit Leiden in the Netherlands in 1987[2]. Such a union is open to two persons of the same sex, not necessarily of the same sexual orientation, but need not confer all the rights on the parties to it as a husband and wife would have conferred on them. In the Netherlands, parties to a same sex marriage (*homohuwelijk*) cannot adopt a child from abroad[3]; in Belgium, they cannot adopt a child at all[4]. In neither of these countries, where marriages are contracted *civilly*[5], though perhaps followed by a religious ceremony or blessing in church, do same sex couples have any legal right to insist on their church recognising, or blessing, their marriage[6]. Same sex marriages are now also recognised, by judicial decision, in British Columbia[7], Ontario[8], Massachusetts[9] and Quebec[10].

1   Greenberg, *The Construction of Homosexuality* (University of Chicago Press, 1998), p 408.
2   See homepage of Kees Waaldijk at athena.leidenuniv.nl/rechten/meijers/index.
3   Ministry of Justice Brochures: 'Trouwen, geregistreerd partnerschap, en samenwonen' and 'U Wilt een kind uit het buitenland adopteren', available at www.justitie.nl or www.postbus51.nl.
4   Burgerlijk Wetboek, art 346.
5   Same sex marriages have been possible in the Netherlands since 1 April 2001, and in Belgium since 1 June 2003. The civil codes in these countries provide that: 'Een huwelijk kan worden aangegaan door twee personen van verschillend of van gelijk geslacht.' (Burgerlijk Wetboek, Nederland, art 30-1) and 'Een huwelijk kan worden aangegaan door twee personen van verschillend of van hetzelfde geslacht' (Burgerlijk Wetboek, Belgie, art 143) – a marriage can be entered into by two persons of a different or the same sex.
6   In the Netherlands, the Burgerlijk Wetboek specifically provides in art 30-2 that: 'De wet beschouwt het huwelijk alleen in zijn burgerljke betrekkingen' – the law is concerned only with the civil effects of marriage. As to 'kerkelijk huwelijk' (church marriage), the original Dutch upon which this text is based reads 'Pas nadat het burgerlijke huwelijk is gesloten, mag een kerkelijk inzegening of bevestiging volgen. Kerkgentootschappen kunnen zelf beslissen of zij het huwelijk willen inzegenen of bevestigen. Zij zijn hiertoe dus niet verplicht.' See further, on religion and the recognition of same sex marriages in the Netherlands: 'The Uniting Protestant Churches in the Netherlands and homosexuality' at www.pkn.nl; and 'The recognition of gay and lesbian relationships in the Remonstrant Church and in Dutch society' at www.wht.nederland.org – click on 'artikelen'.
7   *Barbeau v British Columbia* (2003) 1 May, BC CA, available at www.courts.gov.bc.ca.
8   *Halpern et al v Attorney General of Canada* (2003) 10 June, Ont CA, available at www.ontariocourts.on.ca.
9   *Goodridge v Dept of Public Health* (2003) 18 November, Massachusetts Supreme Judicial Court, available at www.mass.gov/courts/.
10 *Hendricks and Leboeuf v Attorney General of Canada* (2004) 19 March, CA Que, available at www.jugements.qc.ca.

11.03   Although the institution of same sex marriage is contrary to Scots constitutional and family law, the vexed question of whether such marriages should be recognised from abroad, for some or all purposes, may well arise for consideration in the Scottish context. As might be expected, proponents of same sex marriage argue strongly in favour of the recognition of same sex marriages for all legal purposes[1]; yet the fact remains that neither the governments of the Netherlands or Belgium take this view. Both governments counsel their citizens against expecting full recognition of *homohuwelijken*[2] abroad[3]. Parties to these unions cannot therefore legitimately claim any injustice if they cannot obtain the benefits of marriage, be divorced or obtain decrees of nullity of marriage abroad: *homohuwelijken* are not the same as heterosexual marriages since they do not confer the full extent of rights as do heterosexual marriages[4]. Same sex marriage is a new institution in the history of the western world, which does not require to be recognised anywhere abroad[5]. There is no fundamental human right to marriage between persons of the same sex[6]. The introduction of any such right, as in the Netherlands or Belgium, can only, with any pretence to legitimacy, be done by the legislature of the country in question[7]. It follows that same sex marriages introduced by judicial order in North America do not deserve any degree of recognition in Scotland as marriages. Judges are bound to apply the law as it stands, and not to usurp it. The North American cases proceed on the mistaken view that equality requires persons of the same sex to have the right to marry each other and that, in pursuit of this objective, judges have the right to overturn the historically accepted definition of marriage[8].

1   Norrie, 'Would Scots Law Recognise a Dutch Same-Sex Marriage' (2003) 7 Edin LR 147.
2   Same sex marriages.
3   See Jamieson, 'Same Sex Marriages in the Netherlands' (2002)7 SCOLAG, p 220 and www.allesovergay.nl for the position in the Netherlands, and circular of 23 January 2004 by Belgian Federal Government Service, available at www.ejustice.just.fgov.be, 'belgisch staatsblad'.
4   See paras **11.02** and **11.08**.
5   Siehr, 'Family Unions in Private International Law' (2003) 50 NILR 419–435; Nygh, 'The Consequences for Australia of the new Netherlands Law permitting same gender marriages' (2002) 16 Australian Journal of Family Law, pp 139–145. Netherlands same sex marriages are not recognised in the other constituent parts of the Kingdom of the Netherlands – Aruba or the Netherlands Antilles. But, as judgments of courts are valid throughout the Kingdom, orders such as for maintenance on divorce would fall to be recognised in the other parts of the Kingdom: see report at fn 2, para **11.04**, pp 32 and 33.
6   Probert, 'The Right to Marry and the Impact of the Human Rights Act 1998' [2003] IFL 29; McCafferty, 'The Right to Marry – Recent Developments' [2002] HR & UKP 219.
7   Hoge Raad der Nederlanden, Arrest, 19 October 1990 (1992) Nederlandse Jurisprudentie 192; *Lawrence v Texas* (2003) 26 June, Supreme Court of the United States, Scalia J (dissenting); *Bellinger v Bellinger* [2003] 2 AC 467; [2003] 2 WLR 1174.
8   Judgment of Scalia J (dissenting), *Lawrence v Texas* (2003) 26 June, Supreme Court of the United States.

11.04   The question of recognition abroad of *homohuwelijken* has been authoritatively discussed by the Netherlands Private International Law Commission[1]. Its views[2] are that as international private law has never known the institution of *homohuwelijken*, such unions need not be recognised abroad: however, some rights and obligations, principally to aliment, do not depend on the marriage relationship; and to that extent can be recognised and, if necessary, enforced abroad. This is not a surprising result: although, in Scotland, only husband and wife, and parents towards their children, have statutory rights to aliment[3], this does not prevent others from contracting for aliment[4]. Accordingly, unless thought to be contrary, or manifestly contrary to public policy[5], an agreement between two persons of the same sex for aliment, which does not require a Scottish court to recognise their marriage, is a purely private relationship between the two persons concerned and may be enforced as an authentic instrument in Scotland[6]. Similarly, such persons may contract in Scotland for the provision of property owned in common by them in this country. What they cannot do is provide for periodical allowance on divorce in Scotland[7], or for the sharing of pension rights in the United Kingdom, as these depend on them being married to each other. A separation agreement or cohabitation agreement between such persons may therefore be valid in part, and not in the other parts, depending on what it seeks to regulate.

1   Kraan, 'Het huwelijksvermogensrecht' (Boom Jurisdische uitgevers, vierde druk, 2003), para 36.2, pp 346, 347.
2   'Advies van de Staatscommissie voor het Internationaal Privaatrecht inzake het internationaal privaatrecht in verband met de openstelling van het huwelijk voor personen van hetzelfde geslacht', december 2001, available at www.justitie.nl.
3   Family Law (Scotland) Act 1985, s 1(1).
4   *Drummond v Drummond* 1995 SC 321.
5   See para **14.24**.
6   See CHAPTER 14 regarding authentic instruments.
7   Post-divorce maintenance, upon divorce in the Netherlands or Belgium *could*, however, be recognised and enforced in Scotland: see report at fn 2, above, p 21.

2. Effect of Civil Partnership Act 2004

11.05   The Civil Partnership Act 2004 will give to same sex couples the same rights as a married couple if they enter into a registered civil partnership with each other, except for the right to apply for the joint adoption of a child[1].

1   See para **12.03**.

11.06   Parties to a Belgian or Dutch *homohuwelijk* will be treated as parties to a Scottish civil partnership and should therefore frame a separation agreement with reference to the terminology of the Civil Partnership Act 2004[1]. Instead of their marriage, or divorce, they should refer to their marriage, recognised as a civil partnership and, instead of divorce, to its dissolution by a Scottish court, or other court of competent jurisdiction. There would be no post-nuptial 'marriage agreement' but 'an agreement regulating the parties' civil partnership', with a narration of the equivalence of their *homohuwelijk* to a Scottish civil partnership.

1   Civil Partnership Act 2004, Sch 20.

11.07   Other foreign same sex marriages which meet the 'general conditions' of the Civil Partnership Act 2004, s 214 will also be treated as Scottish civil partnerships[1].

1   See para **12.06**.

11.08   The fact that foreign same sex marriages will be recognised as civil partnerships and not marriages is significant. It means that the parties to the union will not be recognised as spouses in Scotland. Rights currently retained for married couples, such as jointly to apply for the adoption of a child, will not be open to such persons. This is a just result as, for example, in Belgium, parties to a *homohuwelijk* cannot apply jointly to adopt a child. They should have no higher right in Scotland *qua* parties to a marriage; for most purposes, including the dissolution of the union, they will enjoy the status of civil partners.

3. Same sex marriage in Europe

11.09　In its resolution of 4 September 2003, the European Parliament called upon the Member States of the European Union 'to abolish all forms of discrimination – whether legislative or de facto – which are still suffered by homosexuals, in particular as regards the right to marry and adopt children[1]'.

1　'Fundamental rights in the EU in 2002': Document (2002/2013/INI).

4. Same sex marriage in North America

11.10　In 1996, the US Congress approved the Defense of Marriage Act[1] which banned federal recognition of same sex marriage. Most States have approved their own bans on same sex marriage[2].

1　110 Stat 2419 (1996).
2　See www.hrc.org.

11.11　As a result of the judicial decisions referred to above[1], Canada is likely to amend the marriage definition to 'the voluntary union for life of two persons to the exclusion of all others' throughout Canada[2].

1　See para **11.02**, fns 7, 8, 10.
2　See www.samesexmarriage.ca.

Further research

11.12　Generally:
— Lehmann, *The Gay and Lesbian Marriage and Family Reader* (Gordian Knot Books, University of Nebraska Press, 2001);
— McEleavy, 'New Belgium (sic) Law on Same Sex Marriage' (2003) 52 ICLQ 1039;
— Norrie, 'Would Scots Law Recognise a Dutch Same-Sex Marriage?' (2003) 7 Edin LR 147;
— Siehr, 'Family Unions in Private International Law' (2003) 50 NLR 419–435.

11.13　The Belgian civil code (Burgerlijk Wetboek) is available at:
— www.juridat.be (in either Dutch or French).

The Dutch civil code (Burgerlijk Wetboek) is available (in Dutch) at:
— www.wetten.overheid.nl by searching on the words 'burgerlijk wetboek'.

An English translation of Book 1 of the Dutch Civil Code (Family Law) is available from Intersentia, Antwerpen by Ian Sumner and Hans Warendorf under the title 'Family Law Legislation of the Netherlands' (2003): this can be ordered online at:
— www.intersentia.com.

11.14   Homosexual websites which give information about marriage for homosexuals in Belgium and the Netherlands include:
— www.coc.nl (Cultuur en Ontspannings-Centrum, Centre for Culture and Leisure);
— wwww.gaysite.nl; and
— www.gayworld.be (Gayworld.be offers a 'Huwelijkgids voor holebi's' – Marriage Guide for ho(mo's), Le(sbo's) and bi(sexueel)s).

11.15   The following website is also of relevance, particularly in relation to same sex marriage in North America:
— www.freedomtomarry.org.

11.16   For the moral dilemmas which same sex marriage may pose, see:
— Mostyn, 'Gay Marriage – The Dilemma for the Catholic Law Maker' [2003] IFL 190.

11.17   For adoption issues in the Netherlands, see:
— www.kinderbescherming.nl;
— www.adoptie.nl;
— www.kidskids.nl; and
— www.homo–ouders.nl.

Chapter 12

Civil partnerships in the United Kingdom

'Marriage is a lawful union of a man and woman. It is a legal relationship between persons of the opposite sex. A man's spouse must be a woman; a woman's spouse must be a man. This is the very essence of the relationship, which need not be loving, sexual, faithful, long-lasting, or contented. Although it may be brought to an end as a legal relationship only by death or an order of the court, its demise as a factual relationship will usually have ended long before that.'

Lord Millet, *Ghaidan v Godin–Mendoza* [2004] UKHL 30 at [78]

Introduction

12.01 The terms 'registered partnership' and 'statutory cohabitation' are used to denote the various arrangements, in various countries or territories, by which cohabiting same or opposite sex couples confer rights on each other akin to those which exist between married partners in their particular country or territory[1].

In the United Kingdom, a registered partnership will apply to same sex cohabitation under the title 'civil partnership' by virtue of the Civil Partnership Act 2004. This chapter examines civil partnerships for their effect on the making of family law agreements.

1 See CHAPTER 13 for registered partnerships and statutory cohabitation in Europe.

1. Civil partnerships as registered partnerships in the United Kingdom

Definition

12.02 A civil partnership is defined as a relationship between two people of the same sex ('civil partners') which is formed when they register as civil partners of each other in accordance with the Civil Partnership Act 2004[1]. It ends only on death, dissolution or annulment[2]. In Scotland, two people are not eligible to register as civil partners of each other if:
(a) they are not of the same sex;
(b) they are related in a forbidden degree;

(c) either has not attained the age of 16;
(d) either is married or already in a civil partnership;
(e) either is incapable of understanding the nature of civil partnership; or
(f) either is incapable of validly consenting to its formation[3].

1   Section 1(1)(a).
2   Civil Partnership Act 2004, s 1(3).
3   Civil Partnership Act 2004, s 86(1).

Consequences

12.03   It is evident from the 264 sections and 30 Schedules of the Civil Partnership Act 2004 that its purpose is to equate civil partnership and marriage for all legal purposes, except, in Scotland, in relation to the right to apply for the joint adoption of a child[1]. Provision is made in the Act for the subsequent application of enactments relating to pensions to civil partners[2].

In practice, civil partnership is a marriage in all but name[3]. It can only be dissolved by the court on grounds similar to those applying to divorce of married couples[4]. The exception is that there is no adultery ground of divorce as persons of the same sex cannot commit adultery in relation to each other. Adultery is by its very nature and definition restricted to a married relationship[5].

A civil partnership confers status on the civil partners and establishes family relations in respect of in-laws and step-children[6].

An agreement to enter into a civil partnership is unenforceable and, like breach of promise of marriage, breach of promise to enter into a civil partnership is unactionable[7].

Civil partnership does not create a community of property between the civil partners and they each retain their individual rights of property in their own property[8]. There will, however, be presumptions of equal shares in household goods, and in money and property derived from a housekeeping allowance[9].

The partners in a civil partnership entered into in the United Kingdom have in relation to the other partner, in the same manner as spouses in a marriage:
(a) the obligation to aliment the other[10];
(b) the obligation to aliment a child of the other accepted by both parties as a child of the family[11];
(c) the ability to enter into an agreement under s 16(1)(a) of the Family Law (Scotland) Act 1985 for periodical allowance on dissolution of the civil partnership[12]; and

(d)   the ability to challenge an agreement under s 16(1)(b) of the Family Law (Scotland) Act 1985 as to financial provision on dissolution of the civil partnership as not fair and reasonable at the time it was entered into[13].

Since same sex couples are most likely only to have step-children, as presently they are not allowed to adopt children jointly in Scotland and thereby obtain recognition as joint parents, the provisions of the Child Support Act 1991 are for most purposes irrelevant to same sex couples[14].

1   A 'couple' may prospectively apply for adoption of a child in England and Wales when the Adoption and Children Act 2002, s 50 is brought into force. Section 144(4) of that Act defines a couple as (a) a married couple, or (b) two people (whether of different sexes or the same sex) living as partners in an enduring family relationship. These sections do not apply in Scotland.
2   Civil Partnership Act 2004, s 255.
3   'Gay marriage in all but name' (Christian Institute, 2004).
4   Civil Partnership Act 2004, s 117(1)–(3). The court has jurisdiction under the Civil Partnership Act 2004, s 225, also to grant decree of declarator of nullity of a civil partnership, or decree of separation in relation to civil partners, but the grounds upon which it may do so are not clarified either by the Act itself or amendment to other relevant Acts such as the Court of Session Act 1830, s 33, the Court of Session Act 1850, s 16, or the Sheriff Courts (Scotland) Act 1907, s 5. Section 123 provides for two grounds of nullity: that two persons were ineligible to become civil partners in Scotland, or did not validly consent to its formation.
5   *MacLennan v MacLennan* 1958 SC 105 at 109, per Lord (Ordinary) Wheatley.
6   Civil Partnership Act 2004, s 246.
7   Civil Partnership Act 2004, s 128.
8   Family Law (Scotland) Act 1985, s 24 (as prospectively amended by the Civil Partnership Act 2004, Sch 28, para 27).
9   Family Law (Scotland) Act 1985, ss 25, 26 (as prospectively amended by the Civil Partnership Act 2004, Sch 28, paras 28, 29).
10   Family Law (Scotland) Act 1985, s 1(1)(bb) (as prospectively inserted by the Civil Partnership Act 2004, Sch 28, para 11).
11   Family Law (Scotland) Act 1985, ss 1(1)(d), 27(1) ('definition of family', as prospectively amended by the Civil Partnership Act 2004, Sch 28, para 30(b)).
12   As prospectively amended by the Civil Partnership Act 2004, Sch 28, para 22.
13   As prospectively amended by the Civil Partnership Act 2004, Sch 28, para 22; see CHAPTER 16 for s 16(1)(b) of the Family Law (Scotland) Act 1985.
14   Human Fertilisation and Embryology Act 1990, s 30 allows only a husband and wife to apply for a parental order. It is not affected by the Civil Partnership Act 2004.

2.   Overseas relationships as civil partnerships in the United Kingdom

12.04   A registered 'overseas relationship' between persons of the same sex is also a 'civil partnership', if:
(a)   it is a relationship specified in the Civil Partnership Act 2004, Sch 20[1]; or
(b)   it meets the 'general conditions' in the Civil Partnership Act 2004, s 214.

1   Civil Partnership Act 2004, ss 212, 213, 215, 216.

12.05   Schedule 20 to the Civil Partnership Act 2004 recognises the following overseas relationships as civil partnerships in Scotland:

Country or territory	*Description*
Belgium	cohabitation légale (statutory cohabitation)
	marriage
Canada: Nova Scotia	domestic partnership
Denmark	registeret partnerskab (registered partnership)
Finland	rekisteröity parisuhde (registered partnership)
France	pacte civile de solidarité (civil solidarity pact)
Germany	lebenspartnerschaft (life partnership)
Iceland	stadfesta samvist (confirmed cohabitation)
Netherlands	geregistreerde partnerschap (registered partnership)
	marriage
Norway	registrert partnerskap (registered partnership)
Sweden	registrerat partnerskap (registered partnership)
United States of America: Vermont	civil union

12.06   The general conditions in s 214 of the Civil Partnership Act 2004, under the law of the country or territory where the relationship is registered (including its rules of private international law)[1], are as follows:
(a)   the relationship may not be entered into if either of the parties is already a party to a relationship of that kind or lawfully married;
(b)   the relationship is of indeterminate duration; and
(c)   the effect of entering into it is that the parties are:
   (i)   treated as a couple either generally or for specified purposes; or
   (ii)   treated as married.

1   Civil Partnership Act 2004, s 212(2), defining 'relevant law'.

12.07   This definition is sufficiently wide to include same sex marriages judicially recognised in Canada and Massachusetts[1], but that recognition will not be *qua* marriage but as a civil partnership so that such persons will not, for example, currently have the right jointly to apply for the adoption of a child in Scotland.

1   Woelke, 'International Aspects of Civil Partnerships' [2004] IFL 111 at 112.

3. Family law agreements in relation to civil partnerships

12.08   For most purposes, it will be possible to approach family law agreements between civil partners, or intended civil partners, as though they were, or are to become a married couple. The following differences should be noted, however:

(a)   There will rarely be any need, if at all, to refer to the Child Support Act 1991 in a separation agreement, as it has no application to step-children[1].

(b)   Some provision should be made in an antenuptial civil partnership agreement as to whether or not one or other of the partners is allowed to have sex outside of the relationship with someone other than his or her civil partner. There is no provision for dissolving the civil partnership on the ground of adultery, or infidelity. However, the civil partnership can be dissolved on the ground that one of the partners' behaviour towards the other is so unreasonable that he or she cannot be expected to continue cohabiting with that partner[2]. If the agreement therefore provides for an exclusive sexual relationship between the civil partners, this part of it will be evidence as to whether or not an unfaithful civil partner has acted unreasonably towards the other. Equally this may not be a ground of dissolution if it is shown in the agreement that either or both of the partners has, with agreement of the other, the right to pursue sexual relationships outside of the civil partnership[3].

(c)   The Conjugal Rights Amendment (Scotland) Act 1861, s 6, is not extended to civil partners[4].

1   See para **12.03**, FOOTNOTE **14**.
2   Civil Partnership Act 2004, s 117(2)(a), (3)(a).
3   See paras **2.20**–**2.23**, regarding data protection issues in connection with these matters.
4   See para **1.09**.

12.09   The pension sharing and earmarking provisions of the Family Law (Scotland) Act 1985, and the pension sharing provisions of the Welfare Reform and Pensions Act 1999[1] are to be extended to civil partners[2].

1   Sections 28, 48.
2   Civil Partnership Act 2004, Sch 27, paras 159, 161, Sch 28, Pt 2; see CHAPTER 10 for pension sharing and earmarking.

12.10   The Married Women's Policies of Assurance (Scotland) Act 1880 will also be extended to civil partners and their children[1].

1   Civil Partnership Act 2004, s 132; see para **4.07**.

Further research

12.11   Generally:

—   'Counterfeit Marriage' (Christian Institute, 2002) (available at www.christian.org.uk);

—   'Gay Marriage in all but name' (Christian Institute, 2004) (available at www.christian.org.uk);

—   Grigolo, 'Sexualities and the ECHR: Introducing the Universal Sexual Legal Subject' (2003) 15 EJIL 1023 (abstract available at www.ejil.org);

—   Jones, 'Androgyny: The Pagan Sexual Ideal', JETS 43/3 (September 2000) 443–469;

—   Quail, 'Radical Change or a Lie in the Law' (2004) 49 JLSS, February, p 24;

—   Waaldijk, 'Taking Same-Sex Partnerships Seriously – European Experiences as British Perspectives?' [2003] IFL 84;

—   Woelke, 'International Aspects of Civil Partnerships' [2004] IFL 111.

Chapter 13

Registered partnerships and statutory cohabitation in Europe

1. Registered partnerships

The Nordic countries

13.01   Registered partnerships in Denmark, Finland, Greenland[1], and Sweden, and confirmed cohabitation in Iceland[2], are open to same sex couples only. They can be dissolved only by the court, on the same grounds as apply in relation to divorce of married couples. They can only be entered into before the civil registrar; there is no right to enter into a civil partnership in church. It is a matter for individual churches to what extent, if any, they will allow blessings for the civil partners in church[3].

Registered partners have equivalent status and the equivalent rights of married partners, save that only in Sweden may they jointly apply for the adoption of a child.

1   The Danish law has been extended to Greenland, but not to the Faroe Islands.
2   In essence, registered partnership and confirmed cohabitation are the same as each other.
3   The Evangelical-Lutheran Church of Denmark has approved church blessings for registered partners, subject to the right of individual ministers to refuse to give such blessings if they consider it wrong to do so: 'Registered Partnership Common Life and Blessing' at www.foelkekirken.dk/udvalg/partnerskab/ENGLISH.htm.

The Netherlands

13.02   Registered partnership in the Netherlands is based on the Nordic model, except it is also open to opposite sex couples. However, opposite sex registered partnerships will not be recognised as civil partnerships in the United Kingdom[1].

1   Civil Partnership Act 2004, s 216.

13.03 A distinctive feature of the Dutch registered partnership is that it may be dissolved by mutual agreement, provided the parties have first resolved any outstanding property and maintenance issues, and have recorded these in a binding separation agreement. This leads to the possibility of married couples (same or opposite sex) setting their marriage into a registered partnership, and then dissolving the registered partnership without going through the court by means of agreement to resolve the registered partnership. If no agreement can be reached to dissolve a registered partnership, either party can apply to the court for its dissolution on the same grounds for divorce as a married couple. A joint application to the court for dissolution, unlike in the case of divorce, is not possible.

Registered partners are permitted jointly to apply for adoption of a child.

Germany

13.04 The German registered lifepartnership is similar in concept to the Nordic registered partnership. Thus it is open only to same sex couples, and may be dissolved only by the court, applying the grounds for granting a divorce to a spouse. The rights acquired by a registered lifepartner are not, however, always identical to those which spouses have. A major difference is that the partners must choose, by formal agreement, one of three property regimes to apply to their partnership.

They do not have the right jointly to apply for the adoption of a child.

2. Statutory cohabitation

France

13.05 The French model is known as a 'Pact Civil de Solidarité' or 'PACS'. A PACS is a formal contract, open to same or opposite sex couples, registered with a district court, which confers various legal rights on the parties to it, obligations of mutual material assistance, and limited inheritance rights after two years of cohabitation. It can be terminated by mutual agreement or by a unilateral decision subject to three months' notice; in the event of disagreement as to property rights or maintenance on dissolution, either party can apply to the court for a determination. The PACS can also be terminated by the marriage of the cohabitants to each other, or one of them to someone else.

The cohabitants have no right jointly to apply for the adoption of a child.

Belgium

13.06   Belgium's version of PACS is the statutory, or legal, cohabitation. It is open to two persons, whether related or not, including same or opposite sex couples. It is entered into by means of a written declaration registered with the local civil status registrar. It confers various property and maintenance rights on the partners which apply in the absence of the parties' 'contracting out' of these. Other rights, for example, in relation to the common household, are mandatory and the partners cannot contract out of these. There are no inheritance or post-termination maintenance rights. The statutory cohabitation can be ended by mutual agreement, unilateral notice, marriage of the partners to each other (where they are not excluded from marrying by reason of being closely related to each other), or marriage of one of the partners to someone else. Legal disputes arising from dissolution can be referred to the local court.

The partners have no entitlement jointly to apply for the adoption of a child.

Spain

13.07   Regional laws in Aragon, the Balearic Islands, Catalonia, and Navarre provide protection for couples in stable unions. Limited rights are conferred on the partners to the union through cohabitation itself, or by drawing up a notarial declaration of cohabitation. In the Balearic Islands, registration in a specific register is a formal condition of the validity of the partnership. The termination of these Spanish arrangements is by mutual agreement, unilateral notification, and marriage of one of the partners. The unions are open to both same and opposite sex couples, and in some of the laws to relatives in various degrees, such as aunt and niece in Catalonia, or cousins in other regions.

Only in Navarre may the couple jointly apply to adopt a child.

13.08   Spanish stable unions are not recognised as 'overseas relationships' for the purposes of Sch 20 to the Civil Partnership Act 2004[1] and are therefore recognisable as civil partnerships in the United Kingdom only if they fulfil the 'general conditions', including the requirement of registration with a responsible authority[2]. This seems only to apply in the case of unions entered into and registered, as a condition of their validity, in the Balearic Islands[3].

1   See para **12.05**.
2   Civil Partnership Act, s 214; see para **12.06**.
3   See para **13.07**.

Further research

13.09   The information in this chapter is derived, in the main, from the conference papers submitted to the Council of Europe Fifth European Conference on Family Law held at The Hague, 15–16 March 1999.

13.10   See also:
— Boele-Woelki and Fuchs (eds), *Legal Recognition of Same-Sex Couples in Europe* (Intersentia, Antwerpen, 2003);
— and the papers on registered partnerships available on the website of the International Commission on Civil Status (ICCS) at www.ciec1.org.

13.11   A useful article on registered partnerships is:
— Sumner, 'Transformers – Marriages in Disguise?' [2003] IFL 15.

Chapter 14

Authentic instruments: enforcement within Europe of maintenance obligations contained in family law agreements

'That extractis of contractis, obligationis, etc registrat in the Buikes of Counsale...and producit in forane countries, before Ordinar Judges thairin, sall make as greit faith as the principallis.'

Act of Sederunt, 17 November 1599

Introduction

14.01 An authentic instrument is an extra-judicial document containing obligations which are enforceable as though those obligations were contained in a court decree[1].

A Scottish family law agreement containing maintenance obligations is an 'authentic instrument' if registered in the books of council and session, or the sheriff court books, for execution, as the warrant for execution contained in an extract renders the agreement equivalent to a Court of Session or sheriff court decree for payment of the maintenance concerned[2]. The agreement is enforceable only in relation to maintenance (aliment and periodical allowance) and not in relation to financial provision concerned with dividing property between spouses[3].

Authentic instruments are also known in other European countries[4]; but not in England and Wales or Ireland[5]. The conditions for their 'authenticity' and thus their enforcement as court decrees, vary from country to country and from what is required to make the instrument 'authentic' in Scotland. But all authentic instruments have in common that, upon satisfying the conditions necessary to establish their authenticity, and being enforceable in their country of origin, they have the privilege of being treated as equivalent to court decrees.

European law makes provision for the mutual enforcement of authentic instruments in the European Union ('EU') and certain other States, which it is the object of this chapter to consider[6].

1   Code civil français, art 1317; Act of Sederunt 17 November 1599 anent extractis of contractis, obligationis, etc registrat in the Buikes of Counsale.
2   Execution of Writs (Scotland) Act 1877, ss 1, 2; Maxwell Report, para 7.2; Schlosser Report, para 226.
3   Case C-220/95 *Van den Boogaard v P M Laumen* [1997] ECR I-1147.
4   The Jenard and Moller Report, para 72, p 80 notes that authentic instruments are not known in the EFTA States of Iceland, Leichtenstein or Norway, though they are known in Austria (now an EU Member State). The Evrigenis and Kerameus Report, para 89, p 22, notes that they are known in Greece. Other countries in which they are known include Benelux, France, Germany and Italy.
5   Schlosser Report, para 226, p 136.
6   Procedural rules by which authentic instruments for maintenance are enforced in Scotland can be made by Act of Sederunt (Civil Jurisdiction and Judgments Act 1982, s 50) under authority of the Civil Jurisdiction and Judgments Act 1982, s 48(2), in connection with the Brussels and Lugano Conventions (as applied to authentic instruments by the CJJ Order 1993, art 8), and in connection with the Council Regulation on Jurisdiction and Judgments (as applied to authentic instruments enforceable under the Council Regulation by the Civil Jurisdiction and Judgments (Authentic Instruments and Court Settlements) Order 2001 (SI 2001/3928), art 4). However, there are in practice no specific sheriff court rules relating to authentic instruments. Where it has been possible to do so in the commentary below, the rules relating to judgments have been adapted so as to relate to authentic instruments.

1. Overview of legal provisions relating to authentic instruments

Applicable legal provisions

14.02   The following instruments contain provisions relating to authentic instruments which include maintenance obligations:
(a)   Convention on jurisdiction and the enforcement of judgments in civil and commercial matters signed at Brussels on 27 September 1968 ('Brussels Convention')[1];
(b)   Convention on jurisdiction and the enforcement of judgments in civil and commercial matters opened for signature at Lugano on 16 September 1988 ('the Lugano Convention')[2]; and
(c)   Council Regulation (EC) No 44/2001 of 22 December 2000 on jurisdiction and the recognition and enforcement of judgments in civil and commercial matters ('Council Regulation on Jurisdiction and Judgments')[3].

The Hague Convention on the recognition and enforcement of decisions relating to aliment obligations of 2 October 1973 applies only to decisions 'rendered' by the court, or settlements which it approves[4] and does not therefore apply to authentic instruments[5].

1   OJ C27/1, 26.6.1998 ; Civil Jurisdiction and Judgments Act 1982, Sch 1.
2   OJ L319, 25.11.1988, p 9; Civil Jurisdiction and Judgments Act 1982, Sch 3C.
3   OJ L12, 16.1.2001, p 1.
4   Hague Convention, art 1.

5   Verwilghen, 'Report of the Special Commission to the Twelfth session of the Hague Conference on Private International Law' (October 1972), Acte et documents, Tome IV, Obligations alimentaries, para 93, pp 129, 130.

Territorial scope

14.03   The territorial scope of these instruments is as follows:

(a)   Brussels Convention – applies between the United Kingdom, Denmark and Aruba[1]. It has also been extended as between the United Kingdom and Gibraltar[2], with power (unexercised) to extend it as between the United Kingdom and any other overseas territory, or Crown dependency[3].

(b)   Lugano Convention – applies between the United Kingdom, Iceland, Norway, and Switzerland[4].

(c)   Council Regulation on Jurisdiction and Judgments – applies between the United Kingdom or Gibraltar[5], and all other Member States[6] of the EU, except for Denmark[7].

The instruments do not apply as between Scotland and the other United Kingdom jurisdictions of England and Wales, and Northern Ireland[8].

1   Council Regulation on Jurisdiction and Judgments, preamble, paras (22), (23), art 68(1); Treaty establishing the European Community, art 299; Cruz, Real and Jenard Report (OJC 189/50, 28.7.1990).
2   Civil Jurisdiction and Judgments Act 1982 (Gibraltar) Order 1997 (SI 1997/2602), arts 2, 3.
3   Civil Jurisdiction and Judgments Act 1982, s 39. The Crown dependencies are the Isle of Man; and the Channel Islands. United Kingdom 'dependent' territories are now known as 'overseas territories': British Overseas Territories Act 2002, s 1(2). The British overseas territories are listed in the British Nationality Act 1981, Sch 6.
4   See para **14.05** regarding Poland.
5   Council Regulation on Jurisdiction and Judgments, Annexes II and III.
6   Including the new Member States from 1 May 2004.
7   Preamble, para (21), art 1(3).
8   Civil Jurisdiction and Judgments Act 1982, s 18(7); CJJ Order 1993, art 7; Civil Jurisdiction and Judgments (Authentic Instruments and Court Settlements) Order 2001 (SI 2001/3928), art 3. But the Maintenance Orders Act 1950 may apply: see *Butterworths Family Law Service*, paras [1029]–[1042].

14.04   The Council Regulation on Jurisdiction and Judgments supersedes the Brussels Convention as between Member States of the EU, other than Denmark[1]. It does not apply to the overseas territories of France or the United Kingdom, or to the territories of the Kingdom of the Netherlands outside Europe[2]. It is for these reasons that the Brussels Convention continues to apply in respect of Denmark and Aruba.

1   Article 68(1).
2   Article 68(1); Treaty establishing the European Community, art 299.

14.05   The Lugano Convention previously applied in respect of the United Kingdom and Poland as well as Iceland, Norway and Switzerland. It ceased to apply in respect of the United Kingdom and Poland on the latter's accession to the EU on 1 May 2004[1].

1   Treaty of Athens, art 2.

Substantive provisions concerning authentic instruments

14.06   Article 50 of the Brussels and Lugano Conventions, and art 57(1) of the Council Regulation on Jurisdiction and Judgments, provide that:

'a document which has been formally drawn up or registered as an authentic instrument and is enforceable in one contracting/Member State shall, in another contracting/Member State, be declared enforceable there',

on application made in accordance with the procedure for enforcement of judgments recognised under the Conventions and the Regulation. Such application may be refused only if enforcement of the instrument:
(a)   'is manifestly contrary to public policy in the Member State addressed' (the Regulation); or
(b)   'is contrary to public policy in the State addressed' (the Conventions).

14.07   An authentic instrument cannot be 'declared enforceable' in the United Kingdom as a whole. It must be registered for enforcement in a particular part of the United Kingdom, whether Scotland, England and Wales, or Northern Ireland[1]. In Scotland, an authentic instrument relating to 'maintenance' must be submitted to the 'sheriff court' for registration on transmission by the Scottish Ministers[2] to the court of the place of the debtor's domicile[3], or the place of enforcement[4]. Transmission to the court of the place of enforcement is only available under the Brussels and Lugano Conventions if the debtor is not domiciled in the United Kingdom[5].

'Domicile' for the purpose of the Conventions and the Regulation is determined in accordance with the Civil Jurisdiction and Judgments Act 1982, s 41 and the Civil Jurisdiction and Judgments Order 2001[6], art 9, which both provide[7] for a presumption of domicile in a particular place in the United Kingdom if a person has resided there for at least the last three months[8]. If the debtor is not domiciled in the United Kingdom in accordance with these rules, then the laws of the contracting or Member States must be applied to determine whether the debtor is domiciled in any of those States as a condition precedent of the applicability of the Convention or Regulation[9]. An individual is domiciled in a State other than a contracting Member State only if resident in that State, and the nature and circumstances of his residence indicate he has a substantial connection with it[10].

1   Brussels and Lugano Conventions, art 31(2). Council Regulation on Jurisdiction and Judgments, art 38(2).
2   Brussels and Lugano Conventions, art 32(1); Council Regulation on Jurisdiction and Judgments, art 39(1), Annex II. The functions of the 'Secretary of State' have been devolved to the Scottish Ministers: Scotland Act 1998, s 53(2). Note that the Scotland Act 1998 (Consequential Modifications) (No 2) Order 1999 (SI 1999/1820), art 2(2) prevents devolution to a department or officer of the Scottish

Administration of the functions of any government department or officer therein, under the Civil Jurisdiction and Judgments Act 1982.
3   Brussels and Lugano Conventions, art 32(2); Council Regulation on Jurisdiction and Judgments, art 39(2).
4   Council Regulation on Jurisdiction and Judgments, art 39(2).
5   Article 32(2).
6   SI 2001/3929.
7   Implementing Brussels and Lugano Conventions, art 52(1); Council Regulation on Jurisdiction and Judgments, art 59(1), respectively.
8   Civil Jurisdiction and Judgments Act 1982, s 41(6); SI 2001/3929, art 9(6)
9   Brussels and Lugano Conventions, art 52(2); Council Regulation on Jurisdiction and Judgments, art 59(2).
10 Civil Jurisdiction and Judgments Act 1982, 41(7); SI 2001/3929, art 9(7).

The conditions which establish a document as an authentic instrument

14.08   'Authentic instrument' might equally have been translated as 'authentic act', from the French 'acte authentique' or Dutch 'authentieke akte'. 'Act' would be understood in Scots legal language as being a formal legal instrument[1].

In the civil law systems of France and Benelux an authentic act (acte authentique/authentieke akte) is drawn up by a notary. He attaches a 'formule exécutoire', which acts as warrant for diligence in respect of a debt both due and liquid. The act is not registered in a public register; the original is kept by the notary and he issues extracts to the interested party[2]. An agreement to pay maintenance is capable of forming an authentic act[3].

An authentic instrument may take a different form from a notarial act in other legal systems. It needs to fulfil the following criteria to qualify as an authentic act:
(a)   its authenticity must be established by a public authority;
(b)   the authenticity must relate to the contents of the document and not only, for example, the signature; and
(c)   it must be enforceable in the State of origin[4].

It must be 'formally drawn up' or registered in accordance with these criteria[5]. An extracted agreement from the books of council and session, or sheriff court books, with warrant for all lawful execution, fulfils all the criteria for recognition of an authentic act, and is an example of an act which derives its authority from registration in a public register[6]. Any settlement occurring outside the court but enforceable in Denmark (*undenretlig forlig*) does not qualify as an authentic instrument as it has not been authenticated by a public authority[7].

The element of intervention by a public official is an important consideration in determining whether the document is an authentic instrument. It must contain the written statement of an agreement reached between the parties, in the presence of a person with official authority, who himself is not a party to the agreement[8]. A German *urkunde* (agreement) for payment of maintenance drawn up in the presence of a public authority, and signed by the payer, was held to be an authentic instrument[9].

The authentic instrument must not only have the intervention of a public authority such as the Keeper of the Registers of Scotland or sheriff clerk in Scotland, a notary in France or Benelux, or a public official in Germany, but it must also be enforceable in the State of origin. The example of the Danish *undenretlig forlig*[10] illustrates how an agreement, while enforceable in Denmark, was not an authentic instrument as it lacked the element of authentication by a public official.

1 As in the 'Register of Acts and Decrees', forming the records of the Court of Session.
2 Maxwell Report, para 7.2; Dalloz, *Nouveau Répertoire de droit* (2éme édn, 1964), vol 3, 'Notair', 37 ff, para 42; Foster, *Dutch Legal Terminology in English: a Practical Reference Guide* (Academic Press, Leiden, 1991), p 37.
3 *Tonon v Office Cantonal de la Jeunesse de tuttlingen*, Rev Crit DIP (1994) 557, Cour de Cassation, First Civil Chamber, 12 January 1994.
4 Jenard and Moller Report, p 80, para 72.
5 Brussels and Lugano Conventions, art 50; Council Regulation on Jurisdiction and Judgments, art 57(1).
6 Maxwell Report, para 7.2; Schlosser Report, para 226.
7 Jenard and Moller Report, p 80, para 72.
8 *Zilken and Weber v Scholl* (1982) NJ 466, President, District Court of Masstricht, 11 November 1981.
9 *Raad voor de Kinderbescherming Middelburg v X* (1986) NJ 512, Court of Appeal 's-Gravenhage, 18 October 1985.
10 See fn 7.

14.09 Article 57(2) of the Council Regulation on Jurisdiction and Judgments provides that agreements relating to maintenance obligations concluded with administrative authorities or authenticated by them are also to be regarded as authentic instruments.

Procedure for registration of an authentic instrument in Scotland

Stage 1: Application to the Scottish Ministers

14.10 The authentic instrument must first be sent to the Scottish Ministers for transmission to the sheriff court referred to above[1]. The party seeking registration must produce a copy of the authentic instrument:

'which satisfies the conditions necessary to establish its authenticity in the [contracting or] Member State of origin'[2].

The functions of the Scottish Ministers in relation to both the Conventions and Council Regulation on Jurisdiction and Judgment are discharged by the Scottish Executive, Justice Department, European Union and Justice and Home Affairs, Private International Law

Branch, St. Andrews House, Regent Road, Edinburgh EH1 3DG (tel: 0131 244 4827/ 4826)

1   Para 14.07; Civil Jurisdiction and Judgments Act 1982, s 5(1)(b); SI 2001/3929, art 3(1)(b).
2   Brussels and Lugano Conventions, arts 46(1), 50(2), (3); Council Regulation on Jurisdiction and Judgment, arts 53, 57(3), (4), first sentence.

14.11   The Council Regulation on Jurisdiction and Judgments, but not the Brussels and Lugano Conventions provides that:

'the competent authority of a Member State where an authentic instrument was drawn up or registered shall issue, at the request of any interested party, a certificate using the standard form in Annex VI to this Regulation[1].'

1   Article 57(4).

14.12   It does not appear to be mandatory under the Regulation to produce the certificate of authenticity of the authentic instrument along with the application for its registration in the sheriff court[1], but there is nothing to prevent this, and it may indeed be helpful, on a practical level, to do so.

1   See the position regarding production of a certificate of authenticity of a judgment under art 53(2) of the Regulation.

APPLICATIONS UNDER THE BRUSSELS AND LUGANO CONVENTIONS

14.13   An application to the Scottish Ministers under the Brussels and Lugano Conventions for transmission of an authentic instrument relating to maintenance obligations for registration in the sheriff court is made under s 5 of the Civil Jurisdiction and Judgments Act 1982 as applied to authentic instruments by the CJJ Order 1993. The application is governed by the CCMR 1997, r 5.38. It must be signed by the applicant, or a solicitor or professional person qualified to act in such matters in the State of origin on the applicant's behalf[1]. Under CCMR 1997, r 5.38(1)[1], the application must specify:
(a)   an address within Scotland for service on the applicant[2];
(b)   the usual and last known address of the person against whom enforcement is sought;
(c)   the place where the applicant seeks to enforce the authentic instrument;
(d)   whether at the date of the application the authentic instrument has been satisfied in whole or in part;
(e)   whether interest is recoverable under the authentic instrument in accordance with the law of the State of origin and, if so, the rate of interest and the date from which interest became due; and
(f)   whether any time for challenging the authentic instrument has expired without an appeal having been brought or whether an appeal against it has been brought and is pending or has been finally disposed of[3].

1   As adapted for application to authentic instruments by the author.
2   This implements the Brussels and Lugano Conventions, art 33(2).

3   See para **14.28**.

14.14   The application under s 5 of the Civil Jurisdiction and Judgments Act 1982 as applied to authentic instruments by the CJJ Order 1993 must be accompanied by various documents prescribed by the CCMR 1997[1]. These are:

(a)   a copy of the instrument authenticated by the competent authority in the State of origin[2];

(b)   documents which establish that, according to the State of origin, the authentic instrument is enforceable;

(c)   documents which establish that the authentic instrument has been served[3];

(d)   where appropriate, a document showing that the applicant is in receipt of Legal Aid in the State of origin; and

(e)   English translations of the authentic instrument and the documents referred to at paras (b), (c) and (d) above (if the originals are not in English), certified by a person qualified to do so in one of the contracting States[4].

1   CCMR, r 5.38(2).
2   This appears to extend beyond the requirements of the Conventions: see para **14.10**.
3   It is not, however, entirely clear whether prior service is necessary in the case of an authentic instrument under the Brussels or Lugano Conventions: see para **14.26**, below.
4   This includes a person in the United Kingdom. It is not necessary to obtain translations from abroad.

APPLICATIONS UNDER THE COUNCIL REGULATION ON JURISDICTION AND JUDGMENTS

14.15   An application to the Scottish Ministers under the Council Regulation on Jurisdiction and Judgments for transmission of an authentic instrument relating to maintenance obligations for registration in the sheriff court is made under art 3 of the Civil Jurisdiction and Judgments Order 2001 ('CJJ Order 2001')[1], as applied to authentic instruments by the Civil Jurisdiction and Judgments (Authentic Instruments and Court Settlements) Order 2001 ('CJJ(AICS) Order 2001')[2]. Rule 5.38 of the CCMR 1997[3] has not explicitly been extended to applications under the Council Regulation on Jurisdiction and Judgments. It is, in any event, difficult to apply exactly, word for word, to applications under art 3 of the CJJ Order 2001 as applied to authentic instruments by the CCJ(AICS) Order 2001.

There are three significant differences between the Conventions and the Council Regulation on Jurisdiction and Judgments so far as enforcement of authentic instruments is concerned:

(a)   There is no requirement for prior service of the authentic instrument; accordingly there is no need to produce evidence of prior service of the authentic instrument as mentioned above[3].

(b)   There is no requirement for a certificate of authenticity in terms of Annex VI of the Regulation, but it would be useful to produce one[4].

(c)   There is no need to produce a document showing, where appropriate, that the applicant has been granted Legal Aid in the State of origin.

The documents which should be produced in connection with an application under art 3 of the CJJ Order 2001 as applied to authentic instruments by the CCJ(AICS) Order 2001 are:

(i)   a copy of the instrument, preferably with a certificate of its authenticity in terms of Annex VI of the Council Regulation on Jurisdiction and Judgments;

(i)   documents which establish that, according to the State of origin, the authentic instrument is enforceable;

(iii)   English translations of the authentic instrument and the documents referred to at paras (i) and (ii) above (if the originals are not in English), certified by a person qualified to do so in one of the Regulation States[5].

1   SI 2001/3929.
2   SI 2001/3928.
3   See para **14.14**, sub-para (c); and see further paras **14.26** and **14.27**.
4   See paras **14.11** and **14.12**. See para **14.14** sub-para (b) regarding the Brussels and Lugano Conventions for production of a document establishing that the authentic instrument is enforceable in the State of origin.
5   Such a person could be in the United Kingdom as 'one of the contracting States'. It is not necessary to obtain translations from abroad.

14.16   The need for production of a copy of the authentic instrument 'satisfying the conditions necessary to establish its authenticity' in the State of origin must also be borne in mind[1].

1   See para **14.10**.

14.17   It would be useful in practice to point out to the Scottish Ministers that the application proceeds under art 3 of the CJJ Order 2001 as applied by the CJJ(AICS) Order 2001, and that as under the Council Regulation on Jurisdiction and Judgments there is no need for prior service of the authentic instrument, no certificate of service has been provided.

14.18   It would also be helpful to appoint an address for service within the area of the jurisdiction of the court applied to, or alternatively, to appoint a representative *ad litem*[1].

1   Council Regulation on Jurisdiction and Judgments, art 40(2).

Stage 2: Procedure in the Sheriff Court

14.19   Article 33 of the Brussels and Lugano Conventions, and art 40(1) of the Council Regulation on Jurisdiction and Judgments, provide that:

'the procedure for making the application shall be governed by the law of the [contracting or] Member State in which enforcement is sought[1].'

1   Articles 33(1), 40(1).

14.20 However, the Conventions and the Regulation make some mandatory provisions about procedure as well. Thus the applicant must give an address for service of process within the area of the jurisdiction of the court applied to or, if the law of the State in which enforcement is sought does not provide for the furnishing of such an address, the applicant must appoint a representative *ad litem*[1]. A copy of the instrument which satisfies the conditions necessary to establish its authenticity must be produced with the application[2]. There must also be produced in respect of the Brussels and Lugano Conventions, where appropriate, a document showing that the applicant is in receipt of Legal Aid in the State of origin; where this is not produced, the court may specify a time for its production or accept an equivalent document or, if it considers it has sufficient information before it, dispense with production[3]. The court may require certified translations of the documents produced[4]. No legalisation or other similar formality may be required of the authentic instrument, their certified translations, or in respect of a document appointing a representative *ad litem*[5]. No security, bond or deposit, however described, may be required of the party seeking registration on the ground that the applicant is a foreign national or that the applicant is not domiciled or resident in the State in which enforcement is sought[6]. A court fee may be charged for the application but not, in respect of the Regulation, by reference to the value of the matter at issue[7]. In practice, no fee is charged in respect of the initial application for enforcement, but a fee would be paid for presenting an initial writ in an appeal against enforcement or its refusal[9].

1 Brussels and Lugano Conventions, art 33(2); Council Regulation on Jurisdiction and Judgments, art 40(2).
2 Brussels and Lugano Conventions, art 33(3), art 46(1); Council Regulation on Jurisdiction and Judgments, arts 40(3), 53(1). For Brussels and Lugano Conventions applications, a document establishing that the instrument is enforceable and has been served must also be produced: art 47(1).
3 Brussels and Lugano Conventions, arts 47(2), 48(1); CCMR 1997, r 5.38(3).
4 Brussels and Lugano Conventions, art 48(2); Council Regulation on Jurisdiction and Judgments, art 55(2). The list in the Brussels and Lugano Conventions also includes the document establishing that the instrument is enforceable and has been served referred to in fn 2.
5 Brussels and Lugano Conventions, art 49; Council Regulation on Jurisdiction and Judgments, art 56.
6 Brussels and Lugano Conventions, art 45; Council Regulation on Jurisdiction and Judgments, art 51; see *Rossmeier (Dieter) v Mounthooly Transport* 2000 SLT 208; *Nguyen v Searchnet Associates Ltd* 2000 SLT (Sh Ct) 83.
7 Council Regulation on Jurisdiction and Judgments, art 52.
8 Sheriff Court Fees Order 1997 (SI 1997/687), Schedule, para 17 prescribes a fee for an application under the Civil Jurisdiction and Judgments Act 1982, ss 12 and 18, but not s 5 of the Council Regulation on Jurisdiction and Judgments.

14.21 The Brussels and Lugano Conventions require the court to make the decision on registration 'without delay'[1]; the Council Regulation on Jurisdiction and Judgments that the authentic instrument be declared enforceable 'immediately' on production of the authenticated copy of the instrument[2]. This decision must be made in respect of both the Conventions and the Regulation without giving the party against whom enforcement is sought an opportunity to make submissions at this stage of the proceedings[3]. The court's decision must 'without delay' (the Conventions) or 'forthwith' (the Regulation) be brought to the notice of the applicant 'in accordance with the procedure laid down by the law of the [contracting or] Member State in which enforcement is sought[4]'. The Regulation additionally provides that:

'the declaration of enforceability shall be served on the party against whom enforcement is sought, accompanied by the judgment, if not already served on that party[5].'

The reference to judgment includes 'authentic instrument'[6].

1   Article 34(1).
2   Article 41.
3   Brussels and Lugano Conventions, art 34(1); Council Regulation on Jurisdiction and Judgments, art 41.
4   Brussels and Lugano Conventions, art 35; Council Regulation on Jurisdiction and Judgments, art 42(1).
5   Council Regulation on Jurisdiction and Judgments, art 42(2).
6   Council Regulation on Jurisdiction and Judgments, art 57(4), first sentence.

14.22   The application for registration under the Brussels and Lugano Conventions is dealt with in the first instance by the sheriff clerk or the 'sheriff court' in applications under the Regulation[1]. If he, or the 'sheriff court' in applications under the Regulation, authorises registration, the debtor may appeal to the sheriff within one month of service of the decision on him[2]. If he is domiciled in a contracting or Member State other than the United Kingdom, he has two months to appeal from the date of service of the decision on him personally, or at his place of residence[3]. No extension of time may be granted on account of distance[4]. During the time specified for the appeal and until any such appeal has been determined, no measures of enforcement may be taken other than protective measures taken against the property of the party against whom enforcement is sought[5]. The declaration of enforceability carries with it the power to proceed to protective measures[6].

1   The Civil Jurisdiction and Judgments Act 1982, s 5(2) and SI 2001/3929, art 3(2) require applications for registration of authentic instruments relating to maintenance obligations to be 'determined in the first instance by the prescribed officer of court having jurisdiction in the matter'. The sheriff clerk has been designated the 'prescribed officer' in respect of applications under the Brussels and Lugano Convention (CCMR 1997, r 5.38(1)(a)), but he has not yet been designated 'prescribed officer' for the purposes of the Regulation.
2   Brussels and Lugano Conventions, arts 36(1), 37(1); Council Regulation on Jurisdiction and Judgments, art 43(1), (2), (5), first sentence, and Annex III.
3   Brussels and Lugano Conventions, art 36(2); Council Regulation on Jurisdiction and Judgments, art 43(5), second sentence.
4   Brussels and Lugano Convention, art 36(2), second sentence; Council Regulation on Jurisdiction and Judgments, art 43(5), third sentence.
5   Brussels and Lugano Conventions, art 39(1); Council Regulation on Jurisdiction and Judgments, art 47(3).
6   Brussels and Lugano Conventions, art 39(2); Council Regulation on Jurisdiction and Judgments, art 47(2).

14.23 If the sheriff clerk, or court, refuses registration, the applicant may appeal to the sheriff within one month of service of the decision in respect of applications under the Brussels and Lugano Conventions and within 21 days after the refusal of registration was communicated in respect of applications under the Regulation[1]. Under the provisions of the Conventions, the party against whom enforcement is sought must be summoned to appear before the sheriff in the appeal[2]. In relation to both the Conventions and the Regulation, the sheriff must sist the proceedings if the debtor does not appear in the appeal proceedings:

> 'so long as it is not shown that the defendant has been able to receive the document instituting the proceedings or an equivalent document in sufficient time to enable him to arrange for his defence, or that all necessary steps have been taken to this end[3].'

This provision is replaced by art 19 of Council Regulation (EC) 1348/2000[4] if the document instituting the proceedings or an equivalent document was transmitted from Scotland to another Member State for service pursuant to that Regulation[5]. If that Regulation is not applicable, then art 15 of the Hague Convention of 15 November 1965 on the service abroad of judicial and extra-judicial documents in civil or commercial matters applies if the document instituting the proceedings[6] had to be transmitted abroad 'pursuant to that Convention'[7]. Article 19(1) of Council Regulation (EC) 1348/2000 and art 15 of the Hague Convention provide that where the document for service was transmitted to another Member or contracting State under the provisions of Regulation 1348/2000 or the Hague Convention, judgment must not be given in the absence of the defender until it is established that:

(a) the document was served by a method prescribed by the internal law of the State addressed for the service of documents in domestic actions upon persons who are within its territory; or

(b) the document was actually delivered to the defender or his residence by another method provided for by the Regulations or Hague Convention;

and that in either of these cases the service or delivery of the document was effected in sufficient time to enable the defender to defend.

1 Brussels and Lugano Conventions, art 40; Council Regulation on Jurisdiction and Judgments, art 43(1). Neither the Conventions nor the Regulation lay down a time limit. This is provided for by the CCMR 1997, r 5.42(1) in relation to applications under the Brussels and Lugano Conventions. As no time limit is specified in the CCMR 1997 for applications under the Regulation, the appeal must be made within 21 days after its intimating to the applicant: Summary Applications, Statutory Applications and Appeals etc Rules 1999 (SI 1999/No 929), r 2.6.

2 Brussels and Lugano Conventions, art 40(2), first sentence.

3 Brussels and Lugano Conventions, arts 20(2), 40(2); Council Regulation on Jurisdiction and Judgments, arts 26(2), 43(4).

4 Council Regulation (EC) 1348/2000 of 29 May 2000 on the service in the Member States of judicial and extra-judicial documents in civil or commercial matters (OJ L160, 30.6.2000, p 37).

5 Council Regulation on Jurisdiction and Judgments, arts 26(3), 43(4).

6　Or an equivalent document, such as a service copy, or notice of the proceedings has to be transmitted abroad. Note that while the terminology differs as between the Conventions, and the Regulation, the meaning is the same.
7　Brussels and Lugano Conventions, art 20(3); Council Regulation on Jurisdiction and Judgments, arts 26(4), 43(4).

Stage 3: Further appeal

14.24　The judgment given by the sheriff on an appeal by the applicant or the person against whom enforcement is sought may be further appealed by either party to the Inner House of the Court of Session[1] on a point of law[2]. No further appeal is permitted[3]. The appeal to the Inner House is treated as a reclaiming motion, for the purpose of regulating procedure in the appeal[4].

1　Civil Jurisdiction and Judgments Act 1982, s 6(3)(b) as applied to authentic instruments by CJJ Order 1993, art 3(1); SI 2001/3929, art 4(3)(b).
2　Brussels and Lugano Conventions, arts 37(2), 41; Council Regulation on Jurisdiction and Judgments, art 44, Annex IV.
3　Brussels and Lugano Conventions, arts 37(2), 41; Council Regulation on Jurisdiction and Judgments, art 44, Annex IV.
4　RCS 1994, r 38.10.

Powers of the sheriff and Court of Session on appeal

14.25　Subject to the exception noted in para **14.26**, the court *must* order the registration of the authentic instrument for enforcement against the maintenance debtor if satisfied that the authentic instrument has been formally drawn up or registered as an authentic instrument and it is enforceable in the State of origin[1]. It has power to order the production and translation of the authentic instrument or other documents[2], and under the Council Regulation on Jurisdiction and Judgments it may receive a certificate of authenticity from the State of origin to satisfy itself as to the authenticity of the document[3].

1　Brussels and Lugano Conventions, art 50; Council Regulation on Jurisdiction and Judgments, art 57(1), (2).
2　Brussels and Lugano Conventions, art 48; Council Regulation on Jurisdiction and Judgments, art 55.
3　Council Regulation on Jurisdiction and Judgments, art 57(4).

14.26　The only ground upon which the court can refuse to order the registration of an authentic instrument which it is satisfied is a proper and enforceable authentic instrument in the State of origin and which, in cases under the Brussels and Lugano Conventions, has previously been served on the person against whom enforcement is sought[1], is if the enforcement of the instrument is contrary to public policy in the State addressed. Under the Regulation, the instrument must be *manifestly* contrary to public policy[2]. The validity of the agreement cannot be challenged on grounds of public policy[3].

The view has been expressed that there is no need for prior service of an authentic instrument under the Brussels or Lugano Conventions[4], but it is respectfully submitted that prior service is appropriate, at least where the national law of the State of origin requires the instrument to be served before enforcement can take place[5].

1 Brussels and Lugano Conventions, art 47(1).
2 Brussels and Lugano Conventions, art 50; Council Regulation on Jurisdiction and Judgments, art 57(1).
3 *Bertrand v CDE* (1992) NIPR 455, District Court of Roermond, 27 August 1992.
4 Maxwell Committee Report, para 7.5.
5 O'Malley and Layton, *European Civil Procedure* (1989, Sweet & Maxwell), para 30.10, p 819.

14.27 There is no requirement for previous service of the authentic instrument under the Regulation but if there has been no previous service, then a copy of the authentic instrument must be served on the person against whom enforcement is sought at the same time as he is served with the notice authorising registration of the authentic instrument in the sheriff court[1].

1 Council Regulation on Jurisdiction and Judgments, art 42(2) applied by art 57(4), first sentence.

14.28 Since it may be possible for an authentic instrument to be challenged in the State of origin, it should be noted that the sheriff (and specifically the Court of Session in cases under the Regulation) has power to sist the application for registration of the authentic instrument if an appeal has been lodged against the authentic instrument in the State of origin or if the time for any appeal has not yet expired[1]. Alternatively, the court might make enforcement conditional on the provision of such security as it may determine[2].

1 Brussels and Lugano Conventions, art 38(1), (2); Council Regulation on Jurisdiction and Judgments, art 46(1), (2); *Bertrand v CDE* (1992) NIPR 455, District Court of Roermond, 27 August 1992.
2 Brussels and Lugano Conventions, art 38(3); Council Regulation on Jurisdiction and Judgments, art 46(3).

Partial enforcement

14.29 The court may order, or may be specifically requested to order, enforcement of only part of an authentic instrument if the instrument relates to several matters[1]. This is particularly important in the case of a family law agreement qualifying as an authentic instrument which governs many different matters as it is only competent to seek its enforcement in relation to matters of maintenance[2].

1 Brussels and Lugano Conventions, art 42; Council Regulation on Jurisdiction and Judgments, art 48.
2 Case C-220/95 *Van den Boogaard v PM Laumen* [1997] ECR I-1147.

Legal Aid and costs

14.30   An applicant who in a State of origin (other than Denmark) has benefited from complete or partial Legal Aid or exemption from costs or expenses or who, in Denmark or Iceland, obtains a statement from the Ministry of Justice to the effect that he or she fulfils the economic requirements to qualify for the grant of complete or partial Legal Aid or exemption from costs or expenses, is entitled in proceedings for enforcement of an authentic instrument:

> 'to benefit from the most favourable Legal Aid or to the most extensive exemption from costs or expenses provided for by the law of the State addressed[1].'

1   Brussels and Lugano Conventions, art 44; Council Regulation on Jurisdiction and Judgments, art 50.

14.31   Unfortunately, these generous provisions extend under the Brussels and Lugano Conventions only to the point where the sheriff clerk makes the initial decision[1]. They do not apply to appeals to the sheriff, or Court of Session. However, the Civil Legal Aid (Scotland) Regulations 2002[2] extend the provisions 'for the purpose of any proceedings following' on an application under s 5 of the Civil Jurisdiction and Judgments Act 1982[3] and, therefore, in appeals to the sheriff and Court of Session the applicant is eligible for Legal Aid without regard to income and capital or payment of a contribution[4]. A simplified form of Legal Aid application may be submitted, and any money then recovered is not required to be paid to the Scottish Legal Aid Board[5]. Similar privileges are obtained in relation to legal advice and assistance, which would be used for the initial application to the sheriff clerk under s 5 of the Civil Jurisdiction and Judgments Act 1982, and in making applications for Legal Aid for making or opposing appeals to the sheriff or Court of Session. As a person in receipt of Legal Aid, the applicant is exempt from payment of sheriff court and Court of Session fees[7]. The initial application to the sheriff does not attract a fee as it is made by letter and not formal pleadings and no fee is otherwise prescribed for the application[8].

1   They apply only to proceedings under arts 32–35. An applicant appeals to the sheriff under art 40 and to the Court of Session under art 41.
2   SSI 2002/494, reg 46(1)(b).
3   SSI 2002/494, reg 46(1)(b)(ii).
4   SSI 2002/494, reg 46(2)(a), (b).
5   SSI 2002/494, reg 46(2)(b)–(d).
6   Advice and Assistance (Scotland) Regulations 1996 (SI 1996/2447).
7   Sheriff Court Fees Order 1997 (SI 1997/687), art 7(1)(c); Court of Session etc Fees Order 1997 (SI 1997/No 688), art 5(c).
8   SI 1997/687, art 2(1)(c) (definition of 'writ'), scheduled Table of Fees, Part II – Sheriff Court Proceedings (while these are fees for applications under ss 12 or 18 of the Civil Jurisdiction and Judgments Act 1982, none is prescribed for applications under s 5 of the Act).

14.32   An applicant under the Council Regulation on Jurisdiction and Judgments is to benefit from the Legal Aid provisions 'in the procedures provided for' by the relevant part of the Regulation[1], which suggests the applicant should receive favourable Legal Aid treatment in an appeal to the sheriff or Court of Session, whether at his or her, or the opponent's, instance. No implemental regulations have been made by the Scottish Ministers, but the applicant is entitled to rely directly on the terms of the Regulation as it takes precedence over domestic law[2].

1   Section 2, ch III: Recognition and Enforcement, applied to authentic instruments by art 54(4), first sentence of the Regulation.
2   *R v Secretary of State for Transport, ex parte Factortame* [1991] AC 603.

14.33   It should be noted that only the applicant, and not the person against whom enforcement is sought, is entitled to benefit from the Legal Aid provisions of the Conventions and the Regulation.

2. Transmitting Scottish authentic instruments abroad for enforcement

14.34   A person seeking to apply for enforcement abroad of an authentic instrument relating to maintenance registered in the books of council and session must apply by letter to the Keeper of the Registers of Scotland for:
(a)   either:
   (i)   a certificate in form 62.40–B, in applications under the Brussels or Lugano Conventions; or
  (ii)   a certificate under art 57 of the Council Regulation on Jurisdiction and Judgments in applications under the Regulation; and
(b)   an extract of the authentic instrument[1].

The Keeper may only issue the certificate referred to above if the applicant produces an affidavit verifying that enforcement has not been suspended and that the time available for enforcement has not expired[2].

1   RCS 1994, rr 62.40(4), 62.40(5).
2   RCS 1994, r 62.40(6).

14.35   There are no equivalent rules of procedure in respect of authentic instruments registered in the sheriff court books. There is no reason, however, why the sheriff clerk cannot be asked to issue a certificate under art 57 of the Council Regulation on Jurisdiction and Judgments, as that Regulation is directly applicable in Scotland, and, if required, a further extract of the authentic instrument.

3. Service of documents in connection with enforcement of authentic instruments

14.36   For service in any EU Member State (other than Denmark), use, if necessary, can be made of Council Regulation (EC) 1348/2000[1].

For service under the Brussels or Lugano Conventions use, if necessary, can be made of the Hague Convention of 15 November 1965 on the service abroad of judicial and extra-judicial documents in civil or commercial matters in relation to service of authentic instruments in Aruba, Denmark, Norway and Switzerland. Iceland is not a party to this Convention. It does not apply in respect of Gibraltar[2].

However, there exists in relation to the Brussels and Lugano Conventions provision for service by sending judicial and extra-judicial documents: 'by the appropriate public officers of the State in which the document has been drawn up directly to the appropriate public officers of the State in which the addressee is to be found' unless this method of service is objected to by any of the contracting States[3]. Of these States, Switzerland has reserved the right, in relation to the Lugano Convention, to require that between public officers, documents sent from and to Switzerland be transmitted by other procedures.

These provisions apply in respect of Gibraltar[4].

1   Council Regulation (EC) 1348/2000 of 29 May 2000 on the service in the Member States of judicial and extra-judicial documents in civil or commercial matters (OJ L160, 30.6.2000, p 37).
2   See in relation to both instruments, Jamieson, *Butterworths Scottish Family Law Service*, 'Service Abroad of Judicial and Extra-Judicial Documents', paras [1501]–[1541]; Jamieson, 'Service of Judicial and Extra-Judicial Documents within the EU' (2000) JLSS, November, p 36; Jamieson, 'Setting Off Abroad: Service in the EU' (2003) JLSS, December, p 29.
3   Brussels Convention, Annexed Protocol, art IV; Lugano Convention, Protocol No 1, art IV.
4   Civil Jurisdiction and Judgments Act 1982 (Gibraltar) Order 1997 (SI 1997/2602).

4. European Enforcement Order

14.37   The European Enforcement Order ('EEO') for uncontested claims will, from its introduction on 21 October 2005, apply also to authentic instruments for maintenance[1].

This provides for an authentic instrument, including one relating to maintenance, to be enforced directly in the other EU Member States (except Denmark) on the force of a certificate issued by the designated authority in the State of origin[2].

There will be no need to submit it to the judicial authorities in the other country, and there is to be no 'possibility of opposing its recognition'[3], or applying to sist enforcement[4].

There appears to be no need for prior service of the EEO[5].

Use of the EEO procedure will be optional to the procedures under the Council Regulation on Jurisdiction and Judgments[6], but as the EEO procedure is far more advantageous to the maintenance creditor, it is difficult to see why use should be made of the more involved procedure under the Regulation.

1   Regulation (EC) 805/2004 of the European Parliament and of the Council of 21 April 2004 creating a European Enforcement Order for uncontested claims (OJ L143, 30.4.2004, p 15).
2   Regulation (EC) 805/2004, arts 5, 25.
3   Regulation (EC) 805/2004, art 5.
4   Regulation (EC) 805/2004, art 19, to this effect, does not apply to authentic instruments: art 25(3). Article 21(1), which also contains grounds for refusal of enforcement, does not apply, also by virtue of art 25(3).
5   Regulation (EC) 805/2004, art 19, as noted in fn 4, does not apply.
6   Regulation (EC) 805/2004, art 27.

Further research

14.38   The most useful textbook is:
—   O'Malley and Layton, *European Civil Procedure* (Sweet & Maxwell, 1989).

14.39   APPENDIX 1 shows the courts to which applications and appeals are made in respect of authentic instruments relating to maintenance obligations in the various countries to which the reciprocal arrangements apply.

14.40   APPENDIX 2 explains how to obtain information on case law relating to the Brussels and Lugano Conventions.

Chapter 15

Diligence, enforcement and protective measures

1. General considerations

15.01 A separation agreement is a contract and most obligations made by that contract are enforceable against the other party. It is possible to sue for breach of contract[1].

The court is unlikely to enforce purely social or personal agreements, such as arrangements for house-keeping and child care arrangements[2].

Agreements in connection with residence and contact in respect of the parties' children are ultimately unenforceable as the court, in the event of a dispute, must consider the interests of the child as paramount, even if that overrides the parties' agreement about the children[3].

Obligations to perform acts, or deliver deeds in relation to heritable or moveable property will unusually be enforceable by specific implement[4]. Negative obligations, to retain from doing an act, may be the subject of an interdict[5].

Money obligations are directly enforceable if the agreement has been registered for execution in the books of council and session, or sheriff court books[6]. If the agreement has not been registered in this way, the court can nonetheless grant decree in terms of the agreement, for example for a sum of aliment agreed to be paid by the husband to the wife[7]. If the agreement is for aliment, but the amount is not specified, the court has jurisdiction to modify a suitable aliment for the party entitled to aliment under the agreement[8]. A decree for payment of aliment, or other money obligation, authorises:

(a) the service of a charge for payment of the sums due, together with any interest thereon;

(b) the execution of an earnings arrestment or of an attachment, after expiry of the days of charge;

(c) an arrestment in execution;

(d)   a current maintenance arrestment in respect of current maintenance[9].

Arrears of aliment due under a decree are enforceable by service of a charge, followed by an earnings arrestment, or attachment; or by an arrestment in execution, without prior service of a charge[10]. Current maintenance is enforceable by a current maintenance arrestment directed against the debtor's earnings, after service of a statutory notice under s 54 of the Debtors (Scotland) Act 1987[11]. The details involved in carrying out diligences are beyond the scope of this book[12].

1   *Darke v Strout* [2003] EWCA Civ 176.
2   Walker, *The Law of Contracts and Related Obligations in Scotland* (3rd edn, 1995), p 141, para 9.2.
3   Children (Scotland) Act 1995, s 11(7)(a).
4   McBryde, *The Law of Contract in Scotland* (2nd edn, 2001), ch 23.
5   *Burn Murdoch on Interdict* (1933), pp 287, 288; Scott Robinson, *The Law of Interdict* (Butterworths, 2nd edn, 1994), p 155; Family Law (Scotland) Act 1985, s 18 in relation to interdicting disposal of assets to defeat claim for aliment.
6   Writs Execution (Scotland) Act 1877, s 3; reproduced in CHAPTER 18; see paras **15.02–15.04**, for the diligences authorised under s 3 of the 1877 Act.
7   *McGlashan on Aliment* (1837), p 6.
8   *Lady Buchannan v The Laird*, July 23, 1629, Durie's Decisions, p 466.
9   Debtors (Scotland) Act 1987, s 87(1), (2) (as amended by the Debt Arrangement and Attachment (Scotland) Act 2002 (asp 17), Sch 3, para 17(9)); Sheriff Courts (Scotland) Extracts Act 1892, s 7(1) (as substituted by the Debtors (Scotland) Act 1987, s 87(3) and amended by the Debt Arrangement and Attachment (Scotland) Act 2002 (asp 17), Sch 3, para 8).
10 Debtors (Scotland) Act 1987, s 73(1) (definition of 'ordinary debt').
11 Debtors (Scotland) Act 1987, s 54(1) (as amended by the Child Support Act 1991, Sch 5, para 8(4)).
12 See Stewart, *A Treatise on the Law of Diligence* (1898); Maher and Cusine, *The Law and Practice of Diligence* (Butterworths, 1990); and the Debt Arrangement and Attachments (Scotland) Act 2002 (asp 17). See also Gretton, *The Law of Inhibitions and Adjudication* (2nd edn, 1996) in relation to inhibitions and adjudication, discussed below at paras **15.07–15.11**, **15.15** and **15.16**.

2.   Payment of money under agreements registered for execution

15.02   It is a great advantage to the creditor if the agreement has been registered for execution in the books of council and session, or sheriff court books. The warrant for execution contained in an extract of such an agreement is equivalent to a court decree[1] and, like a court decree, it authorises:
(a)   the service of a charge for payment of the sums due, together with any interest thereon;
(b)   the execution of an earnings arrestment or of an attachment, after expiry of the days of charge;
(c)   an arrestment in execution;
(d)   a current maintenance arrestment in respect of current maintenance[2].

1   Act of Sederunt 17 November 1599 anent extractis of contractis, obligations, etc, registrat in the Buikes of Counsale; Bell's *Comm* I, 4; *Taylor, Ptr* 1931 SLT 260 at 261, per Lord Pitman; *Commissioner's Case No CSCS/5/97* 1999 FLR 37.
2   Writs Execution (Scotland) Act 1877, s 3.

15.03   Arrears of maintenance are enforceable by service of a charge, followed by an earnings arrestment; or by an arrestment in execution, without prior service of a charge[1]. Current maintenance is enforceable by a current maintenance arrestment, directed against the debtor's earnings, after service of a statutory notice under s 54 of the Debtors (Scotland) Act 1987[2].

1   Debtors (Scotland) Act 1987, s 90.
2   Debtors (Scotland) Act 1987, s 54(1) (as amended by the Child Support Act 1991, Sch 5, para 8(4)): the statutory notice is necessary as the registered agreement is a 'maintenance order' as defined by the Debtors (Scotland) Act 1987, s 106 (definition (h)(i)). It is therefore not one of the types of 'maintenance order' excluded from the Debtors (Scotland) Act 1987, s 54(1) by s 54(2) of that Act.

15.04   The creditor's solicitor must take care to instruct a messenger-at-arms to carry out diligence under an agreement registered for execution in the books of council and session[1], and a sheriff officer if the agreement is registered for execution in the sheriff court books[2]. An advantage of agreements registered in the books of council and session is that diligence proceedings on an extract of the agreement can be carried out edictally on the obligant if he cannot be found, or is furth of Scotland[3].

1   RCS 1994, r 16.12(1), (2).
2   OCR 1993, r 5.4.
3   RCS 1994, r 16.12(1)(b), (4).

3. Payment of maintenance under registered European authentic instruments

15.05   Authentic instruments registered in the sheriff court under s 5 of the Civil Jurisdiction and Judgments Act 1982[1] are entered in the Maintenance Orders Register[2]. The applicant may obtain an extract of a registered order and proceed to:
(a)   arrest in execution[3] (for arrears of maintenance);
(b)   intimate the authentic instrument for the purposes of s 54(1) of the Debtors (Scotland) Act 1987 (statutory notice to be given prior to service of a current maintenance arrestment);
(c)   inhibit; or
(d)   charge and attach thereon[4];

but may not proceed to:
(i)   an action of furthcoming in respect of an arrestment;
(ii)   serve a current maintenance arrestment schedule;
(iii) make application for a conjoined arrestment order[5];

(iv) adjudication in respect of inhibition; or

(v) auction in respect of an attachment

unless the time for appeal against the determination of the sheriff has elapsed and any appeal has been disposed of[6].

1   As applied to authentic instruments by the Civil Jurisdiction and Judgments Order 1993 **(SI 1993/ 604)**, art 3.

2   CCMR 1997, r 5.4.

3   This does not include an earnings arrestment, for which prior service a charge is needed: Debtors (Scotland) Act 1987, s 90(1).

4   No provision is made about service of an earnings arrestment in respect of arrears of maintenance, but see fn 5.

5   This does not prevent an earnings arrestment on its own, but it is submitted that, as the scheme of this rule is to prevent the actual taking of the debtor's money or property until an appeal is disposed of, such an arrestment would not be competent until the expiry of the appeal period and the determination of any appeal.

6   CCMR 1997, r 5.43 (as amended by Act of Sederunt (Debt Arrangement and Attachment) (Scotland) Act 2002) 2002, Sch 3, para 7). An authentic instrument registered in the sheriff court is a 'maintenance order' for the purposes of a current maintenance arrestment: Debtors (Scotland) Act 1987, s 106 (definition (h)(ii) in respect of maintenance).

15.06   An application for inhibition on an extract of an authentic instrument registered in the sheriff court Maintenance Orders Register must be made to the Court of Session. Form 59.1B of the Rules of the Court of Session 1994 (decree granted or foreign judgment registered for execution) should be used for this purpose[1].

1   RCS 1994, r 59.1(1)(b).

4. Letters of inhibition

15.07   Application for letters of inhibition may be made:

(a) where decree has been granted for sums due under a family law agreement which has not been registered for execution;

(b) in respect of a 'foreign judgment registered for execution' which, it is submitted, is apt to include an authentic instrument registered in the sheriff court under s 5 of the Civil Jurisdiction and Judgments Act 1982;

(c) in respect of sums due under a family law agreement registered for execution;

(d) on the dependence of an action in the sheriff court for payment of sums due under a family law agreement which has not been registered for execution;

(e) in respect of future or contingent debts; and

(f) on a contract for the transfer of heritable property[1].

1   RCS 1994, r 59.1(1).

15.08   Inhibitions in execution on decrees, registered authentic instruments, extracts of registered family law agreements, or in respect of contracts for transfer of heritable property, are granted on application to the Deputy Principal Clerk in Forms 59.1B (decrees, registered authentic instruments, and extracts of registered agreements) or 59.1C (contract for transfer of heritable property) of the Rules of the Court of Session 1994, without the need for any judicial intervention[1]. Particular note should be taken of inhibition being granted in respect of contracts for the transfer of heritable property. This is a useful remedy if a party to a separation agreement seeks to sell heritable property contrary to his agreement to transfer it to the other party under the agreement. If in relation to these four types of inhibition the Deputy Principal Clerk refuses to sign and date the warrant for inhibition, the application may, on request, be placed before a Lord Ordinary, whose decision is final and not subject to review[2].

1   RCS 1994, r 59.1(3) (as amended by Act of Sederunt (Rules of the Court of Session Amendment No 6) (Diligence on the Dependence) 2003 para 2(9)(a)).
2   RCS 1994, r 59.1(4) (as amended by Act of Sederunt (Rules of the Court of Session Amendment No 6) (Diligence on the Dependence) 2003, para 2(9)(b)).

15.09   Applications for inhibition on the dependence of a Court of Session action for payment, which are sought by motion, or on the dependence of a sheriff court action for payment, which are sought by application for letters of inhibition in the Court of Session, must be considered by the Lord Ordinary[1]; but a hearing before him is not necessary[2]. There must be cause shown for the granting of inhibition on the dependence of an action for aliment by a spouse or child[3]. The Lord Ordinary's decision is final and not subject to review[4].

1   RCS 1994, r 13.6A (introduced by the Act of Sederunt (Rules of the Court of Session Amendment No 6) (Diligence on the Dependence) 2003, para 2(2)); RCS 1994, r 59.1(4A) (as amended by the Act of Sederunt (Rules of the Court of Session Amendment No 6) (Diligence on the Dependence) 2003, para 2(9)(a)).
2   *Advocate General for Scotland v Taylor* 2003 SLT 1340.
3   Family Law (Scotland) Act 1985, s 19(1).
4   RCS 1994, r 59.1(4B) (as amended by the Act of Sederunt (Rules of the Court of Session Amendment No 6) (Diligence on the Dependence) 2003, para 2(9)(a)); RCS 1994, r 59.1(5).

15.10   Applications for inhibition in respect of future or contingent debts ('inhibitions in security') include claims for payment of future aliment under a separation agreement[1] and are competent where the debtor is *in meditatione fugae* or *vergens ad inopiam* or the circumstances are such that he intends to remove his effects beyond the power of his creditors[2].

1   There appears to be no need for the agreement to have been registered for execution – a document of debt is sufficient: Stewart, *A Treatise on the Law of Diligence* (1898). An adjudication in security, by way of contrast, must proceed on an agreement registered for execution: Debtors (Scotland) Act 1987, s 101.
2   *Symington v Symington* (1875) 3 R 205; *Tweedie v Tweedie* 1966 SLT (Notes) 89; *Gillanders v Gillanders* 1966 SC 54; *Wilson v Wilson* 1981 SLT 101; *Pow v Pow* 1987 SLT 127.

15.11   An application for letters of inhibition in respect of a future or contingent debt is made in Form 59.1-E of the Rules of the Court of Session 1994[1]. It must be considered by a Lord Ordinary[2]. His decision is final and not subject to review[3].

1   RCS 1994, r 59.1(1)(e).
2   RCS 1994, r 59.1(4A).
3   RCS 1994, r 59.1(4B).

5. Letters of arrestment

15.12   Letters of arrestment can be obtained from the Court of Session:
(a)   in execution of a decree;
(b)   in security of a future or contingent debt where the debt is liquid and the debtor is *in meditatione fugae* or *vergens ad inopiam*[1].

1   Stewart, *A Treatise on the Law of Diligence* (1898), pp 22 and 24.

15.13   The first of these functions is superseded by the fact that the warrant in an extract decree, or an extract of an agreement registered for execution in the books of council and session, or sheriff court books, is sufficient warrant for arrestment in execution[1].

1   Debtors (Scotland) Act 1987, s 87(2)(b); Sheriff Courts (Scotland) Extracts Act 1892, s 7(1)(b); Writs Execution (Scotland) Act 1877, s 3(b).

15.14   An application for letters of arrestment is made by Form 59.1-A and is considered by the Deputy Principal Clerk[1]. If he refuses to sign the warrant, it may be considered by a Lord Ordinary at the applicant's request[2]. The Lord Ordinary's decision is final and not subject to review[3].

1   RCS 1994, r 59.1(1)(a).
2   RCS 1994, r 59.1(4).
3   RCS 1994, r 59.1(4).

6. Adjudication

15.15   It is possible to adjudge without having inhibited[1]. An action of adjudication must be raised in the Court of Session, and it can be either in execution of sums due under a separation agreement, or in security of future sums due where the debtor is *in meditatione fugae* or *vergens ad inopiam*. The pursuer, on raising the action, may, and would be well advised to, register a notice of litigiosity under s 159 of the Titles to Land Consolidation (Scotland) Act 1868[2].

1   CCMR, r 5.34, regarding diligence on extracts of registered authentic instruments is misleading in suggesting an adjudication 'proceeds' upon an inhibition.
2   See Gretton, *The Law of Inhibitions and Adjudication* (2nd edn, 1996), ch 13, and RCS 1994, r 7.6 in relation to actions of adjudication.

15.16   An action for adjudication in respect of sums due under a family law agreement is competent only where:

(a)   the debt is constituted by decree; or

(b)   the family law agreement (as 'the document of debt') has been registered for execution in the books of council and session, or sheriff court books[1].

1   Debtors (Scotland) Act 1987, s 101(a), (c).

7.   Civil imprisonment for non-payment of maintenance

15.17   Civil imprisonment is not competent in respect of *aliment, or arrears of aliment*, not decerned for in a decree[1]. It cannot therefore be used to enforce alimentary obligations due under family law agreements, but that does not prevent the creditor obtaining decree for the arrears, and applying for civil imprisonment on the basis of that decree[2].

1   *Purdon v Purdon* (1884) II Guthrie's Select Cases, p 160; *McGeekie v McGeekie* (1897) 13 Sh Ct Rep 357; *Stewart v Scott* 1934 SLT (Sh Ct) 24; *White v White* 1984 SLT (Sh Ct) 30.
2   Civil Imprisonment (Scotland) Act 1882, s 4; see Jamieson, *Summary Applications and Suspensions* (2000), ch 6.

15.18   Civil imprisonment is not competent in respect of periodical allowance[1].

1   *White v White* 1984 SLT (Sh Ct) 30.

8.   Protective measures in respect of foreign family law agreements

Proceedings in other jurisdictions

15.19   Application may be made to the Court of Session for warrant to arrest any assets situated in Scotland, or for warrant of inhibition over any property situated in Scotland, where proceedings have been commenced in another jurisdiction in respect of enforcement of a family law agreement[1]. The warrant must be capable of being granted in equivalent proceedings before a Scottish court[2].

1   Civil Jurisdiction and Judgments Act 1982, s 27(1)(a), (b), (2)(a); Civil Jurisdiction and Judgments Act 1982 (Provisional and Protective Measures) (Scotland) Order 1997 (SI 1997/2780), art 2; Brussels and Lugano Conventions, art 24; Council Regulation on Jurisdiction and Judgments, art 31.
2   Civil Jurisdiction and Judgments Act 1982, s 27(2)(c).

15.20   In addition, application may be made to the Court of Session for interim interdict where proceedings are commenced, or to be commenced, in another jurisdiction in respect of maintenance obligations owed under a family law agreement[1].

1 Civil Jurisdiction and Judgments Act 1982, s 27(1)(c), (2)(a), (b); Civil Jurisdiction and Judgments Act 1982 (Provisional and Protective Measures) (Scotland) Order 1997 (SI 1997/2780), art 3(a); Case 120/79 *De Cavel v De Cavel (No 2)* [1980] ECR 731.

15.21 The proceedings need not have been served on the defender in order to apply for these protective and provisional measures[1]. The proceedings are not limited to those in a State which is a contracting party to the Brussels or Lugano Conventions[2], and may include proceedings in England and Wales or Northern Ireland[3].

1 Civil Jurisdiction and Judgments Act 1982, s 27(2).
2 By virtue of the Civil Jurisdiction and Judgments Act 1982 (Provisional and Protective Measures) (Scotland) Order 1997 (SI 1997/2780), arts 2(a), 3(a). This Order has not been amended to take into account the Council Regulation on Jurisdiction and Judgments: see the Civil Jurisdiction and Judgments Act 1982 (Interim Relief) Order 1997 (SI 1997/302) (as amended by the Civil Jurisdiction and Judgments Order 2001 (SI 2001/3929), Sch 3, para 26), which makes similar provision for England and Wales.
3 Civil Jurisdiction and Judgments Act 1982, s 27(2)(a).

15.22 Procedure is by way of petition[1]; it is necessary to aver a 'colourable case' to justify the granting of the protective measures which are sought[2].

1 RCS 1994, r 14.1; since the proceedings are independent of any judgment to be enforced, RCS 1994, rr 62.1 and 62.27 do not apply to these petitions.
2 *Stancroft Securitues Ltd v McDowall* 1990 SC 274.

Registered authentic instruments for maintenance

15.23 Protective measures may be granted pending registration, and disposal of any appeal, against registration or non-registration of an authentic instrument concerning maintenance. These measures are not defined in the Brussels and Lugano Conventions, the Council Regulation on Jurisdiction and Judgments, or in the Civil Jurisdiction and Judgments Act 1982[1]. There is, however, no reason why the sheriff alone should grant these measures. The Court of Session could grant letters of inhibition, or arrestment; and the sheriff arrestment on the dependence of the action, or interim interdict. The principles governing the granting of these remedies in Scottish proceedings should be applied to the application for protective measures pending registration and enforcement of the authentic instrument.

1 Brussels Convention, art 39; Lugano Convention, art 39; Council Regulation on Jurisdiction and Judgments, art 47.

Chapter 16

Challenging family law agreements

1. Common law challenge

16.01 Any family law agreement may be reduced on proof of error, fraud, force, fear or undue influence, in accordance with ordinary contract law principles[1].

1 *McAfee v McAfee* 1990 SCLR 805 and 808, per Lord Cameron. See McBryde, *The Law of Contract in Scotland* (2nd edn, 2001), chs 13–17.

2. Statutory challenge

16.02 The court has power under s 16(1)(b) of the Family Law (Scotland) Act 1985 to set aside or vary any agreement as to financial provision on divorce, or (prospectively) dissolution of a civil partnership, where the agreement was not fair and reasonable at the time it was entered into[1].

It may make such an order, in relation to any term other than pension sharing, on granting decree or within such time as it may specify on granting decree[2].

If the agreement contains a term as to pension sharing, then the order setting aside or varying the term relating to pension sharing may only be made on the granting of decree[3].

Any term of the agreement purporting to exclude the right to apply for the setting aside or variation of the agreement, or a term of it, as not fair or reasonable at the time it was entered into is void[4].

1 Family Law (Scotland) Act 1985, s 16(1)(b); Civil Partnership Act 2004, sch 28, para 22; *Gillon v Gillon* (No 3) 1995 SLT 678.
2 Family Law (Scotland) Act 1985, s 16(2)(b), (c)(ii), (2A).

3   Family Law (Scotland) Act 1985, s 16(2)(c), (2A).
4   Family Law (Scotland) Act 1985, s 16(4).

16.03   An application for an order setting aside or varying an agreement on financial provision must be made by crave in the initial writ or defences of the family action in which the application is made[1], or by conclusion in the summons or defences of a Court of Session family action[2]. A preliminary proof should be allowed in relation to the relevant averments in support of such an order, before determining any other craves or conclusions for financial provision on divorce[3]. In determining the application, the court should have regard to the following factors:
(a)   both the fairness and reasonableness of the agreement;
(b)   all relevant circumstances, including the quality of any legal advice; and
(c)   any unfair advantage one party has taken of the other.

The court should not be unduly ready to overturn the agreement: an unequal division is not in itself evidence of unfairness and unreasonableness[4].

1   OCR 1993, r 33.48(1)(a).
2   RCS 1994, r 49.46(1)(a).
3   *Gillon v Gillon (No 1)* 1994 SLT 978; *Gillon v Gillon (No 2)* 1994 SLT 984.
4   *Gillon v Gillon (No 1)* 1994 SLT 978; *Gillon v Gillon (No 3)* 1995 SLT 678. See also: *Young v Young (No 2)* 1991 SLT 869; *Worth v Worth* 1994 SLT (Sh Ct) 54; *Short v Short* 1994 GWD 21-1300; *Inglis v Inglis* 1999 SLT (Sh Ct) 59.

16.04   Section 16(1)(b) of the Family Law (Scotland) Act 1985 also applies to an agreement as to financial provision on the granting of decree of nullity of marriage, or (prospectively) civil partnership[1].

1   Family Law (Scotland) Act 1985, s 17; Civil Partnership Act 2004, sch 28 para 23.

Further research

16.05   Generally:
—   Cubie, 'Agreements and Divorcing Clients' 2003 Fam LB 62-2;
—   Junor, 'Challenging Separation Agreements' 1998 SLT (News) 185.

Chapter 17

Resolving disputes

Introduction

17.01 It is important, in the interests of clients, in order to save them time and money, to resolve their disputes as quickly and as amicably as possible[1]. Concluding a separation agreement is in itself often a means of resolving a dispute between spouses, but disputes can arise even after conclusion of a separation agreement: for example, how it is to be interpreted, or applied. Resolving disputes involves both the adoption of measures for reducing the possibility of post-agreement disputes, and, if disputes do arise, the selection of the appropriate method for resolving them. This chapter considers both of these matters.

1   Opinion of Lord Clarke, *AM or W v JW* (24 February 2004, unreported), OH, at [58].

1. Measures for reducing the possibility of post-agreement disputes

Drafting techniques

17.02 Because of the possibility of post-agreement disputes, it is important, in drafting family law agreements, always to think about the possibilities for future disputes and, so far as possible, to minimise these by the following techniques.

Contract out of the right of retention

17.03 The question of retention, or withholding performance of obligations, to compel a party to perform his obligations is often a fruitful source for disputes. The conditions under which this may be done lawfully are very strict, and were considered by Lord Jauncey in *Bank of East Asia Ltd v Scottish Enterprise*[1]. In summary:

(a) the obligations under the contract must be mutual, where performance of the one is conditional on the other;

(b) the corresponding obligations must be exigible or prestable at the same time; and

(c) the mutual obligation must not have been performed after a demand by the creditor that it be fulfilled[2].

It is possible to contract out of the right of retention[3], and style 1 (Separation Agreement) in CHAPTER 19 adopts that approach in the interests of avoiding future disputes based on retention of obligations[4].

1   1997 SLT 1213, HL.
2   1997 SLT 1213, HL, at 1217H–1218C.
3   *Redpath Dorman Long Ltd v Cummins Engine Co Ltd* 1981 SC 370.
4   Clause 15.

17.04   There is never any right of retention:

(i)   to compel contact with a child by withholding aliment for the child or his mother[1]; or

(ii) to detain a child from his parent for the performance of any obligation owed by the parent[2].

1   Simpson, Boath & Co, Petitioners 1981 SC 153.
2   *Kerrigan v Hall* (1901) 4 F 10.

Anticipate disputes and draft accordingly, even if this involves more words

17.05   By way of example to illustrate this problem, take a common provision that the costs of a divorce action are to be borne equally by husband and wife. The party raising the divorce might think that she can demand half of the anticipated costs before she makes a start on raising the proceedings; but the defender has no means of knowing if she is also paying her solicitor in advance, and he has no control over the timescale of the wife's proceedings, or the efficiency of her solicitor. He may think the fairest solution is that he pay one half of the costs, after decree has been issued, with a right to taxation if he considers the amount unreasonable. A provision providing merely that he pays half the costs does not resolve these problems; detailed provision would be better so that each party knows where they stand[1].

1   See CHAPTER 19 style 1, clause 11.2, and note (10) to that style.

Draft the agreement as clearly as possible and define expressions if necessary

17.06   This is perhaps to state the obvious, but it is vitally important that this be done. One simple example of a word replete with the possibility for different meanings is 'execution': does it mean signature of the agreement? Or its implementation[1]? It may be best to avoid the word, and use the word 'signature', with a definition clause that the date of the signature of the agreement means the later of the two dates on which it has been signed by the parties[2].

1   See **3.14**.
2   See **CHAPTER 19** style 1, clause 17.2.

Remember the obligations accessory to the main ones

17.07   Always think about the time in which things are to be done and, if necessary, the place and performance of obligations[1]. Time is a particular problem, for if nothing is specified in the agreement, the time to perform will be a reasonable time[2], which can always be a source, or excuse, for conflict.

1   See paras **3.11–3.14**.
2   *Rodger (Builders) Ltd v Fawdry* 1950 SC 483.

Build dispute resolution mechanisms into the agreement, if possible

17.08   If possible, there should be built into separation, or other family law agreements, mechanisms for the resolution of any future disputes which may arise between the parties. Examples of such dispute resolution mechanisms are provided in styles 5, 6 and 7 of **CHAPTER 19**. Style 5 is an arbitration agreement for aliment; style 6 is a cohabitation agreement which employs arbitration for aliment and mediation and conciliation in respect of the children; and style 7, a parental responsibilities' agreement, which offers conciliation as a means of resolving disputes about the children's upbringing. The notes to these styles give further information about these methods of dispute resolution.

17.09   However, not all cases are suitable for alternative dispute resolutions and, in particular, arbitration may be more expensive than litigation as the parties must pay the arbiter's costs, and Civil Legal Aid will not be available for it. In such cases, particularly for aliment of £70 a week or less[1], the claimant might be better applying to the sheriff for aliment under the summary cause procedure[2].

1   Or £35 a week or less if suing on behalf of a child under 18 years of age.
2   Sheriff Court (Civil Jurisdiction and Procedure (Scotland) Act 1963, s 3; Act of Sederunt (Summary Cause Rules) 2002 (SSI 2002/No 132), rr 32.1, 32.2.

The solicitor's duty to give objective advice[1]

17.10   Solicitors can sometimes fuel the fire of disputes by not giving firm advice to clients that certain conduct on their part is legally unacceptable. Retention of performance of obligations is often an example. A complicated separation agreement will contain many different obligations, but not all of them are mutual and to be performed at the same time. If the separation agreement does not exclude, or limit, the right of retention, solicitors must advise their clients as to the limited circumstances in which they can withhold performance of obligations they are due to perform in respect of the other party to the agreement[2]. A solicitor should never threaten, on behalf of his client, that his client will withhold aliment for a spouse or child as a means of compelling that spouse to allow contact with the child[3]; such action may amount to contempt of court on the solicitor's part[4].

1   See para **2.13**.
2   See paras **17.03** and **17.04**.
3   Cubie, 'Agreements and Divorcing Clients' 2003 Fam LB 62-2, commenting that an earlier sheriff court decision to the contrary can no longer be followed in modern practice: see *Douglas v Douglas* (1931) 47 Sh Ct Rep 303.
4   Simpson, Boath & Co, Petitioners 1981 SC 153.

2. Methods of resolving disputes

The five principal methods

17.11   The five principal methods of resolving disputes are:
(a)   negotiation;
(b)   mediation;
(c)   conciliation;
(d)   arbitration; and
(e)   litigation.

These methods are not necessarily mutually exclusive; mostly litigations will eventually be settled as a result of negotiation, or, increasingly, mediation[1].

1   There may be expenses implications of not agreeing to resort to mediation in order to avoid litigation: *Dunnett v Railtrack* [2002] 2 All ER 850; *Halsey v Milton Keynes General NHS Trust* [2004] EWCA Civ 576.

Negotiation

17.12   Negotiations are usually conducted between the parties' solicitors, and, if successful, will result in a further agreement, or the compromising of a court action.

Mediation

17.13   Family mediation is not used as often as it probably should be in most parts of Scotland. However, it can be a very useful method of resolving family disputes. It is a form of assisted negotiation which, if successful, results in the mediator preparing a non-binding summary of points upon which the parties have agreed, and which is without prejudice to either party's position. Their solicitors are then responsible for drawing up the formal agreement to bind the parties and settle their dispute.

17.14   Information as to what occurred during family mediation is, as a general rule, inadmissible as evidence in civil proceedings[1] if mediation was conducted by a person accredited as a family mediator by an organisation approved for that purpose by the Lord President of the Court of Session[2]. What 'occurred' during family mediation includes a reference to what was said, written or observed during the mediation[3].

The inadmissibility rule does not apply in respect of arbitrations[4], and certain categories of civil proceedings including those in relation to the care and protection of children[5].

The organisations currently accredited by the Lord President are the Law Society of Scotland, and Family Mediation Scotland ('FMS')[6]. The Law Society accredits family mediators if they have successfully passed a training course provided by the organisation CALM[7] to qualify as a family mediator. It is therefore advisable to make use of an FMS or CALM mediator (accredited by the Law Society) in order to take advantage of the inadmissibility rule.

1   Civil Evidence (Family Mediation) (Scotland) Act 1995, s 1(1).
2   Civil Evidence (Family Mediation) (Scotland) Act 1995, s 1(2).
3   Civil Evidence (Family Mediation) (Scotland) Act 1995, s 1(9).
4   Civil Evidence (Family Mediation) (Scotland) Act 1995, s 1(8).
5   Civil Evidence (Family Mediation) (Scotland) Act 1995, s 2(1)(d).
6   See www.familymediationscotland.org.uk.
7   See www.calmscotland.org.uk.

17.15   Family mediation to which the inadmissibility rule applies is mediation:
(a)   between two or more individuals relating to:
    (i)   the residence of a child;
    (ii)   the regulation of personal relations and direct contact between a child and any other person;
    (iii)   the control, direction or guidance of a child's upbringing;
    (iv)   the guardianship or legal representation of a child; or
    (v)   any other matter relating to a child's welfare;
(b)   between spouses or former spouses concerning matters arising out of the breakdown or termination of their marriage;
(c)   between parties to a purported marriage concerning matters arising out of the breakdown or annulment of their purported marriage; or

(d) between cohabitants or former cohabitants concerning matters arising out of the breakdown or termination of their relationship[1].

The Scottish Ministers may also prescribe additional categories of family mediation to which the inadmissibility rule shall apply[2]; but to date no additional category has been prescribed.

Category (d), above applies in respect of a man and a woman who are not married to each other but are living together as though they were husband and wife[3]. It does not therefore apply to same sex cohabitants[4].

The Civil Partnership Act 2004 prospectively adds a further category, being family mediation 'between partners in a civil partnership or persons in a purported civil partnership concerning matters arising out of the breakdown or termination of their relationship'[5].

1 Civil Evidence (Family Mediation) (Scotland) Act 1995, s 1(2)(a)–(d).
2 Civil Evidence (Family Mediation) (Scotland) Act 1995, s 1(2)(e).
3 Civil Evidence (Family Mediation) (Scotland) Act 1995, s 1(7).
4 It would seem difficult, but not impossible, to stretch *Ghaidan v Godin-Mendoza* [2004] UKHL 30 so as to require category (d) also to apply to same sex couples: in that case it was held possible to construe a 'person' in a cohabiting relationship as including a same sex partner for the purpose of statutory succession to a tenancy under English law. Category (d), as it applies only to a man and a woman, would seem to preclude its similar extension to same sex couples.
5 Civil Partnership Act 2004, Sch 28, para 59.

17.16 There are various exceptions to the inadmissibility rule[1]. These include information that the participants to the mediation (other than the mediator) agree should be admitted as evidence. If the information relates to a child who is capable of understanding the nature and significance of the matters to which the information sought to be admitted as evidence relates, he too must agree to the evidence being admitted[2].

1 Civil Evidence (Family Mediation) (Scotland) Act 1995, s 2.
2 Civil Evidence (Family Mediation) (Scotland) Act 1995, s 2(1)(c), (2), (3).

17.17 Evidence of what occurred during the family mediation is also admissible in relation to:
(a) information as to any contract entered into during it;
(b) the fact no such contract was entered into; and
(c) the subject matter of any challenge to a contract entered into as a result of the mediation[1].

The Scottish Ministers may prescribe additional exceptions to the inadmissibility rule[2], but to date have not done so.

1 Civil Evidence (Family Mediation) (Scotland) Act 1995, s 2(1)(a), (b).
2 Civil Evidence (Family Mediation) (Scotland) Act 1995, s 2(4).#FootnoteE

Conciliation

17.18   Sometimes conciliation means no more than mediation. If so, it is best not to use the term conciliation lest the protection of the inadmissibility rule described above[1], in relation to accredited mediators, is lost.

1   See paras **17.14–17.17**.

17.19   However, conciliation may sometimes be a quite distinct form of alternative dispute resolution; usually the conciliator will have additional powers of investigation, and an ability to make recommendations for settlement in the absence of agreement. However, his recommendations will not be binding and it may be appropriate, if the dispute has to be referred to litigation, for what occurred during the conciliation to be admissible before the court, at the very least in relation to any question of expenses[1].

1   See CHAPTER 19, style 7.

Arbitration

17.20   Arbitration results in a binding settlement, but is generally competent only in respect of aliment, and other matters relating to money or property[1]. If, however, entitlement to aliment depends on proof of any particular fact, such as maltreatment of the other spouse, that fact may also be determined by arbitration[2]. Disputes concerning the upbringing of children cannot be finally determined by arbitration as, in the final analysis, these matters are for determination by the court, based on considerations of the child's best interests[3]. As these matters cannot finally be dealt with by contract, arbitration is not possible in relation to them[4].

The topic of 'arbitration for aliment' is further considered elsewhere[5]. It will be recollected from the above discussion about mediation, that what occurs during the family mediation *is* admissible evidence in connection with an arbitration[6]. This may determine whether parties wish to agree to arbitrate in the first place.

1   *Shand v Shand* (1832) 10 S 384.
2   *Vallance v Lady Touch* 3 May 1707, Lothian's Consistorial Law, p 100.
3   Children (Scotland) Act 1995, s 11(7)(a).
4   Bankton, *Institute* I, 23, 17.
5   Jamieson, 'Arbitration and Conciliation for Aliment' 2003 SLT (News) 47.
6   Civil Evidence (Family Mediation) (Scotland) Act 1995, s 1(8).

17.21   The Civil Evidence (Scotland) Act 1988 applies to arbitrations for aliment except in so far as, in relation to the conduct of the arbitration, specific provision has been made as regards to the rules of evidence which are to apply[1].

1   Civil Evidence (Scotland) Act 1988, s 9, definition of 'civil proceedings', part (b).

Litigation

When it is appropriate

17.22 Litigation is not always to be avoided. It will always be needed to secure urgent protective and provisional orders, such as interdict, and arrestment or inhibition on the dependence. Its existence may be necessary to persuade the other party to negotiate or mediate; most litigations will eventually settle in one of these ways. Only a few cases will ever go to proof.

17.23 As a general rule litigation should be avoided in cases where there is no urgency of this kind, or where it has not been possible to resolve the dispute by means of alternative dispute resolution.

Litigation is always necessary to obtain a decree of divorce, declarator of nullity of marriage, or separation; often most of the ancillary issues concerning the children, maintenance and the matrimonial property, will first have been resolved in the separation agreement.

Suspending charges for payment and recalling inhibitions proceeding on registered agreements

17.24 Litigation is necessary to challenge diligence carried out on a warrant for execution contained in an extract of an agreement registered for execution in the books of council and session, or sheriff court books.

The appropriate remedy to challenge a charge to pay money is for suspension of that charge, which proceeds by way of petition in the Court of Session, or summary application in the sheriff court. The details of such proceedings are discussed further elsewhere[1]. The sheriff has jurisdiction to suspend a charge proceeding on a warrant issuing from an agreement registered in the books of council and session[2].

The only competent remedy for recall of an inhibition in execution proceeding on a registered agreement is by petition for recall of that inhibition to the Outer House of the Court of Session[3]. Recall of such an inhibition will be competent on proof of payment, or where there is a defect or irregularity in the warrant or execution of the inhibition[4].

1 Jamieson, *Summary Applications and Suspensions* (2000), paras 27-11 to 27-16; 28-06 to 28-13; 29-05 to 29-09.
2 Sheriff Courts (Scotland) Act 1907, s 5(5).
3 RCS 1994, r 14.2(g).
4 Stewart, *A Treatise on the Law of Diligence* (1890), p 568.

17.25 If both a charge for payment and inhibition have been served in relation to an agreement registered for execution in the books of council and session, it would seem prudent to combine the applications for suspension of the charge, and recall of the inhibition, in the one Court of Session petition. As the sheriff does not have jurisdiction to recall the inhibition, it seems pointless applying by petition to the Court of Session for recall of the inhibition, and separately to the sheriff court for suspension of the charge, though such a course of action would be competent.

17.26   The possibility of challenging diligence in this way is not entirely remote, given the scope for dispute as to whether aliment was paid under a registered agreement, or payment waived by the creditor for any period of time but in the absence of a formal variation of the agreement by the parties or the court.

Further research

17.27   Generally:
— Brown and Marriott, *ADR Principles and Practice* (Sweet & Maxwell, 2nd edn, 1999);
— Hunter, *The Law of Arbitration in Scotland* (Butterworths, 2nd edn, 2002);
— Jamieson, 'Arbitration and Conciliation for Aliment' 2003 SLT (News) 47;
— Jamieson, *Summary Applications and Suspensions* (2000), chs 27–29;
— Parkinson, *Family Mediation* (Sweet & Maxwell, 1997).

Chapter 18

Extracts from relevant legislation and international instruments

Contents

1. **UNITED KINGDOM**
Acts of Parliament
    Confession of Faith Ratification Act 1690, s 1   **18.01**
    Protestant Religion and Presbyterian Church Act 1707   **18.02**
    Union with England Act 1707   **18.03**
    Conjugal Rights Amendment (Scotland) Act 1861, s 6   **18.04**
    Titles to Land Consolidation (Scotland) Act 1868, s 138   **18.05**
    Writs Execution (Scotland) Act 1877, s 3   **18.06**
    Civil Jurisdiction and Judgments Act 1982, ss 5–8, 11, 12, 15   **18.07**
    Family Law (Scotland) Act 1985, ss 2, 7   **18.14**
    Debtors (Scotland) Act 1987, ss 73, 106   **18.16**
    Child Support Act 1991, ss 9, 10   **18.18**
    Welfare Reform and Pensions Act 1999, ss 28, 48   **18.20**
Statutory instruments and Scottish statutory instruments
    Pensions on Divorce etc (Pension Sharing) (Scotland) Regulations 2000, regs 1–5   **18.22**
    Civil Jurisdiction and Judgments (Authentic Instruments and Court Settlements) Order 2001, arts 1, 2   **18.27**
    Civil Jurisdiction and Judgments Order 2001, Sch 1   **18.29**
Acts of sederunt
    Act of Sederunt (Rules of the Court of Session 1994) 1994, r 62.40(4)–(6) Form 62.40-B   **18.30**
    Act of Sederunt (Child Care and Maintenance Rules) 1997, rr 5.1–5.5, 5.38–43, Sch 1   **18.32**

2. EUROPEAN COMMUNITY LEGISLATION

Council Regulation (EC) 44/2001 of 22 December 2000 on jurisdiction and the recognition and enforcement of judgments in civil and commercial matters, arts 1, 38–57, 59, 68, 69, Annex II–IV, VI   **18.44**

3. INTERNATIONAL TREATIES

Convention on jurisdiction and the enforcement of judgments in civil and commercial matters, signed at Brussels on 27 September 1968, arts 1, 31–42, 44–50, Annexed protocol   **18.72**

Convention on jurisdiction and the enforcement of judgments in civil and commercial matters, concluded at Lugano on 16 September 1988, arts 1, 31–42, 44–50, Protocols No 1 and 2   **18.93**

4. COUNCIL OF EUROPE RECOMMENDATION

Recommendation R(88)3 of the Committee of Ministers to Member States on the validity of contracts between persons living together as an unmarried couple and their testamentary dispositions   **18.115**

1. United Kingdom

Acts of Parliament

Confession of Faith Ratification Act 1690

(aps) c 7

Chapter XXIV
of marriage and divorce

18.01   1   Marriage is between one man and one woman; neither is it lawful for any man to have more than one wife, nor for any woman to have more than one husband, at the same time.

Protestant Religion and Presbyterian Church Act 1707

(aps) c 6

18.02   OUR Sovereign Lady and the Estates of Parliament...Ratifies Approves and for ever confirms the [Confession of Faith Ratification Act 1690][1]...And it is hereby Statute and Ordained that this Act of Parliament...shall be held and observed in all time comeing as a fundamental and essential condition of any Treaty or Union to be concluded betwixt [Scotland and England] without any alterations thereof or derogation thereto for ever As also that this Act of Parliament...shall be insert and repeated in any Act of Parliament that shall pass for agreeing and concluding the foresaid Treaty or Union betwixt the two Kingdoms And that the same shall be therein expressly Declared to be a fundamental and essential Condition of the said Treaty or Union in all time comeing[2].

1   Short title inserted here according to the Statute Law Revision (Scotland) Act 1964; Sch 2.
2   This Act is incorporated with the Treaty of Union as an essential condition thereof by virtue of the Union with England Act 1707, (aps) c 7.

Union with England Act 1707

(aps) c 7

18.03   ...WHICH ARTICLES OF UNION and Act [Protestant Religion and Presbyterian Church Act 1707]... to be and Continue in all time coming the sure and perpetuall foundation of one compleat and intire Union of the Two Kingdoms of Scotland and England...

Conjugal Rights (Scotland) Amendment Act 1861

1861 c 86

18.04   6   After a decree of separation *a mensa et thoro* obtained at the instance of the wife, all property which she may acquire, or which may come to or devolve upon her, shall[1] on her decease[2], in case she shall die intestate, pass to [the persons entitled to succeed to her property on intestacy[3]] in like manner as if her husband had been then dead[4].

1, 2   Words rendered obsolete by virtue of the Married Women's Property (Scotland) Act 1920, and repealed by the Family Law (Scotland) Act 1985, Sch 2.
3   Words substituted by virtue of the Succession (Scotland) Act 1964, s 34, Sch 2, para 1.
4   Words rendered obsolete by virtue of the Married Women's Property (Scotland) Act 1920, ss 1, 3, and repealed by the Family Law (Scotland) Act 1985, Sch 2 have been omitted.

Titles to Land Consolidation (Scotland) Act 1868[1]

1868 c 101

18.05 138 The short Clauses of Consent to Registration for Preservation, and for Preservation and Execution, contained in Forms Numbers 1 and 2 of Schedule (B.) hereto annexed[2], when occurring in... any Deed or Writing or Document of whatsoever nature, and whether relating to Lands or not, shall unless specifically qualified import a Consent to Registration and a Procuratory of Registration in the Books of Council and Session, or other Judges Books competent, therein to remain for preservation; and also, if for Execution, upon the issue of an extract containing a warrant for execution, all lawful execution shall pass thereon'.

1 As amended by the Debtors (Scotland) Act 1987, Sch 6, para 7.
2 The clauses provided in these schedules read: 'and I consent to Registration hereof for Preservation [*or* for Preservation and Execution'].

Writs Execution (Scotland) Act 1877

1877 c 40

18.06   3[1]   Power to execute diligence by virtue of warrant

The warrant inserted in an extract of a document registered in the Books of Council and Session or in sheriff court books which contains an obligation to pay a sum of money shall have the effect of authorising:

(a)   in relation to an ordinary debt within the meaning of the Debtors (Scotland) Act 1987, the charging of the debtor to pay to the creditor within the period specified in the charge the sum specified in the extract and any interest accrued on the sum and, in the event of failure to make such payment within that period, the execution of an earnings arrestment and the attachment of articles belonging to the debtor and, if necessary for the purpose of executing the attachment, the opening of shut and lockfast places;

(b)   in relation to an ordinary debt within the meaning of the Debtors (Scotland) Act 1987, an arrestment other than an arrestment of the debtor's earning in the hands of his employer; and

(c)   if the document is a maintenance order within the meaning of the Debtors (Scotland) Act 1987, a current maintenance arrestment in accordance with Part III of that Act[2].

1   As substituted by the Debtors (Scotland) Act 1987, s 87(4); and amended by the Debt Arrangements and Attachment (Scotland) Act 2002 (asp 17), Sch 3, para 7.
2   See, for the definitions of 'ordinary debt' and 'maintenance order', the Debtors (Scotland) Act 1987, ss 73(1) and 106, reproduced at paras **18.16** and **18.17**.

Civil Jurisdiction and Judgments Act 1982

1982 c 27

18.07 5[1]   Recognition and enforcement of [authentic instruments concerning maintenance]

(1)   The function of transmitting to the appropriate court an application under Article 31 [of the 1968 Convention or of the Lugano Convention] for the recognition or enforcement in the United Kingdom of [an authentic instrument concerning maintenance] shall be discharged:

(a)   ...

(b)   as respects Scotland, by the Secretary of State[2].

In this subsection 'the appropriate court' means the sheriff court having jurisdiction in the matter in accordance with the second paragraph of Article 32.

(2)   Such an application shall be determined in the first instance by the prescribed officer of that court.

(3)   Where on such an application the enforcement of the [authentic instrument] is authorised to any extent, the [authentic instrument] shall to that extent be registered in the prescribed manner in that court.

(4)   [An authentic instrument concerning maintenance] registered under this section shall, for the purposes of its enforcement, be of the same force and effect, the registering court shall have in relation to its enforcement the same powers, and proceedings for or with respect to its enforcement may be taken, as if it was an order which had been originally made by the registering court.

(5)   Subsection (4) is subject to Article 39 (restriction on enforcement where appeal pending or time for appeal unexpired), to section 7 and to any provision made by rules of court as to the manner in which and conditions subject to which an order registered under this section may be enforced[3].

1   As applied and modified for authentic instruments concerning maintenance by the Civil Jurisdiction and Judgments (Authentic Instruments and Court Settlements) Order 1993 (SI 1993/604), arts 3–6. Only the provisions relating to Scotland are reproduced.
2   Now the Scottish Ministers: Scotland Act 1998, s 53(1), (2)(c).
3   'Rules of court' includes an Act of Sederunt (this Act, s 50). For the relevant rule concerning enforcement, see CCMR 1997, r 5.43.

18.08   6   Appeals under Article 37, second paragraph and Article 41

...

(3)   The single further appeal on a point of law referred to [in each of [the] Conventions] in Article 37, second paragraph and Article 41 in relation to the recognition or enforcement of [an authentic instrument concerning maintenance] lies:

(a)   ...

    (b) in Scotland, to the Inner House of the Court of Session.

18.09   7   Interest on registered [authentic instruments]
(1) Subject to subsection (4), where in connection with an application for registration of [an authentic instrument] under section 5 the applicant shows:
    (a) that the authentic instrument provides for the payment of a sum of money; and
    (b) that in accordance with the law of the Contracting State interest on that sum is recoverable under the [authentic instrument] from a particular date or time,
    (c) the rate of interest and the date or time from which it is so recoverable shall be registered with the [authentic instrument] and, subject to any provision made under subsection (2), the debt resulting from the registration of the [authentic instrument] shall carry interest in accordance with the registered particulars.
(2) Provision may be made by rules of court as to the manner in which and the periods by reference to which any interest payable by virtue of subsection (1) is to be calculated and paid, including provision for such interest to cease to accrue as from a prescribed date[1].
...
(5) Debts under judgements registered under section 4 shall carry interest only as provided by this section.

1   No such rules have been made in Scotland in relation to authentic instruments concerning maintenance.

18.10   8   Currency of payment under registered [authentic instruments concerning maintenance]
(1) Sums payable in the United Kingdom under [an authentic instrument concerning maintenance] by virtue of its registration under section 5, including any arrears so payable, shall be paid in the currency of the United Kingdom.
(2) Where the order is expressed in any other currency, the amounts shall be converted on the basis of the exchange rate prevailing on the date of registration of the [authentic instrument].
(3) For the purposes of this section, a written certificate purporting to be signed by an officer of any bank in the United Kingdom and stating the exchange rate prevailing on a specified date shall be sufficient evidence of the facts stated.

...

18.11   11   Proof and admissibility of certain [authentic instruments] and related documents
(1) For the purposes of the 1968 Convention [and the Lugano Convention]:
    (a) a document, duly authenticated, which purports to be a copy of [an authentic instrument] of a Contracting State other than the United Kingdom shall without further proof be deemed to be a true copy, unless the contrary is shown; and

(b) the original or a copy of any such document as is mentioned in Article 47 (supporting documents to be produced by a party seeking recognition or enforcement of [an authentic instrument] shall be sufficient evidence of any matter to which it relates.

(2) A document purporting to be a copy of an authentic instrument drawn up or registered, and enforceable, in a Contracting State other than the United Kingdom is duly authenticated for the purposes of this section if it purports to be a true copy of such an instrument by a person duly authorised in that Contracting State to do so.

(3) Nothing in this section shall prejudice the admission in evidence of any document which is admissible apart from this section.

18.12 12 Provision for issue of copies of, and certificates in connection with, UK judgments[1]

The Court of Session may by Act of Sederunt make provision for enabling any interested party wishing to secure under the 1968 Convention [or the Lugano Convention] the recognition or enforcement in another Contracting State of a judgment within section 18(2)(c) to obtain, subject to any conditions specified in the rules:

(a) a copy of the judgement; and

(b) a certificate giving particulars relating to the judgement.

1 The word 'judgment' is used here in the sense of s 18(2)(c) of this Act to mean: 'any document which has been registered for execution in the Books of Council and Session or in the sheriff court books kept for any sheriffdom.' The Court of Session has made provision for documents registered for execution in the books of council and session (see RCS 1994, r 62.40(3)–(4); but no similar provision has been made in the CCMR (or in any other Act of Sederunt) for documents registered for execution in any sheriff court books.

...

18.13 15 Interpretation of Part I and consequential amendments

...

(2) References in this Part to a judgment registered under section 5 include, to the extent of its registration, references to a judgment so registered to a limited extent only.

Family Law (Scotland) Act 1985

1985 c 37

18.14   2   Actions for Aliment

...

(8) It shall be a defence to an action for aliment by or on behalf of a person other than a child under the age of 16 years that the defender is making an offer, which it is reasonable to expect the person concerned to accept, to receive that person into his household and to fulfil the obligation of aliment.

(9) For the purposes of subsection (8) above, in considering whether it is reasonable to expect a person to accept an offer, the court shall have regard among other things to any conduct, decree or other circumstances which appear to the court to be relevant: but the fact that a husband and wife have agreed to live part shall not of itself be regarded as making it unreasonable to expect a person to accept such an offer.

...

18.15   7   Agreements on aliment

(1) Any provision in an agreement which purports to exclude future liability for aliment or to restrict any right to bring an action for aliment shall have no effect unless the provision was fair and reasonable in all the circumstances of the agreement at the time it was entered into.

(2) Where a person who owes an obligation of aliment to another person has entered into an agreement to pay aliment to or for the benefit of the other person, on a material change of circumstances application may be made to the court by or on behalf of either person for variation of the amount payable under the agreement or for termination of the agreement.

(2A) Without prejudice to the generality of subsection (2) above, the making of a maintenance calculation with respect to a child to whom or for whose benefit aliment is payable under such an agreement is a material change of circumstances for the purposes of that subsection.

(3) Subsections (8) and (9) of section 2 of this Act (which afford a defence to an action for aliment in certain circumstances) shall apply to an action to enforce such an agreement as is referred to in subsection (2) above as they apply to an action for aliment.

(4) In subsection (2) above 'the court' means the court which would have jurisdiction and competence to entertain an action for aliment between the parties to the agreement to which the application under that subsection relates.

(5) In this section 'agreement' means an agreement entered into before or after the commencement of this Act and includes a unilateral voluntary obligation.

Debtors (Scotland) Act 1987

1987 c 18

18.16 73   Interpretation of Part III

(1) In this Part of this Act:

'current maintenance' means maintenance being deducted from earnings in accordance with [a current maintenance arrestment or conjoined arrestment order].

'ordinary debt' means any debt (including...arrears of maintenance and the expenses of current maintenance arrestments) other than current maintenance.

...

18.17 106   Interpretation

'maintenance order' means:

(h) an alimentary bond or agreement (including a document providing for the maintenance of one party to a marriage by the other after the marriage has been dissolved or annulled):

(i)   registered for execution in the Books of Council and Session or sheriff court books; or

(ii) registered in Scotland under an Order in Council made under section 13 of the Civil Jurisdiction and Judgments Act 1982[1].

(i) 'ordinary debt' has the meaning given to it in section 73(1) of this Act.

1   This refers to authentic instruments registered under the provisions of the Civil Jurisdiction and Judgments (Authentic Instruments and Court Settlements) Order 1993 (SI 1993/604).

Child Support Act 1991[1]

1991 c 48

18.18   9   Agreements about maintenance

(1)   In this section 'maintenance agreement' means any agreement for the making, or for securing the making, of periodical payments by way of aliment to or for the benefit of any child.

(2)   Nothing in this Act shall be taken to prevent any person from entering into a maintenance agreement.

(3)   Subject to section 4(10)(a) and section 7(10) the existence of a maintenance agreement shall not prevent any party to the agreement, or any other person, from applying for a maintenance calculation with respect to any child to or for whose benefit periodical payments are to be made or secured under the agreement[2].

(4)   Where any agreement contains a provision which purports to restrict the right of any person to apply for a maintenance calculation, that provision shall be void.

(5)   Where section 8 would prevent any court from making a maintenance order in relation to a child and a non-resident parent of his, no court shall exercise any power that it has to vary any agreement so as:

   (a)   to insert a provision requiring that non-resident parent to make or secure the making of periodical payments by way of aliment to or for the benefit of that child; or

   (b)   to increase the amount payable under such a provision.

(6)   In any case in which section 4(10) or 7(10) prevents the making of an application for a maintenance calculation, and:

   (a)   no parent has been treated under section 6(3) as having applied for a maintenance calculation with respect to the child; or

   (b)   a parent has been so treated but no maintenance calculation has been made,

   subsection (5) shall have effect with the omission of paragraph (b).

1   As applicable to Scotland.

2   These sections provide that no application may be made for a maintenance calculation if 'there is in force a written maintenance agreement made before 5 April 1993, or a maintenance order made before a prescribed date, in respect of [the] child and the…non-resident parent'. The prescribed date for the purposes of ss 4(10)(a) and 7(10) is 3 March 2003: Child Support (Applications: Prescribed Date) Regulations 2003 (SI 2003/194), art 2. A maintenance order, in Scotland, includes an agreement for aliment registered for execution in the books of council and session or sheriff court books (*Commissioner's Case No CSCS/5/97* 1999 Fam L R 37) and if registered before 3 March 2003 will effectively oust the jurisdiction of the Child Support Agency ('CSA') (except if the parent is on benefits and is required to apply for a maintenance calculation under s 6 of the Act). If the agreement is registered after that date, it ousts CSA jurisdiction for a year only (see CHAPTER 9 for further details).

18.19 10   Relationship between maintenance calculations and certain court orders and related matters

...

(2)   Where an agreement of a kind prescribed for the purposes of this subsection is in force with respect to any qualifying child with respect to whom a maintenance calculation is made, the agreement:

    (a)   shall, so far as it relates to the making or securing of periodical payments, be unenforceable to such extent as may be determined in accordance with regulations made by the Secretary of State; or

    (b)   where the regulations so provide, shall, so far as it so relates, have effect subject to such modifications as may be so determined[1].

(3)   Any regulations under this section may, in particular, make such provision with respect to:

    (a)   any case where any person with respect to whom an order or agreement of a kind prescribed for the purposes of subsection (1) or (2) has effect applies to the prescribed court, before the end of the prescribed period, for the order or agreement to be varied in the light of the maintenance calculation and of the provisions of this Act;

    (b)   the recovery of any arrears under the order or agreement which fell due before the coming into force of the maintenance calculation;

    as the Secretary of State considers appropriate and may provide that, in prescribed circumstances, an application to any court which is made with respect to an order of a prescribed kind relating to the making or securing of periodical payments to or for the benefit of a child shall be treated by the court as an application for the order to be revoked[2].

1   The Child Support (Maintenance Arrangements and Jurisdiction) Regulations 1992 (SI 1992/2645), art 4(1) provides that maintenance agreements within the meaning of s 9(1) of the Act are prescribed agreements for the purposes for this subsection. Articles 4(2) and (3) make provision for partial unenforceability of an agreement concerning more than one child in the event of a maintenance calculation being made in respect of one or more, but not all, of these children (see CHAPTER 9 for these provisions).

2   No such provisions have been made.

Welfare Reform and Pensions Act 1999

1999 c 30

18.20   28[1]   Activation of pension sharing

(1)   Section 29 applies[2] on the taking effect of any of the following relating to a person's shareable rights under a pension arrangement:

...

    (f)   provision which corresponds to the provision which may be made by [a pension sharing order under the Family Law (Scotland) Act 1985] and which:

        (i)   is contained in a qualifying agreement between the parties to a marriage,

        (ii)   is in such form as the Secretary of State may prescribe by regulations, and

        (iii)   takes effect on the grant, in relation to the marriage, of decree of divorce under the Divorce (Scotland) Act 1976 or of declarator of nullity.

...

(3)   For the purposes of subsection (1)(f), a qualifying agreement is one which:

    (a)   has been entered into in such circumstances as the Secretary of State may prescribe by regulations, and

    (b)   is registered in the Books of Council and Session.

...

(6)   Subsection (1)(f) does not apply if there is in force an order under section 12A(2) or (3) of the Family Law (Scotland) Act 1985 which relates to benefits or future benefits to which the party who is the transferor is entitled under the pension arrangement to which the provision relates.

(7)   For the purposes of this section, an order or provision falling within subsection (1)(f) shall be deemed never to have taken effect if the person responsible for the arrangement to which the order or provision relates does not receive before the end of the period of 2 months beginning with the relevant date:

    (a)   copies of the relevant matrimonial documents, and

    (b)   such information relating to the transferor and transferee as the Secretary of State may prescribe by regulations under section 34(1)(b)(ii)[3].

(8)   The relevant date for the purposes of subsection (7) is:

    (a)   in the case of provision falling within subsection (f), the date of the extract of the decree or declarator responsible for the divorce or annulment to which the order or provision relates.

...

(9)   The reference in subsection (7)(a) to the relevant matrimonial documents is:

...

    (b)   in the case of provision falling within subsection (1)(f), to:

(i) copies of the provision and the order, decree or declarator responsible for the divorce or annulment to which it relates, and

(ii) documentary evidence that the agreement containing the provision is one to which subsection (3)(a) applies.

(10) The sheriff may, on the application of any person having an interest, make an order:

(a) extending the period of 2 months referred to in subsection (7), and

(b) if that period has already expired, providing that, if the person responsible for the arrangement receives the documents and information concerned before the end of the period specified in the order, subsection (7) is to be treated as never having applied.

1   Sections 28 and 48, below, though similar, apply respectively to shareable rights in a pension arrangement other than an excepted public service pension scheme, and to shareable State scheme rights.

2   Section 29 makes provision for creating pension credits and debits in respect of a person's shareable rights under a pension arrangement other than an excepted public service pension scheme, and is not reproduced here. Section 28 is reproduced only in so far as it applies to Scottish separation agreements.

3   See the Pensions on Divorce etc (Provision of Information) Regulations 2000 (SI 2000/1048), reg 5.

18.21   **48**   Activation of benefit sharing

(1) Section 49 applies[1] on the taking effect of any of the following relating to a person's shareable state scheme rights:

...

(f) provision which corresponds to the provision which may be made by [a pension sharing order under the Family Law (Scotland) Act 1985] and which:

(i) is contained in a qualifying agreement between the parties to a marriage,

(ii) is in such form as the Secretary of State may prescribe by regulations, and

(iii) takes effect on the grant, in relation to the marriage, of decree of divorce under the Divorce (Scotland) Act 1976 or of declarator of nullity.

...

(3) For the purposes of subsection (1)(f), a qualifying agreement is one which:

(a) has been entered into in such circumstances as the Secretary of State may prescribe by regulations, and

(b) is registered in the Books of Council and Session.

...

(6) For the purposes of this section, provision falling within subsection (1) shall be deemed never to have taken effect if the Secretary of State does not receive before the end of the period of 2 months beginning with the relevant date:

(a) copies of the relevant matrimonial documents, and

(b) such information relating to the transferor and transferee as the Secretary of State may prescribe by regulations under section 34(1)(b)(ii)[2].

(7) The relevant date for the purposes of subsection (6) is:

(a)   in the case of provision falling within subsection (1)(f), the date of the extract of the decree or declarator responsible for the divorce or annulment to which the order or provision relates;

...

(8)   The reference in subsection (6)(a) to the relevant matrimonial documents is:

(b)   in the case of provision falling within subsection (1)(f), to:

(i)   copies of the provision and the order, decree or declarator responsible for the divorce or annulment to which it relates, and

(ii)   documentary evidence that the agreement containing the provision is one to which subsection (3)(a) applies.

(9)   The sheriff may, on the application of any person having an interest, make an order:

(a)   extending the period of 2 months referred to in subsection (6), and

(b)   if that period has already expired, providing that, oif the Secretary of State receives the documents and information concerned before the end of the period specified in the order, subsection (6) is to be treated as never having applied.

1   Section 49 makes provision for creating pension credits and debits in respect of a person's shareable State scheme rights under a pension arrangement other than an excepted public service pension scheme, and is not reproduced here. Section 48 is reproduced only in so far as it applies to Scottish separation agreements.

2   See the Pensions on Divorce etc (Provision of Information) Regulations 2000 (SI 2000/1048), reg 5.

Statutory instruments and Scottish statutory instruments

SI 2000/1051

Pensions on Divorce etc (Pension Sharing) (Scotland) Regulations 2000

Made 13th April 2000

Coming into force 1st December 2000

18.22   1   Citation, commencement and interpretation
(1) These Regulations may be cited as the Pensions on Divorce etc (Pension Sharing) (Scotland) Regulations 2000 and shall come into force on 1st December 2000.
(2) In these Regulations:
'the 1985 Act' means the Family Law (Scotland) Act 1985;
'the 1999 Act' means the Welfare Reform and Pensions Act 1999;
'pension arrangement' has the meaning given by section 46(1) of the 1999 Act;
'qualifying arrangement' has the meaning given by paragraph 6 of Schedule 5 to the 1999 Act;
'transferee' and 'transferor' have, in regulations 2 and 3, the meaning given by section 29(8), and, in regulations 4 and 5, the meaning given by section 49(6), of the 1999 Act.

Sharing of Rights under Pension Arrangements

18.23   2   Prescribed form of provision corresponding to provision in a pension sharing order under the 1985 Act

For the purposes of section 28(1)(f)(ii) of the 1999 Act, the provision which corresponds to the provision which may be made by a pension sharing order under the 1985 Act shall be in a form which contains in an annex to, and which is separable from, the qualifying agreement referred to in section 28(1)(f)(i) of the 1999 Act, the following information:
   (a) in relation to the party who is the transferor:
       (i) all names by which the transferor has been known;
       (ii) date of birth;
       (iii) address;
       (iv) national insurance number;
       (v) the name and address of the pension arrangement to which the pension sharing provision relates; and
       (vi) the transferor's membership number or policy number in that pension arrangement;

(b) in relation to the party who is the transferee:
    (i) all names by which the transferee has been known;
    (ii) date of birth;
    (iii) address;
    (iv) national insurance number; and
    (v) if the transferee is a member of the pension arrangement from which a pension credit is derived, his membership number in that pension arrangement;

(c) details of:
    (i) the amount to be transferred to the transferee; or
    (ii) the specified percentage of the cash equivalent of the relevant benefits on the valuation day to be transferred to the transferee;

(d) where the transferee has given his consent, in accordance with paragraph 1(3)(c), 3(3)(c) or 4(2)(c) of Schedule 5 to the 1999 Act (mode of discharge of liability for a pension credit), to the payment of a pension credit to the person responsible for a qualifying arrangement:
    (i) the full name of that qualifying arrangement;
    (ii) its address;
    (iii) if known, the transferee's membership number or policy number in that arrangement; and
    (iv) the name or title, business address, business telephone number and, where available, the business facsimile number and electronic mail address of a person who may be contacted in respect of the discharge of liability for the pension credit;

(e) details of the provision about the apportionment (if any) made by the transferor and the transferee of liability for any charges levied by the person responsible for the pension arrangement in relation to pension sharing under Chapter I of Part IV of the 1999 Act; and

(f) confirmation by the transferor that he has intimated to the pension arrangement his intention with respect to pension sharing and that the pension arrangement has acknowledged receipt of the intimation.

18.24   3   Circumstances in which an agreement is to be entered into, in order to be considered a 'qualifying agreement' under section 28(1)(f) of the 1999 Act

A qualifying agreement is, for the purposes of section 28(1)(f) of the 1999 Act, one which the transferor and transferee have entered into in order to determine the financial settlement on divorce and in respect of which the transferor has intimated to the person responsible for a pension arrangement prior to the making of the agreement the intention to have the transferor's pension rights under the pension arrangement shared with the transferee.

Sharing of State Scheme Rights

18.25   4   Prescribed form of provision corresponding to provision in a pension sharing order under the 1985 Act

For the purposes of section 48(1)(f)(ii) of the 1999 Act, the provision which corresponds to the provision which may be made by a pension sharing order under the 1985 Act shall be in a form which contains in an annex to, and which is separable from, the qualifying agreement referred to in section 48(1)(f)(i) of the 1999 Act, the following information:

(a)   in relation to the party who is the transferor:
    (i)   full name;
    (ii)   date of birth;
    (iii)   address;
    (iv)   national insurance number; and
    (v)   details of the specified amount or, as appropriate, the specified percentage of the cash equivalent on the transfer day of the transferor's relevant state scheme rights immediately before that day;

(b)   in relation to the party who is the transferee:
    (i)   full name by which the transferee is or will be known;
    (ii)   date of birth;
    (iii)   address; and
    (iv)   national insurance number; and

(c)   a statement by the transferor and the transferee that they have received confirmation from the Secretary of State that shareable state scheme rights are held in the name of the transferor and that on the grant of decree of divorce or declarator of nullity of marriage a pension-sharing agreement will be implemented.

18.26   5   Circumstances in which an agreement is to be entered into, in order to be considered a 'qualifying agreement' under section 48(1)(f) of the 1999 Act

A qualifying agreement is, for the purposes of section 48(1)(f) of the 1999 Act, one which the transferor and transferee have entered into in order to determine the financial settlement on divorce and in respect of which they have received confirmation from the Secretary of State that shareable state scheme rights are held in the name of the transferor.

SI 2001/3928

Civil Jurisdiction and Judgments (Authentic Instruments and Court Settlements) Order 2001

Made 11th December 2001

Coming into force 1st March 2002

18.27   1
(1)   This Order may be cited as the Civil Jurisdiction and Judgments (Authentic Instruments and Court Settlements) Order 2001 and shall come into force on 1st March 2002.

(2)   In this Order:
'the Act' means the Civil Jurisdiction and Judgments Act 1982;
'the Regulation' means Council Regulation (EC) No 44/2001 of 22nd December 2000 on jurisdiction and the recognition and enforcement of judgments in civil and commercial matters;
'Regulation State' in any provision, in the application of that provision in relation to the Regulation, has the same meaning as 'Member State' in the Regulation, that is all Member States except Denmark;
'the 2001 Order' means the Civil Jurisdiction and Judgments Order 2001.

(3)   In this Order:
references to authentic instruments are references to those instruments referred to in Chapter IV of the Regulation; and
references to maintenance orders are references to maintenance orders to which the Regulation applies.

18.28   2
(1)   Subject to the modifications specified in paragraphs (2) and (3), paragraphs 1 to 6 of Schedule 1 to the 2001 Order shall apply, as appropriate, to authentic instruments which:
(a)   ...
(b)   concern maintenance as if they were maintenance orders.
...
(4)   Paragraph 8 of Schedule 1 to the 2001 Order shall apply to authentic instruments as if they were judgments.

SI 2001/3929

Civil Jurisdiction and Judgments Order 2001

Made 11th December 2001

Coming into force 1 March 2002

18.29

Schedule 1[1]
The Regulation

1   Interpretation
(1)   In this Schedule:
'court', without more, includes a tribunal;
'judgment' has the meaning given by Article 32 of the Regulation;
'maintenance order' means a maintenance judgment within the meaning of the Regulation;
'part of the United Kingdom' means England and Wales, Scotland or Northern Ireland;
'payer', in relation to [an authentic instrument which concern[s]maintenance], means the person liable to make the payments for which the order provides;
'prescribed' means prescribed by rules of court[2].
(2)   In this Schedule, any reference to a numbered Article or Annex is a reference to the Article or Annex so numbered in the Regulation, and any reference to a sub-division of a numbered Article shall be constructed accordingly.
(3)   References in paragraphs 2 to 8 to [an authentic instrument] registered under the Regulation include, to the extract of its registration, references to [an authentic instrument] so registered to a limited extent only.
...

3   Recognition and enforcement of [authentic instruments concerning maintenance] (section 5)
(1)   The Secretary of State's function (under Article 39 and Annex II) of transmitting an application for the recognition or enforcement in the United Kingdom of [an authentic instrument concerning maintenance] (made under Article 38) to a magistrates' court[3] shall be discharged:
(a)   ...

(b)   as respects Scotland, by the Scottish Ministers.

(2)   Such an application shall be determined in the first instance by the prescribed officer of the court having jurisdiction in the matter[4].

(3)   [An authentic instrument] registered under the Regulation shall, for the purposes of its enforcement, be of the same force and effect, the registering court shall have in relation to its enforcement the same powers, and proceedings for or with respect to its enforcement may be taken, as if it was an order which had been originally made by the registering court.

(4)   Sub-paragraph (3) is subject to Article 47 (restriction on enforcement where appeal pending or time for appeal unexpired), and to any provision made by rules of court as to the manner in which and conditions subject to which an order registered under the Regulation may be enforced[5].

4   Appeal under Article 44 and Annex IV (section 6)

...

(3)   The single further appeal on a point of law referred to in Article 44 and Annex IV in relation to the recognition or enforcement of [an authentic instrument which concern[s] maintenance] lies:

(a)   ...

(b)   in Scotland, to the Inner House of the Court of Session.

5   Interest on registered judgments (section 7)

(1)   Subject to sub-paragraph (3), where in connection with an application for registration of [an authentic instrument] under the Regulation the applicant shows:

(a)   that the [authentic instrument] provides for the payment of a sum of money; and

(b)   that in accordance with the law of the Regulation State in which the [authentic instrument] was given interest on that sum is recoverable under the [authentic instrument] from a particular date or time,

the rate of interest and the date or time from which it is so recoverable shall be registered with the [authentic instrument] and, subject to rules of court, the debt resulting from the registration of the [authentic instrument] shall carry interest in accordance with the registered particulars[6].

...

(4)   Debts under [authentic instruments] registered under the Regulation shall carry interest only as provided by this paragraph.

6   Currency of payment under registered [authentic instruments concerning maintenance] (section 8)

(1)   Sums payable in the United Kingdom under [an authentic instrument concerning maintenance] by virtue of its registration under the Regulation, including any arrears so payable, shall be paid in the currency of the United Kingdom.

(2) Where the [authentic instrument] is expressed in any other currency, the amounts shall be converted on the basis of the exchange rate prevailing on the date of registration of the [authentic instrument].

(3) For the purposes of this paragraph, a written certificate purporting to be signed by an officer of any bank in the United Kingdom and stating the exchange rate prevailing on a specified date shall be sufficient evidence of the facts stated.

...

8 Proof and admissibility of certain and related documents (section 11)

(1) For the purposes of the Regulation:

(a) a document, duly authenticated, which purports to be a copy of [an authentic instrument] of a Regulation State other than the United Kingdom shall without further proof be deemed to be a true copy, unless the contrary is shown; and

(b) a certificate obtained in accordance with Article 57 and Annex VI shall be sufficient evidence that the [authentic instrument] is enforceable in the Regulation State of origin.

(2) A document purporting to be a copy of an authentic instrument drawn up or registered, and enforceable, in a Regulation State other than the United Kingdom is duly authenticated for the purposes of this paragraph if it purports to be certified to be a true copy of such an instrument by a person duly authorised in that Regulation State to do so.

(3) Nothing in this paragraph shall prejudice the admission in evidence of any document which is admissible apart from this paragraph.

1 As modified for authentic instruments concerning maintenance by the Civil Jurisdiction and Judgments (Authentic Instruments and Court Settlements) Order 2001 (SI 2001/3928). Only provisions relating to Scotland are reproduced here. Paragraph 2 of this Schedule is not reproduced as it relates to authentic instruments other than those concerning maintenance.

2 'Rules of court' includes an Art of Sederunt (Civil Jurisdiction and Judgments Act 1982, ss 48, 50).

3 No mention is made of the sheriff court, though the sheriff court is mentioned in Council Regulation (EC) 44/2001: see para **18.68**.

4 There is no prescribed officer in Scotland for the purposes of the Regulation as the CCMR 1997 have not been applied to it.

5 No rules of court have been made in Scotland concerning enforcement of an authentic instrument concerning maintenance.

6 No rules of court have been made in Scotland concerning interest due under an authentic instrument concerning maintenance.

Acts of sederunt

Act of Sederunt (Rules of the Court of Session 1994) 1994

18.30   62.40 Enforcement in another Contracting State or Member State of Court of Session judgments etc

...

(4)   Where a person seeks to apply under Article 50 of the [Brussels or Lugano Conventions] for enforcement of an authentic instrument...registered for execution in the Books of Council and Session, he shall apply by letter to the Keeper of the Registers for:

    (a)   a certificate in Form 62.40–B; and

    (b)   an extract of the authentic instrument...

(5)   Where a person seeks to apply under Article 57...of the Council Regulation for enforcement in another Member State of an authentic instrument...registered for execution in the Books of Council and Session, he shall apply by letter to the Keeper of the Registers for:

    (a)   a certificate under Article 57...of the Council Regulation; and

    (b)   an extract of the authentic instrument...

(6)   The Keeper of the Registers shall not issue a certificate under paragraph (4) or (5) unless there is produced to him an affidavit verifying that enforcement has not been suspended and that the time available for enforcement has not expired.

...

18.31

Rule 62.40(3)

Form 62.40–B

Form of certificate by Keeper of the Registers of writ registered for execution in the Books of Council and Session for registration under Article 50 of [the Brussels or Lugano Conventions]

REGISTERS OF SCOTLAND

CERTIFICATE

UNDER THE CIVIL JURISDICTION AND JUDGMENTS ACT 1982

OF

DEED [*OR OTHER WRIT*]

BETWEEN

[AB] (*ADDRESS*)

AND

[CD] (*ADDRESS*)

REGISTERED FOR EXECUTION IN THE BOOKS OF COUNCIL AND SESSION

I,   , the Keeper of the Registers of Scotland, and as such, Keeper of the Register of Deeds, Bonds, Protests, Judgments and other writs registered for execution in the Books of Council and Session, do hereby certify:

1   That [AB] registered in the Books of Council and Session on the   day of   for execution against [CD] a (*describe writ and state terms of writ for which enforcement is to be sought*).
2   That the extract of the deed [*or other writ*] attached hereto is a true copy of the deed [*or other writ*] registered for execution by [AB].
[3   That the deed [*or other writ*] carries interest at the rate of   per cent a year from the   day of   until payment].
[4   That enforcement of the deed] [*or other writ*] has not for the time being been suspended and that the time available for its enforcement has not expired.
5   That this certificate is issued under Article 50 of Schedule 1 [*or* 3C] to the Civil Jurisdiction and Judgments Act 1982[1] and rule 62.40(3) of the Rules of the Court of Session 1994.

Dated the   day of

(Signed)

Keeper of the Registers of Scotland

1   These contain English language texts of the Brussels and Lugano Convention respectively.

Act of Sederunt (Child Care and Maintenance Rules) 1997

Chapter 5
Maintenance Orders

Part I
General

18.32   5.1   Interpretation

In this Chapter, unless the context otherwise requires:
'the 1982 Act' means the Civil Jurisdiction and Judgments Act 1982;
'court in a specified state' includes any judicial or administrative authority in a specified state,
'order' includes decree.

18.33   5.2   Application
...
(5)   Part VI of this Chapter shall have effect in relation to the registration in the sheriff court of orders made by courts outwith the United Kingdom to which the 1982 Act applies and such orders are referred to in this Chapter as 'incoming orders under the 1982 Act'.

18.34   5.3   Prescribed officer
(1)   The sheriff clerk shall be:
    (a)   the prescribed officer for the purposes of the 1982 Act;
    ...
(2)   Unless otherwise provided, all communications which the prescribed officer is required to send to:
    (a)   an addressee in the United Kingdom shall be sent by first class recorded delivery post; and
    (b)   an addressee outwith the United Kingdom shall be sent by registered letter or the nearest equivalent which the available postal service permits.

18.35   5.4   Maintenance Orders Register
(1)   The sheriff clerk shall maintain a Register called 'the Maintenance Orders Register' for the purpose of [*inter alia*] the 1982 Act, Part I of which shall relate to outgoing orders and Part II to incoming orders.

(2) The sheriff clerk shall make appropriate entries in the Maintenance Orders Register in respect of any action taken by him or notified to him in accordance with the provisions of those Acts, and shall keep in such manner as he considers appropriate any documents sent to him in connection with any such action.

(3) Every entry registering a maintenance order shall specify the section of the Act and where appropriate any Order in Council under which the maintenance order in question is registered.

(4) When a registered maintenance order is varied, revoked or cancelled, the sheriff clerk shall make an appropriate entry against the entry for the original order.

18.36   5.5   Inspection

(1) The sheriff clerk shall, on an application by:
   (a) any person entitled to, or liable to make, payments under an order in respect of which any entry has been made in the Maintenance Orders Register; or
   (b) a solicitor acting on behalf of any such person,
   permit that person or his solicitor, as the case may be, to inspect any such entry and any document in his possession relating to that entry and to take copies of any such entry or document.

(2) On an application by or on behalf of any other person, the sheriff clerk may, on being satisfied of that person's interest, grant that person or his solicitor permission to inspect or take copies of any such entry or document.

...

Part VI
Incoming Orders under the 1982 Act

18.37   5.38   Applications under section 5 of the 1982 Act[1]

(1) An application under section 5 of the 1982 Act shall be in writing addressed to the Secretary of State[2], signed by the applicant, or a solicitor or professional person qualified to act in such matters in the Contracting State of origin on his behalf, and shall specify:
   (a) an address within Scotland for service on the applicant;
   (b) the usual and last known address of the person against whom judgment was granted;
   (c) the place where the applicant seeks to enforce the judgment;
   (d) whether at the date of the application the judgment has been satisfied in whole or in part;
   (e) whether interest is recoverable under the judgment in accordance with the law of the country in which it was granted and, if so, the rate of interest and the date from which interest became due; and
   (f) whether the time for bringing an appeal against the judgment has expired without an appeal having been brought or whether an appeal has been brought against the judgment and is pending or has been finally disposed of.

(2) An application under paragraph (1) shall be accompanied by:
  (a) a copy of the judgment authenticated by the court which made the order;
  (b) documents which established that, according to the law of the country in which the judgment has been given, the judgment is enforceable and has been served;
  (c) in the case of a judgment given in default, documents which establish that the party in default was served with the documents instituting the proceedings[3];
  (d) where appropriate, a document showing that the applicant is in receipt of legal aid in the country in which the judgment was given; and
  (e) where the judgment or any of the documents specified in sub-paragraphs (b) to (d) are in a language other then English, a translation into English certified by a person qualified to do so in one of the Contracting States.
(3) Where the applicant does not produce a document required under paragraph 2(c) or (d), the sheriff clerk may:
  (a) fix a time within which the document is to be produced;
  (b) accept an equivalent document; or
  (c) dispense with production of the document.

1   Section 5 of the 1982 Act applies to an authentic instrument concerning maintenance as though it were a maintenance order to which the Brussels or Lugano Convention applies: Civil Jurisdiction and Judgments (Authentic Instruments and Court Settlements) Order 1993 (SI 1993/604), art 3(1).
2   This function is transferred to the Scottish Ministers by the Scotland Act 1998, s 53.
3   This requirement is not relevant to authentic instruments.

18.38   5.39   Address of applicant's solicitor for service

Where the sheriff clerk is informed by a solicitor practising in Scotland that he is acting on behalf of the applicant, the business address of the solicitor shall thereafter be treated as the address for service on the applicant.

18.39   5.40   Notice of determination of application

Immediately after determination of an application for the recognition or enforcement of an order, the sheriff clerk shall serve, in accordance with the Ordinary Cause Rules so far as not inconsistent with the terms of this Chapter, a notice in Form 73 on the applicant and on the person against whom enforcement is sought.

18.40   5.41   Appeal by party against whom enforcement is authorised
(1) Where enforcement of a maintenance order is authorised to any extent, the party against whom enforcement is authorised may appeal by way of summary application to the sheriff against the decision of the sheriff clerk:
  (a) within one month from the date of service of the notice under rule 5.40; or
  (b) if the person against whom enforcement is sought is domiciled in a Contracting State other than the United Kingdom, within two months from the date of service of such notice.

(2) The determination of the sheriff of such a summary application shall be subject to a final appeal on a point of law to the Inner House of the Court of Session in accordance with the Ordinary Cause Rules.

18.41   5.42   Appeal by applicant

(1) Where the application for enforcement of a maintenance order is refused, the applicant may appeal by way of summary application to the sheriff within one month from the date of service of the notice under rule 5.40.

(2) The determination of the sheriff of such a summary application shall be subject to a final appeal on a point of law to the Inner House of the Court of Session in accordance with the Ordinary Cause Rules.

18.42   5.43   Enforcement of registered order[1]

The applicant may obtain an extract of a registered order and proceed to arrest in execution, to intimate the order (for the purposes of section 54(1) if the Debtors (Scotland) Act 1987), to inhibit and to charge and attach thereon, but may not proceed to an action of furthcoming in respect of an arrestment, serve a current maintenance arrestment schedule, make application for a conjoined arrestment order, proceed to adjudication in respect of inhibition or sale in respect of an attachment until the time for appeal against the determination of the sheriff under rules 5.41 or 5.42 has elapsed and any appeal has been disposed of.

1   As amended by the Act of Sederunt ((Debt Arrangement and Attachment) (Scotland) Act 2002) 2002, SSI 2002, No 5560, Sch 3, para 7.

18.43   Schedule 1

Rule 5.40

FORM 73

Notice of Determination by Sheriff Clerk of Application under Section 5 of the Civil Jurisdiction and Judgments Act 1982

Sheriff Court (Address)

....(Applicant) v. ....……….(Respondent)

TAKE NOTICE that the application by [name and address], for the recognition and/or enforcement of a maintenance order granted by [state Court or Tribunal] on the day of   ; has been *GRANTED/REFUSED (state reasons in brief for refusal); and has been registered in the Books of Court to the extent that (state the extent)[1].

(Signed)

Sheriff Clerk

Date

NOTE:
1   If the application has been granted to any extent, the person against whom enforcement is sought may appeal against this decision within one month from the date of service of this Notice, unless he is domiciled in another Contracting State in which case he may appeal within two months from the date of service.
2   If the application has been refused or not granted in full the Applicant may appeal against the decision within one month from the date of service of this Notice.
3   A solicitor qualified in Scots law should be consulted for the purposes of any appeal.

* Delete as appropriate

1   The sheriff clerk should suitably amend this in the case of authentic instruments; it is suggested the words 'authentic instrument' be used in place of 'maintenance order'.

2. European Community legislation

Council Regulation (EC) 44/2001

of 22 December 2000[1]

on Jurisdiction and the Recognition and Enforcement of Judgments in Civil and Commercial Matters

Chapter I
Scope

18.44   Article 1

1   This Regulation shall apply in civil and commercial matters whatever the nature of the court or tribunal. It shall not extend, in particular, to revenue, customs or administrative matters.

2   The Regulation shall not apply to:
   (a)   the status or legal capacity of natural persons, rights in property arising out of a matrimonial relationship, wills and succession;
   (b)   bankruptcy, proceedings relating to the winding-up of insolvent companies or other legal persons, judicial arrangements, compositions and analogous proceedings;
   (c)   social security;
   (d)   arbitration.

3   In this Regulation, the term 'Member State' shall mean Member States with the exception of Denmark.

1   OJ L12, 16.1.2001, p 1. This regulation has been amended/corrected by (a) Corrigendum (OJ L307, 22.11.2001, p 28); (b) Commission Regulation (EC) 1496/2002 (OJ L225, 28.8.2002, p 13); and (c) Treaty of Athens, Annex II, Pt 18.A.3.

...

Chapter III
Recognition and Enforcement

Section 2
Enforcement

18.45   Article 38
1   A judgment given in a Member State and enforceable in that State shall be enforced in another Member State when, on the application of any interested party, it has been declared enforceable there.
2   However, in the United Kingdom, such a judgment shall be enforced in England and Wales, in Scotland, or in Northern Ireland when, on the application of any interested party, it has been registered for enforcement in that part of the United Kingdom.

18.46   Article 39
1   The application shall be submitted to the court or competent authority indicated in the list in Annex II.
2   The local jurisdiction shall be determined by reference to the place of domicile of the party against whom enforcement is sought, or to the place of enforcement.

18.47   Article 40
1   The procedure for making the application shall be governed by the law of the Member State in which enforcement is sought.
2   The applicant must give an address for service of process within the area of jurisdiction of the court applied to. However, if the law of the Member State in which enforcement is sought does not provide for the furnishing of such an address, the applicant shall appoint a representative ad litem.
3   The documents referred to in Article 53 shall be attached to the application.

18.48   Article 41
The judgment shall be declared enforceable immediately on completion of the formalities in Article 53 without any review under Articles 34 and 35. The party against whom enforcement is sought shall not at this stage of the proceedings be entitled to make any submissions on the application.

18.49   Article 42
1   The decision on the application for a declaration of enforceability shall forthwith be brought to the notice of the applicant in accordance with the procedure laid down by the law of the Member State in which enforcement is sought.

2   The declaration of enforceability shall be served on the party against whom enforcement is sought, accompanied by the judgment, if not already served on that party.

18.50   Article 43

1   The decision on the application for a declaration of enforceability may be appealed against by either party.

2   The appeal is to be lodged with the court indicated in the list in Annex III.

3   The appeal shall be dealt with in accordance with the rules governing procedure in contradictory matters.

4   If the party against whom enforcement is sought fails to appear before the appellate court in proceedings concerning an appeal brought by the applicant, Article 26(2) to (4) shall apply even where the party against whom enforcement is sought is not domiciled in any of the Member States.

5   An appeal against the declaration of enforceability is to be lodged within one month of service thereof. If the party against whom enforcement is sought is domiciled in a Member State other than that in which the declaration of enforceability was given, the time for appealing shall be two months and shall run from the date of service, either on him in person or at his residence. No extension of time may be granted on account of distance.

18.51   Article 44

The judgment given on the appeal may be contested only by the appeal referred to in Annex IV.

18.52   Article 45

1   The court with which an appeal is lodged under Article 43 or Article 44 shall refuse or revoke a declaration of enforceability only on one of the grounds specified in Articles 34 and 35. It shall give its decision without delay.

2   Under no circumstances may the foreign judgment be reviewed as to its substance.

18.53   Article 46

1   The court with which an appeal is lodged under Article 43 or Article 44 may, on the application of the party against whom enforcement is sought, stay the proceedings if an ordinary appeal has been lodged against the judgment in the Member State of origin or if the time for such an appeal has not yet expired; in the latter case, the court may specify the time within which such an appeal is to be lodged.

2   Where the judgment was given in Ireland or the United Kingdom, any form of appeal available in the Member State of origin shall be treated as an ordinary appeal for the purposes of paragraph 1.

3   The court may also make enforcement conditional on the provision of such security as it shall determine.

18.54   Article 47

1   When a judgment must be recognised in accordance with this Regulation, nothing shall prevent the applicant from availing himself of provisional, including protective, measures in accordance with the law of the Member State requested without a declaration of enforceability under Article 41 being required.

2   The declaration of enforceability shall carry with it the power to proceed to any protective measures.

3   During the time specified for an appeal pursuant to Article 43(5) against the declaration of enforceability and until any such appeal has been determined, no measures of enforcement may be taken other than protective measures against the property of the party against whom enforcement is sought.

18.55   Article 48

1   Where a foreign judgment has been given in respect of several matters and the declaration of enforceability cannot be given for all of them, the court or competent authority shall give it for one or more of them.

2   An applicant may request a declaration of enforceability limited to parts of a judgment.

18.56   Article 49

A foreign judgment which orders a periodic payment by way of a penalty shall be enforceable in the Member State in which enforcement is sought only if the amount of the payment has been finally determined by the courts of the Member State of origin.

18.57   Article 50

An applicant who, in the Member State of origin has benefited from complete or partial legal aid or exemption from costs or expenses, shall be entitled, in the procedure provided for in this Section, to benefit from the most favourable legal aid or the most extensive exemption from costs or expenses provided for by the law of the Member State addressed.

18.58   Article 51

No security, bond or deposit, however described, shall be required of a party who in one Member State applies for enforcement of a judgment given in another Member State on the ground that he is a foreign national or that he is not domiciled or resident in the State in which enforcement is sought.

18.59   Article 52

In proceedings for the issue of a declaration of enforceability, no charge, duty or fee calculated by reference to the value of the matter at issue may be levied in the Member State in which enforcement is sought.

Section 3
Common provisions

18.60 Article 53
1 A party seeking recognition or applying for a declaration of enforceability shall produce a copy of the judgment which satisfies the conditions necessary to establish its authenticity.
2 A party applying for a declaration of enforceability shall also produce the certificate referred to in Article 54, without prejudice to Article 55.

18.61 Article 54

The court or competent authority of a Member State where a judgment was given shall issue, at the request of any interested party, a certificate using the standard form in Annex V to this Regulation.

18.62 Article 55
1 If the certificate referred to in Article 54 is not produced, the court or competent authority may specify a time for its production or accept an equivalent document or, if it considers that it has sufficient information before it, dispense with its production.
2 If the court or competent authority so requires, a translation of the documents shall be produced. The translation shall be certified by a person qualified to do so in one of the Member States.

18.63 Article 56

No legalisation or other similar formality shall be required in respect of the documents referred to in Article 53 or Article 55(2), or in respect of a document appointing a representative ad litem.

Chapter IV
Authentic Instruments and Court Settlements

18.64 Article 57
1 A document which has been formally drawn up or registered as an authentic instrument and is enforceable in one Member State shall, in another Member State, be declared enforceable there, on application made in accordance with the procedures provided for in Articles 38, et seq. The court with which an appeal is lodged under Article 43 or Article 44 shall refuse or revoke a declaration of enforceability only if enforcement of the instrument is manifestly contrary to public policy in the Member State addressed.

2 Arrangements relating to maintenance obligations concluded with administrative authorities or authenticated by them shall also be regarded as authentic instruments within the meaning of paragraph 1.

3 The instrument produced must satisfy the conditions necessary to establish its authenticity in the Member State of origin.

4 Section 3 of Chapter III shall apply as appropriate. The competent authority of a Member State where an authentic instrument was drawn up or registered shall issue, at the request of any interested party, a certificate using the standard form in Annex VI to this Regulation.

...

Chapter V
General Provisions

18.65 Article 59

1 In order to determine whether a party is domiciled in the Member State whose courts are seised of a matter, the court shall apply its internal law.

2 If a party is not domiciled in the Member State whose courts are seised of the matter, then, in order to determine whether the party is domiciled in another Member State, the court shall apply the law of that Member State.

...

Chapter VII
Relations with Other Instruments

18.66 Article 68

1 This Regulation shall, as between the Member States, supersede the Brussels Convention, except as regards the territories of the Member States which fall within the territorial scope of that Convention and which are excluded from this Regulation pursuant to Article 299 of the Treaty[1].

2 In so far as this Regulation replaces the provisions of the Brussels Convention between Member States, any reference to the Convention shall be understood as a reference to this Regulation.

1 Treaty establishing the European Community 1950.

18.67 Article 69

Subject to...Article[1] 70, this Regulation shall, as between Member States, supersede the following conventions and treaty concluded between two or more of them:

[the various bilateral or multilateral treaties superseded by the Regulation are here specified]

...

1   Reference is also made to art 66(2), which deals with transitional provisions.

18.68   Annex II

The courts or competent authorities to which the application referred to in Article 39 may be submitted are the following:
— in Belgium, the 'tribunal de première instance' or 'rechtbank van eerste aanleg' or 'erstinstanzliches Gericht';
— in the Czech Republic, the 'okresní soud' or 'soudní exekutor';
— in Germany:
   (a) ...
   (b) by a notary in a procedure of declaration of enforceability of an authentic instrument;
— in Estonia, the 'maakohus' or the 'linnakohus';
— in Greece, the 'Μονομελές Πρωτοδικειο';
— in Spain, the 'Juzgado de Primera Instancia';
— in France, the presiding judge of the 'tribunal de grande instance';
— in Ireland, the High Court;
— in Italy, the 'Corte d'appello';
— in Cyprus, the 'Επαρχιακό Δικαστηριο' or in the case of a maintenance judgment the 'Οικογενειακο Δικαστηριο';
— in Latvia, the 'rajona (pilsetas) tiesa';
— in Lithuania, the 'Lietuvos apeliacinis teismas'
— in Luxembourg, the presiding judge of the 'tribunal d'arrondissement';
— in Hungary, the 'megyei bíróság székhelyén muködo helyi bíróság' and in Budapest the 'Budai Központi Kerületi Bíróság';
— in Malta, the 'Prim' Awla tal-Qorti Civili' or 'Qorti tal-Magistrati ta' Ghawdex fil-gurisdizzjoni superjuri taghha', or, in the case of a maintenance judgment, the 'Registratur tal-Qorti' on transmission by the 'Ministru responsabbli ghall-Gustizzja';
— in the Netherlands, the 'voorzieningenrechter van de rechtbank';
— in Austria, the 'Bezirksgericht';
— in Poland, the 'Sad Okregowy';
— in Portugal, the 'Tribunal de Comarca';
— in Slovenia, the 'Okranjo sodišce';
— in Slovakia, the 'okresny súd' or 'exekútor';
— in Finland, the 'käräjäoikeus/tingsrätt';
— in Sweden, the 'Svea hovrätt';
— in the United Kingdom:
   (a) in England and Wales, the High Court of Justice, or in the case of a maintenance judgment, the Magistrate's Court on transmission by the Secretary of State;

(b)   in Scotland, the Court of Session, or in the case of a maintenance judgment, the Sheriff Court on transmission by the Secretary of State;

(c)   in Northern Ireland, the High Court of Justice, or in the case of a maintenance judgment, the Magistrate's Court on transmission by the Secretary of State;

(d)   in Gibraltar, the Supreme Court of Gibraltar, or in the case of a maintenance judgment, the Magistrates' Court on transmission by the Attorney General of Gibraltar[1].

1   See United Kingdom declaration concerning Gibraltar (OJ C13, 16.1.2001, p 1) and European Union Council document 'Gibraltar authorities in the context of EU and EC instruments and related treaties' (Document 7998/2000, 19.4.2000) for procedure relating to Gibraltar.

18.69   Annex III

The courts with which appeals referred to in Article 43(2) may be lodged are the following:
—   in Belgium:
(a)   as regards appeal by the defendant: the 'tribunal de première instance' or 'rechtbank van eerste aanleg' or 'erstinstanzliches Gericht';
(b)   as regards appeal by the applicant: the 'Cour d'appel' or 'hof van beroep';
—   in the Czech Republic, the 'okresní soud.';
—   in the Federal Republic of Germany, the 'Oberlandesgericht';
—   in Estonia, the 'ringkonnakohus';
—   in Greece, the 'Εφετειο';
—   in Spain, the 'Audiencia Provincial';
—   in France, the 'cour d'appel';
—   in Ireland, the High Court;
—   in Italy, the 'corte d'appello';
—   in Cyprus, the 'Επαρχιακο Δικαστηριο' or in the case of a maintenance judgment the 'Οικογενειακο Δικαστηριο';
—   in Latvia, the 'Apgabaltiesa';
—   in Lithuania, the 'Lietuvos Aukščiausiasis Teismas';
—   in Luxembourg, the 'Cour supérieure de Justice' sitting as a court of civil appeal;
—   in Hungary, the 'megyei bíróság'; in Budapest, the 'Fovárosi Bíróság';
—   in Malta, the 'Qorti ta' l-Appell' in accordance with the procedure laid down for appeals in the 'Kodici ta' Organizzazzjoni u Procedura Civili – Kap.12' or in the case of a maintenance judgment by 'citazzjoni' before the 'Prim' Awla tal-Qorti ivili jew il-Qorti tal-Magistrati ta' Ghawdex fil-gurisdizzjoni superjuri taghha';
—   in the Netherlands:
(a)   for the defendant: the 'arrondissementsrechtbank';
(b)   for the applicant: the 'gerechtshof';
—   in Austria, the 'Bezirksgericht';
—   in Poland, the 'Sad Apelacyjny';
—   in Portugal, the 'Tribunal de Relação';
—   in Slovenia, the 'Višje sodišce';

— in Slovakia, 'odvolanie' to the 'krajský súd' or 'námietka' or the 'okresný súd' in cases of execution ordered by the 'exekútor';
— in Finland, the 'hovioikeus/hovrätt';
— in Sweden, the 'Svea hovrätt';
— in the United Kingdom:
   (a) in England and Wales, the High Court of Justice, or in the case of a maintenance judgment, the Magistrate's Court;
   (b) in Scotland, the Court of Session, or in the case of a maintenance judgment, the Sheriff Court;
   (c) in Northern Ireland, the High Court of Justice, or in the case of a maintenance judgment, the Magistrate's Court;
   (d) in Gibraltar, the Supreme Court of Gibraltar, or in the case of a maintenance judgment, the Magistrates' Court[1].

1 See United Kingdom declaration concerning Gibraltar (OJ C13, 16.1.2001, p 1) and European Union Council document 'Gibraltar authorities in the context of EU and EC instruments and related treaties' (Document 7998/2000, 19.4.2000) for procedure relating to Gibraltar.

18.70   Annex IV

The appeals which may be lodged pursuant to Article 44 are the following:
— in Belgium, Greece, Spain, France, Italy, Luxembourg and the Netherlands, an appeal in cassation;
— in the Czech Republic, a 'dovolání' and a '•aloba pro zmatecnost';
— in Germany, a 'Rechtsbeschwerde';
— in Estonia, a 'kassatsioonkaebus';
— in Ireland, an appeal on a point of law to the Supreme Court;
— in Cyprus, an appeal to the supreme Court;
— in Latvia, an appeal to the 'Augstaka tiesa';
— in Lithuania, by a retrial, only in cases prescribed by statute;
— in Hungary, 'felülvizsgálati kérelem';
— in Malta, no further appeal lies to any other court; in the case of a maintenance judgment the 'Qorti ta' l-Appell' in accordance with the procedure laid down for appeal in the 'kodici ta' Organizzazzjoni u Procedura Civili—Kap.12';
— in Austria, a 'Revisionsrekurs';
— in Poland, by an appeal to the 'Sad Najwyzszy;
— in Portugal, an appeal on a point of law;
— in Slovenia, the 'retrial, only in cases prescribed by statute';
— in Slovakia 'odvolanie' in cases of execution ordered by the 'exekútor' to the 'Krajsky súd';
— in Finland, an appeal to the 'korkein oikeus/högsta domstolen';
— in Sweden, an appeal to the 'Högsta domstolen';
— in the United Kingdom, a single further appeal on a point of law.

18.71   Annex VI

Certificate referred to in Article 57(4) of the Regulation on authentic instruments
1   Member State of origin
2   Competent authority issuing the certificate
    2.1   Name
    2.2   Address
    2.3   Tel./fax/e-mail
3   Authority which has given authenticity to the instrument
    3.1   Authority involved in the drawing up of the authentic instrument (if applicable)
        3.1.1 Name and designation of authority
        3.1.2 Place of authority
    3.2   Authority which has registered the authentic instrument (if applicable)
        3.2.1 Type of authority
        3.2.2 Place of authority
4   Authentic instrument
    4.1   Description of the instrument
    4.2   Date
        4.2.1 on which the instrument was drawn up
        4.2.2 if different: on which the instrument was registered
    4.3   Reference number
    4.4   Parties to the instrument
        4.4.1 Name of the creditor
        4.4.2 Name of the debtor
5   Text of the enforceable obligation as annexed to this certificate

The authentic instrument is enforceable against the debtor in the Member State of origin (Article 57(1) of the Regulation)

Done at ...., date ....
Signature and/or stamp ....

3. International treaties

Convention on Jurisdiction and the Enforcement of Judgments in Civil and Commercial Matters

signed at Brussels on 27 September 1968

Brussels Convention

Title 1
Scope

18.72   Article 1

This Convention shall apply in civil and commercial matters whatever the nature of the court or tribunal. It shall not extend, in particular, to revenue, customs or administrative matters.

The Convention shall not apply to:
1   The status or legal capacity of natural persons, rights in property arising out of a matrimonial relationship, wills and succession[1]...

1   Despite this exclusion, the Convention *does* apply to maintenance obligations, including those arising out of a matrimonial relationship: Case C-220/95 *Van den Boogaard v PM Laumen* [1997] ECR I-1147, [1997] All ER (EC) 517, ECJ.

...

Title III
Recognition and Enforcement

Section 2
Enforcement

18.73   Article 31

A judgment given in a Contracting State and enforceable in that State shall be enforced in another Contracting State when, on the application of any interested party, it has been declared enforceable there.

However, in the United Kingdom, such a judgment shall be enforced in England and Wales, in Scotland, or in Northern Ireland when, on the application of any interested party, it has been registered for enforcement in that part of the United Kingdom.

18.74   Article 32
1   The application shall be submitted:
   — in Denmark, to the byret;
   — in the United Kingdom:
     (a)   ...
     (b)   in Scotland, in the case of a maintenance judgment to the Sheriff Court on transmission by the Secretary of State.
2   The jurisdiction of local courts shall be determined by reference to the place of domicile of the party against whom enforcement is sought. If he is not domiciled in the State in which enforcement is sought, it shall be determined by reference to the place of enforcement.

18.75   Article 33

The procedure for making the application shall be governed by the law of the State in which enforcement is sought.

The application must give an address for service of process within the area of jurisdiction of the court applied to. However, if the law of the State in which enforcement is sought does not provide for the furnishing of such an address, the applicant shall appoint a representative *ad litem.*

The documents referred to in Articles 46[1] and 47 shall be attached to the application.

1   Article 46(2) is not relevant to authentic instruments, and has been omitted from this text.

18.76   Article 34

The court applied to shall give its decision without delay; the party against whom enforcement is sought shall not at this stage of the proceedings be entitled to make any submissions on the application.

The application may be refused only for one of the reasons specified in Articles 27 and 28[1].

Under no circumstances may the foreign judgment be reviewed as to its substance.

1   Paragraph 2 of this article does not apply to authentic instruments: see art 50, second sentence.

18.77   Article 35

The appropriate officer of the court shall without delay bring the decision given on the application to the notice of the applicant in accordance with the procedure laid down by the law of the State in which enforcement is sought.

18.78   Article 36

If enforcement is authorised, the party against whom enforcement is sought may appeal against the decision within one month of service thereof.

If that party is domiciled in a Contracting State other than that in which the decision authorising enforcement was given, the time for appealing shall be two months and shall run from the date of service, either on him in person or at his residence. No extension of time may be granted on account of distance.

18.79   Article 37
1   An appeal against the decision authorising enforcement shall be lodged in accordance with the rules governing procedure in contentious matters:
— in Denmark, with the landsret;
— in the United Kingdom:
    (a)   ...
    (b)   in Scotland, in the case of a maintenance judgment with the Sheriff Court
2   The judgment given on the appeal may be contested only:
— in Denmark, by an appeal to the højesteret, with the leave of the Minister of Justice;
— in the United Kingdom, by a single further appeal on a point of law[1].

1   In Scotland, the single further appeal on a point of law is to the Inner House of the Court of Session: Civil Jurisdiction and Judgments Act 1982, s 6(3)(b).

18.80   Article 38

The court with which the appeal under Article 37(1) is lodged may, on the application of the appellant, stay the proceedings if an ordinary appeal has been lodged against the judgment in the State of origin or if the time for such an appeal has not yet expired; in the latter case, the court may specify the time within which such an appeal is to be lodged.

Where the judgment was given in Ireland or the United Kingdom, any form of appeal available in the State of origin shall be treated as an ordinary appeal for the purposes of the first paragraph.

The court may also make enforcement conditional on the provision of such security as it shall determine.

18.81   Article 39

During the time specified for an appeal pursuant to Article 36 and until any such appeal has been determined, no measures of enforcement may be taken other than protective measures taken against the property of the party against whom enforcement is sought.

The decision authorising enforcement shall carry with it the power to proceed to any such protective measures.

18.82   Article 40

1   If the application for enforcement is refused, the applicant may appeal:
    — in Denmark, to the landsret,
    — in the United Kingdom:
       (a)   ...
       (b)   in Scotland, in the case of a maintenance judgment to the Sheriff Court.
2   The party against whom enforcement is sought shall be summoned to appear before the appellate court. If he fails to appear, the provisions of the second and third paragraphs of Article 20[1] shall apply even where he is not domiciled in any of the Contracting States.

1   The provisions of art 20 are considered at Para 14.23.

18.83   Article 41

A judgment given on appeal provided for in Article 40 may be contested only:
    — in Denmark, by an appeal to the højesteret, with the leave of the Minister of Justice;
    — in the United Kingdom, by a single further appeal on a point of law[1].

1   In Scotland, the single further appeal on a point of law is to the Inner House of the Court of Session: Civil Jurisdiction and Judgments Act 1982, s 6(3)(b).

18.84   Article 42

Where a foreign judgment has been given in respect of several matters and enforcement cannot be authorized for all of them, the court shall authorize enforcement for one or more of them.

An applicant may request partial enforcement of a judgment.

...

18.85   Article 44

An applicant who, in the State of origin has benefited from complete or partial legal aid or exemption from costs or expenses, shall be entitled, in the procedures provided for in Articles 32 to 35, to benefit from the most favourable legal aid or the most extensive exemption from costs or expenses provided for by the law of the State addressed.

However, an applicant who requests the enforcement of a decision given by an administrative authority in Denmark in the respect of a maintenance order may, in the State addressed, claim the benefits referred to in the first paragraph if he presents a statement from the Danish Ministry of Justice to the effect that he fulfils the economic requirements to qualify for the grant of complete or partial legal aid or exemption from costs or expenses.

18.86   Article 45

No security, bond or deposit, however described, shall be required of a party who in one Contracting State applies for enforcement of a judgment given in another Contracting State on the ground that he is a foreign national or that he is not domiciled or resident in the State in which enforcement is sought.

Section 3
Common Provisions

18.87   Article 46

A party seeking recognition or applying for enforcement of a judgment shall produce:
1   a copy of the judgment which satisfied the conditions necessary to establish its authenticity;
2   ...

18.88   Article 47

A party applying for enforcement shall also produce:
1   documents which establish that, according to the law of the State of origin the judgment is enforceable and has been served;
2   where appropriate, a document showing that the applicant is in receipt of legal aid in the State of origin.

18.89   Article 48

If the documents specified in […]¹ Article […] 42(2) are not produced, the court may specify a time for their production, accept equivalent documents or, if it considers that it has sufficient information before it, dispense with their production.

If the court so requires, a translation of the documents shall be produced; the translation shall be certified by a person qualified to do so in one of the Contracting States.

1   Words omitted (shown by square brackets) are not relevant in the case of authentic instruments.

18.90   Article 49

No legalization or other similar formality shall be required in respect of the documents referred to in Articles 46 and 47 or the second paragraph to Article 48, or in respect of a document appointing a representative *ad litem*.

Title IV
Authentic Instruments and Court Settlements

18.91   Article 50

A document which has been formally drawn up or registered as an authentic instrument and is enforceable in one Contracting State shall, in another Contracting State, be declared enforceable there, on application made in accordance with the procedures provided for in Article 31 *et seq*. The application may be refused only if enforcement of the instruments is contrary to public policy in the State addressed.

The instrument produced must satisfy the conditions necessary to establish its authenticity in the State of origin.

The provisions of Section 3 of Title III shall apply as appropriate.

18.92   Annexed protocol

The High Contracting Parties have agreed upon the following provisions, which shall be annexed to the Convention.

Article IV

Judicial and extrajudicial documents drawn up in one Contracting State which have to be served on persons in another Contracting State shall be transmitted in accordance with the procedures laid down in the conventions and agreements concluded between the Contracting States.

Unless the State in which service is to take place objects by declaration to the Secretary General of the Council of the European Communities, such documents may also be sent by the appropriate public officers of the State in which the document has been drawn up directly to the appropriate public officers to the State in which the addressee is to be found. In this case the officer of the State of origin shall send a copy of the document to the officer of the State applied to who is competent to forward it to the addressee. The document shall be forwarded in the manner specified by the law of the State applied to. The forwarding shall be recorded by a certificate sent directly to the officer of the State of origin.

Article Va

In matters relating to maintenance, the expression 'court' includes the Danish administrative authorities.

Convention on Jurisdiction and the Enforcement of Judgments in Civil and Commercial Matters

concluded at Lugano on 16 September 1988

Lugano Convention

Title 1
Scope

18.93   Article 1

This Convention shall apply in civil and commercial matters whatever the nature of the court or tribunal. It shall not extend, in particular, to revenue, customs or administrative matters.

The Convention shall not apply to:
1   The status or legal capacity of natural persons, rights in property arising out of a matrimonial relationship, wills and succession[1]...

1   Despite this exclusion, the Convention *does* apply to maintenance obligations, including those arising out of a matrimonial relationship: Case C-220/95 *Van den Boogaard v PM Laumen* [1997] ECR I-1147, [1997] All ER (EC) 517, ECJ.

...

Title III
Recognition and Enforcement

Section 2
Enforcement

18.94   Article 31

A judgment given in a Contracting State and enforceable in that State shall be enforced in another Contracting State when, on the application of any interested party, it has been declared enforceable there.

However, in the United Kingdom, such a judgment shall be enforced in England and Wales, in Scotland, or in Northern Ireland when, on the application of any interested party, it has been registered for enforcement in that part of the United Kingdom.

18.95 Article 32

1   The application shall be submitted:
— in Iceland, to the (héra d sdómari);
— in Norway, to the herredsrett or byrett as namsrett;
— in Switzerland:
  (a) in respect of judgments ordering the payment of a sum of money, to the juge de la mainlevée/Rechtsöffnungsrichter/giudice competente a pronunciare sul rigetto dell'opposizione, within the framework of the procedure governed by Articles 80 and 81 of the loi fédérale sur la poursuite pour dettes et la faillite/Bundesgesetz über Schuldbetreibung und Konkurs/ legge federale sulla esecuzione e sul fallimento;

    ...
— in the United Kingdom:
  (a) ...
  (b) in Scotland, in the case of a maintenance judgment to the Sheriff Court on transmission by Secretary of States.
2   The jurisdiction of local courts shall be determined by reference to the place of domicile of the party against whom enforcement is sought. If he is not domiciled in the State in which enforcement is sought, it shall be determined by reference to the place of enforcement.

18.96 Article 33

The procedure for making the application shall be governed by the law of the State in which enforcement is sought.

The applicant must give an address for service of process within the area of jurisidiction of the court applied to. However, if the law of the State in which enforcement is sought does not provide for the furnishing of such an address, the applicant shall appoint a representative *ad litem*.

The documents referred to in Articles 46[1] and 47 shall be attached to the application.

1   Article 46(2) is not relevant to authentic instruments, and has been omitted from this text.

18.97 Article 34

The court applied to shall give its decision without delay; the party against whom enforcement is sought shall not at this stage of the proceedings be entitled to make any submissions on the application.

The application may be refused only for one of the reasons specified in Articles 27 and 28[1].

Under no circumstances may the foreign judgment be reviewed as to its substance.

1   Paragraph 2 of this article does not apply to authentic instruments: see art 50, second sentence.

18.98   Article 35

The appropriate officer of the court shall without delay bring the decision given on the application to the notice of the applicant in accordance with the procedure laid down by the law of the State in which enforcement is sought.

18.99   Article 36

If enforcement is authorised, the party against whom enforcement is sought may appeal against the decision within one month of service thereof.

If that party is domiciled in a Contracting State other than that in which the decision authorising enforcement was given, the time for appealing shall be two months and shall run from the date of service, either on him in person or at his residence. No extension of time may be granted on account of distance.

18.100   Article 37

An appeal against the decision authorising enforcement shall be lodged in accordance with the rules governing procedure in contentious matters:
— in Iceland, with the (héra d sdómari);
— in Norway, to the lagmannsrett;
— in Switzerland, with the tribunal cantonal / Kantonsgericht / tribunale cantonale;
— in the United Kingdom:
  (a)   ...
  (b)   in Scotland, in the case of a maintenance judgment with the Sheriff Court.
2   The judgment given on the appeal may be contested only:
— in Iceland, by an appeal to the Haestiréttur;
— in Norway, by an appeal...to the Hoyesteretts Kjaeremalsutvalg or Hoyesterett;
— in Switzerland, by a recours de droit public devant le tribunal fédéral / staatsrechtliche Beschwerde beim Bundesgericht / ricorso di diritto pubblico davanti al tribunale federale;
— in the United Kingdom, by a single further appeal on a point of law[1].

1   In Scotland, the single further appeal on a point of law is to the Inner House of the Court of Session: Civil Jurisdiction and Judgments Act 1982, s 6(3)(b).

18.101   Article 38

The court with which the appeal under the first paragraph of Article 37 is lodged may, on the application of the appellant, stay the proceedings if an ordinary appeal has been lodged against the judgment in the State of origin or if the time for such an appeal has not yet expired; in the latter case, the court may specify the time within which such an appeal is to be lodged.

Where the judgment was given in Ireland or the United Kingdom, any form of appeal available in the State of origin shall be treated as an ordinary appeal for the purposes of the first paragraph.

The court may also make enforcement conditional on the provision of such security as it shall determine.

18.102   Article 39

During the time specified for an appeal pursuant to Article 36 and until any such appeal has been determined, no measures of enforcement may be taken other than protective measures taken against the property of the party against whom enforcement is sought.

The decision authorising enforcement shall carry with it the power to proceed to any such protective measures.

18.103   Article 40

1   If the application for enforcement is refused, the applicant may appeal:
— in Iceland, to the (héra d sdómari);
— in Norway, to the lagmannsrett;
— in Switzerland, to the tribunal cantonal / Kantonsgericht / tribunale cantonale;
— in the United Kingdom:
   (a)   ...
   (b)   in Scotland, in the case of a maintenance judgment to the Sheriff Court.

2   The party against whom enforcement is sought shall be summoned to appear before the appellate court. If he fails to appear, the provisions of the second and third paragraphs of Article 20 shall apply even where he is not domiciled in any of the Contracting States[1].

1   The provisions of art 20 are considered at PARA 14.23.

18.104   Article 41

A judgment given on an appeal provided for in Article 40 may be contested only:
— in Iceland, by an appeal to the Haestiréttur;
— in Norway, by an appeal…to the Hoyesteretts kjaeremalsutvalg or Hoyesterett,;

— in Switzerland, by a recours de droit public devant le tribunal fédéral /
     staatsrechtliche Beschwerde beim Bundesgericht / ricorso di diritto pubblico
     davanti al tribunale federale;
— in the United Kingdom, by a single further appeal on a point of law[1].

1   In Scotland, the single further appeal on a point of law is to the Inner House of the Court of
Session: Civil Jurisdiction and Judgments Act 1982, s 6(3)(b).

18.105   Article 42

Where a foreign judgment has been given in respect of several matters and enforcement
cannot be authorised for all of them, the court shall authorise enforcement for one or more
of them.

An applicant may request partial enforcement of a judgment.

...

18.106   Article 44

An applicant who, in the State of origin, has benefited from complete or partial legal aid or
exemption from costs or expenses, shall be entitled, in the procedures provided for in
Articles 32 to 35, to benefit from the most favourable legal aid or the most extensive
exemption from costs or expenses provided for by the law of the State addressed.

However, an applicant who requests the enforcement of a decision given by an administrative
authority in Denmark or in Iceland in respect of a maintenance order may, in the State
addressed, claim the benefits referred to in the first paragraph if he presents a statement
from, respectively, the Danish Ministry of Justice or the Icelandic Ministry of Justice to the
effect that he fulfils the economic requirements to qualify for the grant of complete or
partial legal aid or exemption from costs of expenses.

18.107   Article 45

No security, bond or deposit, however described, shall be required of a party who in one
Contracting State applies for enforcement of a judgment given in another Contracting
State on the ground that he is a foreign national or that he is not domiciled or resident in the
State in which enforcement is sought.

Section 3
Common Provisions

18.108   Article 46

A party seeking recognition or applying for enforcement of a judgment shall produce:
1   a copy of the judgment which satisfies the conditions necessary to establish its authenticity;
2   ...

18.109   Article 47

A party applying for enforcement shall also produce:
1   documents which establish that, according to the law of the State of origin, the judgment is enforceable and has been served;
2   where appropriate, a document showing that the applicant is in receipt of legal aid in the State of origin.

18.110   Article 48

If the documents specified in...[1] Article 47(2) are not produced, the court may specify a time for their production, accept equivalent documents or, if it considers that it has sufficient information before it, dispense with their production.

If the court so requires, a translation of the documents shall be produced; the translation shall be certified by a person qualified to do so in one of the Contracting States.

1   Words omitted are not relevant in the case of authentic instruments.

18.111   Article 49

No legislation or other similar formality shall be required in respect of the documents referred to in Article 46 and 47 or the second paragraph of Article 48, or in respect of a document appointing a representative *ad litem*.

Title IV
Authentic Instruments and Court Settlements

18.112   Article 50

A document which has been formally drawn up or registered as an authentic instrument and is enforceable in one Contracting State shall, in another Contracting State, be declared enforceable there, on application made in accordance with the procedures provided for in Articles 31 *et seq.* The application may be refused only if enforcement of the instrument is contrary to public policy in the State addressed.

The instrument produced must satisfy the conditions necessary to establish its authenticity in the State of origin.

The provisions of Section 3 of Title III shall apply as appropriate.

18.113

PROTOCOL NO 1
ON CERTAIN QUESTIONS OF JURISDICTION, PROCEDURE AND ENFORCEMENT

The High Contracting Parties have agreed upon the following provisions, which shall be annexed to the Convention:

Article IV

Judicial and extrajudicial documents drawn up in one Contracting State which have to be served on persons in another Contracting State shall be transmitted in accordance with the procedures laid down in the conventions and agreements concluded between the Contracting States.

Unless the State in which service is to take place objects by declaration to the Swiss Federal Council, such documents may also be sent by the appropriate public officers of the State in which the document has been drawn up directly to the appropriate public officers of the State in which the addressee is to be found. In this case the officer of the State of origin shall send a copy of the document to the officer of the State applied to who is competent to forward it to the addressee. The document shall be forwarded in the manner specified by the law of the State applied to. The forwarding shall be recorded by a certificate sent directly to the officer of the State of origin.

Article Va

In matters relating to maintenance, the expression 'court' includes the Icelandic and Norwegian administrative authorities.

18.114

PROTOCOL NO 2
ON THE UNIFORM INTERPRETATION OF THE CONVENTION

Preamble

The High Contracting Parties
Having regard to Article 65 of this Convention,

Considering the substantial link between this Convention and the Brussels Convention,

Considering that the Court of Justice of the European Communities by virtue of the Protocol of 3 June 1971 has jurisdiction to give rulings on the interpretation of the provisions of the Brussels Convention,

Being aware of the rulings delivered by the Court of Justice of the European Communities on the Interpretation of the Brussels Convention up to the time of signature of this Convention,

Considering that the negotiations which led to the conclusion of the Convention were based on the Brussels Convention in the light of these rulings,

Desiring to prevent, in full deference to the independence of the courts, divergent interpretations and to arrive at as uniform an interpretation as possible of the provision of the Convention, and of these provisions and those of the Brussels Convention which are substantially reproduced in this Convention,

Have agreed as follows:

Article 1

The courts of each Contracting State shall, when applying and interpreting the provisions of the Convention, pay due account to the principles laid down by any relevant decision delivered by courts of the other Contracting States concerning provisions of this Convention.

Article 2

1   The Contracting Parties agree to set up a system of exchange of information concerning judgments delivered pursuant to this Convention as well as relevant judgments under the Brussels Convention. This system shall comprise:

— transmission to a central body by the competent authorities of judgments delivered by courts of last instance and the Court of Justice of the European Communities as well as judgments of particular importance which have become final and have been delivered pursuant to this Convention or the Brussels Convention;

— classification of these judgments by the central body including, as far as necessary, the drawing-up and publication of translations and abstracts;

— communication by the central body of the relevant documents to the competent national authorities of all signatories and acceding States to the Convention and to the Commission of the European Communities.

2   The central body is the Registrar of the Court of Justice of the European Communities.

Article 3
1   A Standing Committee shall be set up for the purposes of this Protocol.
2   The Committee shall be composed of representatives appointed by each signatory and acceding State.
3   The European Communities (Commission, Court of Justice and General Secretariat of the Council) and the European Free Trade Association may attend the meetings as observers.

Article 4
1   At the request of a Contracting Party, the depositary of the Convention shall convene meetings of the Committee for the purpose of exchanging views on the functioning of the Convention and in particular on:
— the development of the case-law as communicated under the first paragraph first indent of Article 2,
...
2   The Committee, in the light of these exchanges, may also examine the appropriateness of starting on particular topics a revision of the Convention and make recommendations.

4. Council of Europe recommendation

Recommendation R(88)3

adopted by the Committee of Ministers on 7 March 1988, at the 415th meeting of the Ministers' Deputies

Recommendation of the Committee of Ministers to Member States on the validity of contracts between persons living together as an unmarried couple and their testamentary dispositions[1]

18.115   The Committee of Ministers, under the terms of Article 15.b of the Statute of the Council of Europe,

Considering that the aim of the Council of Europe is to achieve a greater unity between its members, in particular by promoting the adoption of common rules in legal matters;

Considering that many problems concerning persons living together as an unmarried couple may be resolved by the conclusion of contracts between such persons or by testamentary dispositions made by one in favour of the other;

Noting that in some countries such contracts and testamentary dispositions might be considered to be contrary to public policy or morality,

Recommends that the governments of member states take the necessary measures:

(i)   to ensure that contracts relating to property between persons living together as an unmarried couple, or which regulate matters concerning their property either during their relationship or when their relationship has ceased, should not be considered to be invalid solely because they have been concluded under these conditions;

(ii)   to apply the same principle to testamentary dispositions.

1   When this recommendation was adopted, and in application of art 10.2.c. of the Rules of Procedure for the meetings of the Ministers' Deputies, the Representative of Luxembourg reserved the right of his Government to comply with it or not.

Chapter 19

Style family law agreements

Style 1

Separation agreement (continuing after divorce)

19.01

AGREEMENT

BETWEEN

MRS ANNABEL LEE OR ALLAN, 5 RUE MORGUE, PAISLEY

AND

EDGAR ALLAN, 'THE RAVEN', WILLIAM WILSON ROAD, PAISLEY

WHEREAS:

The parties married at Edinburgh on 1 July 1990; have two children under the age of 16 years: Annabel Allan, born 14 February 1992; and Catherine Allan, born 26 August 1994; and separated on 2 May 1997.

The parties agree that their marriage has broken down irretrievably, and that there is no prospect of them reconciling; wish to enter into an agreement in contemplation of them divorcing; and wish the agreement to concern (1) the matrimonial and other property; (2) the children; and (3) related matters.

THEREFORE the parties AGREE as follows:

Part 1   The Matrimonial Home

Option 1   Transfer of title to one spouse

1.1   In regard to the matrimonial home the parties agree that:

(a)   Mr Allan will join with Mrs Allan in executing such deeds and other documents as may be required to vest the whole right, title and interest in the matrimonial home in the name of Mrs Allan alone for no consideration, and to revoke any special destination.

(b)   The transfer of title to Mrs Allan will be completed as soon as practicable but not later than three months from the date of the signature of this agreement.

(c)   In exchange for the deed transferring title to Mrs Allan:

(i)   the parties will sign, and Mrs Allan's agents will register, the necessary Deed of Variation (*or Discharge* (*if discharging the existing standard security*)) of any existing standard security over the matrimonial home, in order to discharge Mr Allan from all future liability and obligation in respect of any existing loan secured by the standard security; and

(ii)   Mrs Allan will free and relieve Mr Allan of any unimplemented obligations due by the parties under the standard security.

(d)   At settlement, Mr Allan will deliver to Mrs Allan's solicitors:

(i)   the deeds and other documents as referred to in clause 1.1(a);

(ii)   a signed and notarised renunciation of his occupancy rights in the matrimonial home;

(iii)   the endowment policies referred to in clause 4.2; and

(iv)   pay to Mrs Allan the capital sum referred to in clause 6.1.

(e)   Likewise Mrs Allan will deliver to Mr Allan's solicitors the Deed of Variation referred to in clause 1.1(c)(i) and any other documents necessary to effect settlement.

1.2   Mrs Allan will assume responsibility from the date of signature of this agreement for payment of:

(a)   the instalments in respect of the loan secured over the matrimonial home;

(b)   the premiums for the endowment policies referred to in clause 4.2; and

(c)   the household accounts including council tax, fuel and telephone bills and household insurance.

Option 2   Sale of matrimonial home

1.1   The matrimonial home will be sold at the best price that can reasonably be obtained, and both parties will co-operate in achieving this.

1.2   It will be exposed for sale (immediately after the signature of this agreement).

1.3   Mrs Allan's solicitors will act for both parties in the sale, and the parties will grant to them an irrevocable mandate to distribute the proceeds of sale in accordance with this agreement.

1.4   Neither party will instruct an arrestment of the sale proceeds.

1.5   There will be deducted from the sale price:
  (a)   the sum required to redeem [*specify the existing standard securities*] at the date of settlement;
  (b)   all fees incurred in the sale including any estate agents' fees, advertising costs, and solicitors' fees and outlays; and
  (c)   any council tax, fuel and telephone bills, and household insurance outstanding at the date of settlement.

1.6   The balance remaining will be divided (equally).

1.7   Until the sale of the matrimonial home, Mr Allan will pay [*specify*].

Option 3   Transfer of tenancy

1.1   Mrs Allan continues to reside in the matrimonial home, the tenancy of which [*has been/will be*] transferred to her, it [*having been formerly/being presently*] jointly tenanted by her and Mr Allan.

1.2   No payment is due to Mr Allan in respect of this transfer of tenancy and he waives any right of compensation which [*might otherwise have been due/may be due*] to him under section 13 of the Matrimonial Homes (Family Protection) (Scotland) Act 1981.

Part 2   The Parties' Other Property and Debts

2.1   The household goods will subject to the exceptions in clauses 3.1 and 3.2 become Mrs Allan's sole property from [*specify date of signature of this agreement*].

2.2   'Household goods' has the same meaning as in section 25 of the Family Law (Scotland) Act 1985 ('the 1985 Act').

3.1   The following goods [*specify*], will become Mr Allan's sole property from the date of signature of this agreement. [*Specify any arrangements for their uplifting by Mr Allan.*]

3.2   The second exception from clause 2.1 is goods on hire purchase. The parties' agreement in relation to these is contained in clause 5.4.

4.1   The ONE THOUSAND POUNDS (£1,000) to credit of the parties' account number [*specify*] with the Bank of Scotland, High Street, Paisley will be divided equally (six days after the date of signature of this agreement). Until then neither party will draw on or add to the account.

4.2   The parties' endowment policies [*specify*] with [*specify*] will be assigned to Mrs Allan no later than three months from the date of signature of this agreement.

4.3   The parties' joint shareholding of 1,000 shares in the Royal Dutch Overseas Company will be sold as soon as reasonably practicable after signature of this agreement and the net proceeds divided equally. They will be sold by a stockbroker instructed by Mrs Allan's agents, and the parties will sign any necessary forms connected with the sale.

4.4 The motor vehicle [*specify*], registration number [*specify*] is Mr Allan's sole property, and will remain his sole property. Mrs Allan renounces any claim in respect of it.

4.5 The motor vehicle [*specify*], registration number [*specify*] will become Mrs Allan's sole property. Mr Allan will transfer ownership of it to Mrs Allan, and deliver the log book and other documents to her at the date of this agreement, from which date Mrs Allan will be liable for insurance for it.

4.6 The dog 'Hugo' is the children's property.

4.7 The other items held by each party in their own name remains their sole property, and the other party renounces any claim to such items.

5.1 The parties will pay their own debts, except as otherwise provided in this agreement.

5.2 The following are joint and several debts:

  (a) hire purchase contract [*specify*] with [*specify*] for the purchase of the parties' three piece suite; and

  (b) Amsterdam Bank loan [*specify*] with [*specify*] for ONE THOUSAND POUNDS (£1,000).

5.3 Mr Allan will repay the joint and several debts in addition to his obligations to maintain the children and Mrs Allan. He frees and relieves Mrs Allan of these debts.

5.4 On payment of the final hire purchase instalment for the three piece suite, the parties will exercise their option to purchase it. Immediately after it becoming the parties' property, Mr Allan agrees that it will pass from property in the common ownership of him and Mrs Allan to property in the sole ownership of Mrs Allan. Mr Allan will sign and deliver to Mrs Allan any documents necessary to confer sold ownership on Mrs Allan.

Part 3   Capital Sum

Option 1   Immediate capital payment

6.1 Mr Allan will pay Mrs Allan a capital sum of TEN THOUSAND POUNDS (£10,000) due on [*specify*], with interest at 15% a year from the due date of payment until paid.

6.2 [*Option A*] Mrs Allan's entitlement to this sum has been calculated with reference to the scheduled statement of matrimonial property, which both parties warrant is a full and frank disclosure of what they own, and it does not include any element of aliment for the children.

or

6.2 [*Option B*] Mrs Allan's entitlement to this sum has been calculated with reference to the whole matrimonial property at the date of separation as disclosed by each party in correspondence through their solicitors prior to the date of signature of this agreement.

Both parties warrant that disclosure as a full and frank disclosure of what they owned at the date of their separation.

Option 2   Capital sum and pension order on divorce

6.1   Mr Allan will consent to Mrs Allan obtaining any necessary order under section 12A of the 1985 Act in respect of his entitlement to a lump sum from his pension scheme [*specify*] with [*specify*] and her payment of a capital sum from it of TEN THOUSAND POUNDS (£10,000) and interest thereon at 8% a year from the date of the order until the date of payment of the lump sum.

Part 4   Succession and Pension Rights

7.1   The parties hereby renounce and discharge all succession rights, including their prior rights and legal rights, and claims to mournings, aliment, or aliment *ex jure representationis,* in the other's estate and they hereby discharge each other's executors accordingly.

7.2   They hereby revoke the survivorship destination contained in the title to the matrimonial home referred to in clause 1.1.

8.1   They hereby renounce their rights as surviving spouse under any pension scheme.

Part 5   The Children

9.1   Annabel and Catherine will live with Mrs Allan and Mr Allan will have contact with them on a residential and non-residential basis as provided herein or as otherwise from time to time agreed by the parties.

9.2   Mrs Allan will be responsible for day to day decisions in relation to the children but will consult with Mr Allan regarding major parenting decisions, and will not reside with the children outside of the United Kingdom without the consent of Mr Allan or in the event of a disagreement in this regard, without obtaining a relevant court order to that effect.

9.3   The children will have their own passports, and Mrs Allan will have custody of the passports. However, Mrs Allan will hand over the passports to Mr Allan if he is taking the children on an agreed trip abroad.

9.4   Mr Allan will have contact with the children one weekend in two between [*specify*], for two weeks in their summer school holidays as agreed each year and each alternate Christmas and Boxing Day commencing [*specify*].

9.5   Notwithstanding the generality of this contact, Mrs Allan will have the right to have the children on holiday with her for a period of up to three weeks in total during each year, provided only this does not in any year interfere with Mr Allan's entitlement to contact on Christmas and Boxing Day.

Part 6   Aliment and Periodical Allowance

10.1 Mr Allan will aliment Annabel and Catherine at the rate of FIFTY POUNDS (£50.00) a week for each child until each child respectively attains the age of 18 years. But these obligations will cease from the effective date of any Child Support Agency maintenance assessment, and the parties acknowledge that the Agency may overturn their agreement as to aliment for the children. Further, these sums have been calculated with reference to the scheduled statement of the parties' income and outgoings, which they warrant is a full and frank disclosure thereof, and they undertake to disclose to each other annually a full and frank statement of their income and outgoings.

10.2 Mr Allan will pay Mrs Allan aliment for herself at the rate of ONE HUNDRED POUNDS (£100) a week until the date of the parties' divorce. Thereafter, he will pay her a periodical allowance of SEVENTY-FIVE POUNDS (£75.00) a week for a period of three years from the date of the parties' divorce. However, in the event of a Child Support Agency maintenance assessment providing that Mr Allan pay more money than in total agreed under clause 10.1, the amounts in this clause will be decreased by the amount of such increase, and if such increase equals or exceeds the amounts provided herein, then Mr Allan will pay no aliment for or periodical allowance to Mrs Allan.

10.3 The following apply in respect of aliment and periodical allowance:
  (a) All payments of aliment and of periodical allowance will be in advance each week.
  (b) They will be made by credit transfer into such bank or other account as Mrs Allan may from time to time nominate or by any other method designated by her.
  (c) Payments of aliment will commence on [*specify*].
  (d) Payments of aliment for Annabel and Catherine will be made to Mrs Allan for the maintenance of the children, and will be increased each year as the children get older and in line with inflation, subject to the parties' respective incomes and resources and obligations. Such increase will be agreed each year, and failing agreement either party may make application to the Child Support Agency, failing which either party may apply to the President of the Law Society of Scotland to nominate an arbiter to determine whether any increase is justified and, if so, how much. It will be in the option of either party whether to apply for the nomination of an arbiter, but on an arbiter being nominated both parties will be bound to arbitrate. If, however, the parties reach agreement on an increase, such agreement will be recorded in a formal writing registered for execution in the books of council and session. The decision of any arbiter will be registered for execution in the books of council and session, and the parties will pay the arbiter's costs equally, with neither being found liable for the expenses of the other.

10.4 Mr Allan will pay interest on each instalment of aliment and periodical allowance from its due date until paid at 15% a year.

10.5 Subject to clause 10.3(d), a competent court exercising jurisdiction and the power to do so may vary the foregoing amounts of aliment and periodical allowance on there being a material change of circumstances, not including the transfer or sale of the matrimonial home. In this regard, the parties prorogate the non-exclusive jurisdiction of the sheriff of North Strathclyde at Paisley.

Part 7   Divorce

Option 1   Two years separation and consent

11.1 Either party may after a period of two years in which the parties have not cohabited as husband and wife raise an action of divorce on the ground that the marriage has broken down irretrievably as established by that non-cohabitation and the other's party's consent and:

(a)   the other party will give his or her consent to the divorce;

(b)   the party who has not raised the divorce proceedings will provide to the party raising them such affidavits as required by that party in satisfying the court that decree of divorce should be granted; and

(c)   subject to a Scottish court retaining jurisdiction, proceedings will be raised in Scotland.

11.2 The parties will share the costs of the divorce proceedings contemplated by clause 11.1 according to the following arrangement:

(a)   The party wishing to raise the proceedings ('the pursuer') will be initially responsible for paying all the costs of the divorce proceedings ('the costs') to his or her own solicitor. The other party ('defender') will not be required to contribute any share of the costs until the court has issued the extract decree of divorce.

(b)   Upon the issuing of the extract decree of divorce, the pursuer will be entitled to recover one half of the costs from the defender. The pursuer or his solicitor will send a copy of the pursuer's solicitor's invoice for the costs to the defender or his or her solicitor. The defender then has 14 days in which to pay half of the costs, or raise any objection to the costs. The defender does not have the right to insist on a detailed account of expenses.

(c)   Any objection as to costs will be referred to the final determination of the auditor of Paisley Sheriff Court ('the auditor'). The auditor will tax the pursuer's solicitor's account on the basis of a solicitor-client account. He will certify the reasonable amount of costs which should have been charged for the work.

(d)   The auditor will have power to determine whether the pursuer or defender should be responsible for his audit fee.

(e)   However, the defender must in the first instance pay the auditor's fee. He must do so seven days in advance of the date set down by the auditor for taxation of the pursuer's costs. If he does not do so, then he will be held to have abandoned his objections to the pursuer's costs.

(f)   The defender will be liable to pay one half of the pursuer's costs:

      (i)   Fourteen days from the date the defender, or his solicitor, is notified of the costs if the defender does not object to the costs within that period.

      (ii)   Seven days from the date of the auditor's taxation certificate if the pursuer's costs are taxed by the auditor following upon the defenders objection to the pursuer's costs as provided for in clause 11.2(b).

      (iii) Seven days from the date assigned for taxation of the pursuer's costs if the defender is held to have abandoned his objection to the pursuer's costs under clause 11.2(e).

  (g) The amount of the costs of which the defender must pay one half is:

      (i)   the amount of the pursuer's costs as incurred to his or her solicitor if the defender does not object to those costs within the 14-day period referred to in clause 11.2(b) or is held to have abandoned his objections as provided for by clause 11.2(e); or

      (ii)   the amount of the costs as certified by the auditor under clause 11.2(c).

  (h) The amount of costs for which the defender is liable under the agreement is enforceable by summary diligence by virtue of registration of this agreement in terms of clause 19.1.

  (i) 'Costs' in this clause, includes outlays, but not the costs of affidavits referred to in clause 11.3.

11.3 Without prejudice to clause 11.2 if the pursuer needs to obtain affidavits from the defender and/or the defender's witnesses pursuant to clause 11.1(b), then the pursuer must reimburse the defender one half of the cost of those affidavits 14 days after their delivery to the pursuer's solicitors. The pursuer may, however, within that period object to the cost of the affidavits in which case the provisions of clause 11.2(c)–(g) will apply *mutatis mutandis* to the determination of the pursuer's objection to the cost of the defender's affidavits.

11.4 The defender is not entitled to insist on his or her solicitor accepting service of the pursuer's summons, initial writ or application for divorce, but the auditor may take into account any such offer, whether it would have been reasonable for the pursuer to have accepted it, and its effect on the costs of the litigation.

Option 2   Adultery

11.1 Mr Allan acknowledges that he has committed adultery with (here specify the name and address of the paramour) and he undertakes to provide affidavits from him and his paramour confessing their adultery with each other.

11.2 Mrs Allan may raise an action of divorce on the ground that the marriage has broken down irretrievably as established by Mr Allan's adultery, in which event Mr Allan will be obliged to pay to Mrs Allan her legal costs and outlays involved in the raising of such proceedings, subject to taxation of costs and outlays in the event of disagreement as to the amount.

Option 3   Simplified divorce application

11.1 Either party may after a period of two years in which the parties have not cohabited as husband and wife raise an action of divorce under the simplified procedure on the ground that the marriage has broken down irretrievably as established by that non-cohabitation and the other parties consent and:

(a)   the other party will give his or her consent to the divorce; and

(b)   the party who has raised the divorce proceedings will pay the outlays due to the Sheriff Clerk's office (currently understood to be [*specify amount*]) for lodging the application, and [*for service by Sheriff Officers if required*], without entitlement to reimbursement of all or part of those costs from the other party.

Part 8   Final Provisions

12.1 [*Option A*] The cost of registering this agreement and obtaining two extracts will be borne equally by the parties. Mrs Allan's solicitors will attend to the registration and obtaining two extracts of the agreement. Mr Allan's solicitors will reimburse one half of the cost involved to Mrs Allan's solicitors whereupon Mrs Allan's solicitors will send one of the extracts to him.

or

12.1 [*Option B*] The cost of registering this agreement and obtaining two extracts will be borne by Mrs Allan. Her solicitors will send one of the extracts to Mr Allan's solicitors.

13.1 Except as otherwise provided in this agreement, each party will be responsible for his or her own legal costs and outlays in respect of the negotiation, preparation, execution and implementation of his agreement including expenses incurred in the transfer of the title of the matrimonial home, but excluding any costs of litigation arising in connection with the implementation of his agreement.

14.1 The parties acknowledge and agree:

(a)   That except as provided by this agreement (*and without prejudice to an application for the necessary order under s 12A of the Family Law (Scotland) Act 1985, or any order incidental thereto, to give effect to clause 6.1*), the terms of this agreement represent a full and final settlement of all claims that either party has against the other for financial provision arising on divorce (*and under s 13 of the Matrimonial Homes (Family Protection) (Scotland) Act 1981* if applicable).

(b)   That this agreement operates to discharge each party (including that party's estate) of the obligation to aliment the other party, but not the children, which obligation is governed by clauses 10.1 and 10.3–10.5. (*This cannot apply if clause 10.2 applies.*) Aliment includes aliment *pendente lite* and interim aliment.

(c)   That in reaching the terms of this agreement both parties have had the opportunity and benefit of separate legal advice and in particular that they have been fully advised about the terms of the Family Law (Scotland) Act 1985.

(d) That having regard to the whole circumstances prevailing at the date of execution of this agreement, the terms of settlement set out in this agreement are fair and reasonable.

(e) That without prejudice to the provisions of any other part of this agreement, the parties will sign and deliver to the other party or that party's solicitor all deeds, documents, or forms, and will take such steps, necessary to give effect to the terms of this agreement.

(f) That any notice required in terms of this agreement will be sufficiently given, sent or served on the other party at his or her last known address, or at the address of his solicitors at the date of signature of this agreement.

(g) That this agreement comprises all the express terms of the parties contract. However, if any subsequent dispute arises in relation to what the parties disclosed in connection with clause 6.2 or the parties matrimonial debts at the date of their separation, either party may in connection with that dispute rely on evidence extrinsic or prior to this agreement (including any correspondence between thier solicitors).

15.1 Except in relation to the mutual obligations constituted in respect of the sale or transfer of the matrimonial home, neither party will be entitled to withhold performance of an obligation owed to the other party by reason of the other's non-performance of an obligation.

16.1 This agreement will continue to have effect after the parties are divorced.

17.1 This agreement will be governed by and construed in accordance with the law of Scotland.

17.2 The expression 'date of signature' or 'signature' in relation to this agreement means the later of the two dates on which it has been signed by the parties.

17.3 References in this agreement to any enactment are to that enactment as re-enacted or amended at any date after execution of this agreement.

18.1 'Matrimonial home' means the property at 5 Rue Morgue, Paisley (registered in the Land Register of Scotland under Title No REN 1845) (or disponed in favour of the parties by Disposition in their favour dated [*specify*] and recorded in the General Register of Sasines for the County of Renfrew on [*specify*]).

19.1 The parties consent to registration of this agreement for execution in the books of council and session:

IN WITNESS WHEREOF

Notes to Style 1

Instance

1   This identifies the parties to the agreement, but it is preferable in the actual agreement to refer to them as 'Mr Allan' or 'Mrs Allan' to avoid confusion or mistakes.

Preamble

2   This represents essential facts which should be stated. It helps to avoid disputes, eg about the date of the parties' separation (which is important for fixing the relevant date under the Family Law (Scotland) Act 1985). It also defines the purposes and intended scope of the agreement, eg is it intended to regulate the position on divorce, or is it a temporary agreement, valid only until the parties decide to divorce? It is stylistically useful for it avoids unnecessary repetition later on, eg references to the 'children' will be to those identified in the preamble.

Headings

3   These are useful in identifying the different parts of the agreement and what each is about.

The matrimonial home

4   The matrimonial home is most often the main asset, and the place where at least one of the parties will be in occupation for a period after a separation. The main issues are whether the home should be sold or transferred, the right to occupy it, and what is to happen about outgoings in respect of the property.

In Option 1, clause 1.1 addresses the situation where the matrimonial home is transferred to one of the parties. It is essential, in order to evacuate any survivorship destination, that the property is conveyed by both spouses from joint to sole title. Do not simply convey a one half *pro indiviso* share as that does not evacuate the survivorship destination in the other half share. It is also preferable to give a short conveyancing description (eg title number or details of the recording of a sasine title in favour of the parties) so that if one party fails to implement this part of the agreement, the crave for specific implement can more precisely relate to the property agreed to be transferred. Further, it is wise to check that the lenders will agree to a transfer of title. If Mr and Mrs Allan can afford to do so, another option is to discharge the existing loan and for Mrs Allan to grant a new standard security. Any extra legal costs might well be balanced by getting a fixed or discounted rate. Clause 1.1(d) specifies what is to be delivered or paid at settlement. Of course, the capital sum may be payable then, or later.

In Option 2, clauses 1.1–1.6 import the obligation to sell. It may be advisable to obtain a redemption statement prior to concluding the agreement so as to avoid any later nasty surprises. The parties will agree necessary variants on clauses 1.2 and 1.6; clause 1.5(c) is optional, but is purely an example and the parties must agree specifically what deductions are to be made. All other parts are essential; in particular, to comply with the Law Society of Scotland's Practice Guideline 1994 No 1 (February 1994) about solicitors acting in the sale of matrimonial homes on separation, clause 1.3 should specify which firm (if not a third firm) is to act. See 1993 FLB 3-7 and 1995 FLB 17-2 regarding arrestments, the reason for recommending clause 1.4.

The remaining clause in either option is an example, rather than a style. There are too many possible variants. The main thing is to do something about regulating payment for the outgoings of the matrimonial home until and after its transfer (Option 1) or until its sale (Option 2). In Option 1, clause 1.2(a) is unnecessary if the standard security is discharged and a new one signed by Mrs Allan.

The parties' other property and debts

5   The scheme of this part is to disturb the rules of the law of property and obligations as little as possible. The main rule is that each party owns their own property (including pension rights) and is liable to pay their own debts. The general disclaimer at clause 4.1 is enough to confirm, post-divorce, that this is to continue to be so. Special treatment is needed of property owned in common, or jointly, and of debts of which the parties are jointly or jointly and severally liable.

Clauses 2.1, 2.2, 3.1 and 3.2 start from the presumption in the Family Law (Scotland) Act 1985, s 25 that the parties have equal shares in the household goods. It gives ownership of these goods to one of the parties, with exceptions, and an example of how ownership to excepted items might be dealt with. There are other possible variants.

Clauses 4.1–4.7 give a list of common examples of common or joint property, says what is to happen to it and when. None of these things are household goods. Clauses 4.3–4.6 are examples of things specifically exempted as 'household goods' from the definition in the Family Law (Scotland) Act 1985, s 25. Clauses 4.4 and 4.5 remove doubts. Clause 4.6 is an example of property not owned by either of the parties: perhaps this is a useful compromise if custody of the dog cannot be agreed?

Clause 5.1 states and provides for the exceptions to the rule that the parties pay their own debts. Clauses 5.2(a) and 5.4 explain why hire purchase goods are to be exempted from Clause 2.1.

Capital sum

6   The amount should be calculated with reference to what the parties own, and the principles in the Family Law (Scotland) Act 1985, s 9(1). A schedule of these assets might be provided as this protects agents from allegations that some items were omitted or not advised on, and it also helps if there is a later challenge that the agreement was not fair and reasonable. Interest should be at a penal rate to encourage payment, unless it is agreed that payment be deferred, eg to the maturity of a pension when the rate might be agreed at eg 8% a year or at some rate perhaps fixed (in the agreement) after instructing an actuary. An earmarking order in relation to the pension is not binding on the scheme manager unless a court order is obtained; the agreement must provide for it if this is intended. Do not forget the question of interest, which could be substantial.

Succession and pension rights

7   'Legal rights' and 'prior rights' have specific legal meanings, and there is no need to refer to the statute in respect of prior rights. It is best to evacuate a special destination expressly: see *Redfern's Trustees v Redfern* 1996 SLT 900 and 1996 FLB 20.

The children

8   Parties who have been married continue to exercise their responsibilities for their children, and have their parental rights in respect of them, even after divorce. There should normally be no need for a court to intervene. In one view, nothing need be said; but there is no harm in setting out with which parent the children are to reside. This helps to avoid certain changes without agreement and to establish that the parent without the day-to-day care is one who is to pay money to aliment the children.

But such clauses can be elaborated as needed, and might regulate holidays, including to which countries the children may or may not be taken. Beware of clauses in terms of which children stay outwith Scotland 'for a trial period': habitual residence can easily be lost (cf *Cameron v Cameron* 1996 SLT 306). The clauses given here are purely examples.

Aliment and periodical allowance

9   *Stair* (I, 17, 18–20) reminds us that there are obligations accessory to the main ones: time, place and manner of performance being chief among these. This clause attempts to state the main obligations, distinguishing clearly between aliment and periodical allowance (see *Drummond v Drummond* 1985 SCLR 428), and attempting to take into account the effect of the child support legislation. It then adds some relevant accessory obligations common to all three obligations of maintenance. Finally, it provides for variation and allows the court to exercise a residual discretion if there is a change of circumstances. In the case of periodical allowance such a clause is necessary to confer jurisdiction on the court (*Ellerby v Ellerby* 1991 SCLR 608). 'Competent' is intended to refer to either the Court of Session or the sheriff; 'jurisdiction' to the ground upon which either court will exercise its power in a given case. The test is a material change of circumstances, but excludes the transfer or sale of the matrimonial home to put a stop to Mr Allan trying to get away with less than he has agreed to pay. It is open to the parties to agree a reduction on any given event.

Under the Child Support Act 1991, s 9(5), (6) there are certain restrictions on the court's power to vary aliment for children, the most important of which is that in respect of agreements made after 4 April 1993, the court may not exercise any power it has to increase the amount of aliment payable. In that regard the reference must be to an obligation to aliment 'each' child, and not 'both children'. A grammatical error here will halve the amount of aliment payable! Interest should be at a penal rate to encourage payment.

In appropriate cases separate provision may require to be made for school fees, or more rarely a disabled child. These are areas in respect of which the court retains jurisdiction by virtue of the Child Support Act 1991, ss 8, 9.

Divorce

10   The parties might wish to divorce before two years. If adultery is the ground, perhaps the adulterer and paramour can be asked to provide affidavits. Since there are children, and affidavits about their welfare will be needed, the cost of the divorce (the simplified procedure is not available) may be reasonably significant. The parties may wish to agree in advance what is to be done about costs. What is suggested are only examples of what might happen. In the first option, clause 11.1(c) is not legally binding since jurisdiction cannot be prorogated in divorces (*Singh v Singh* 1988 SCLR 541) but it might be useful in relation to costs or the sisting of an action raised in another jurisdiction. It may not be desired.

Experience shows it may be necessary to include very detailed provisions about costs. Some agreements provide merely that the other party pay one half of the costs, taxed if required; but in one actual case, the pursuer demanded her husband pay her own solicitor a sum of money (allegedly one half of her costs) to raise her divorce action. The detailed provisions provide for the fairest solution: the party wanting the divorce pays in the first instance. The other party is then put under tight obligations to make sure he or she can be forced to repay half the costs if necessary. Taxation is provided for if there are genuine disputes. The parties could always vary these terms to suit their own circumstances at a later date, but these provisions would be the starting point and they are intended to put beyond doubt who is responsible for what costs, and when. Because service of notices or objections is required, consequential provision has been made for that in clause 14.1(f).

A third option, for a simplified divorce application, has been added. Because this is a 'do it yourself procedure' and the costs are minimal, it may be simpler just to provide that the party raising the proceedings is not entitled to reimbursement of a share of the costs from the other. The other party may, if he or she feels like it, do this on a voluntary basis at the appropriate time.

Final provisions

11   Clause 12.1 concerns perhaps a trivial point, but one that often gives rise to concern. It is not unusual for a client's solicitor to pay the registration and extract costs, and to fail immediately to be reimbursed by the other party's solicitor. The clause may either be more trouble than it is worth, or it could be varied so that a particular party pays these costs. If it is kept in, it is designed to avoid lawyers falling out over minor matters.

Clause 13.1 is variable too, but it is usual for both to pay their own way. Litigation costs are excluded, which will follow the normal rules for awards of judicial expenses.

Clause 14.1 contains some usual disclaimers and discharges. Clause 14.1(b) is appropriate only where spouses do not ever seek to be alimented by the other. If a capital sum is paid in discharge of aliment, this clause is essential. It should not be used routinely.

Clause 15.1 is to put a stop to Mr Allan refusing Mrs Allan the house simply because she hasn't given him his CD collection, and any such nonsense. The law on retention is stated by the House of Lords in *Bank of East Asia v Scottish Enterprise* 1997 SLT 1213 but why risk litigation over these matters?

Clause 16.1 states the continued effect of the agreement after divorce.

Clause 17.1 states applicable law and clause 17.2 can be used to define any frequently used term in the agreement. It is best to avoid 'execution of the agreement' (rather 'signature') because the term has more than one meaning. Clause 17.3 has been inserted because the Interpretation Act 1978, s 17 (repeal and re-enactment) does not apply to 'deeds and other instruments'.

Clause 19.1 is essential if there are monetary obligations involved as it cuts out the need to litigate for the decree. Execution can proceed on the warrant granted in the extract: Writs Execution (Scotland) Act 1877, s 3. It is professionally improper to insert this clause after signature (decision of Scottish Solicitors' Discipline Tribunal, case 798/90): it is no mere formal clause. There is no need to provide for registration for preservation: see the Requirements of writing (Scotland) Act 1995, s 6(4). Registration will usually be in the books of council and session; registration in the sheriff court books is rare in practice. The practical effects are that any diligence must be carried out by messengers-at-arms instead of sheriff officers, except to the extent permitted by the Execution of Diligence (Scotland) Act 1926. A suspension of any charge may nevertheless be made in the sheriff court: Sheriff Courts (Scotland) Act 1907, s 5(5).

In witness whereof

12   The testing clause should contain the information required to make the agreement self-proving and registrable for the purposes of the Requirements of Writing (Scotland) Act 1995.

Style 2

Separation agreement (terminating on divorce)

19.02

AGREEMENT

BETWEEN

MRS ANNABEL LEE OR ALLAN, 5 RUE MORGUE, PAISLEY

AND

EDGAR ALLAN, 'THE RAVEN', WILLIAM WILSON ROAD, PAISLEY

WHEREAS:

The parties married at Edinburgh on 1 July 1990; have two children under the age of 16 years: Annabel Allan, born 14 February 1992; and Catherine Allan, born 26 August 1994; and separated on 2 May 1997.

The parties wish to enter into an agreement concerning their separation, to last until their divorce.

THEREFORE the parties AGREE as follows:

Part 1   Occupancy of the Matrimonial Home

1.1   Mrs Allan has the right to occupy the matrimonial home at 5 Rue Morgue, Paisley along with the children but without Mr Allan, who will not enter or occupy it except with the permission of Mrs Allan.

2.1   Mr Allan will pay:
   (a)   [*specify which household accounts*];
   (b)   the instalments of the loan secured over the matrimonial home; and
   (c)   the premiums for the endowment policies [*specify*].

3.1   Mrs Allan has the right to use all of the household goods (within the meaning of section 25 of the Family Law (Scotland) Act 1995) presently situated in the matrimonial home, and Mr Allan will not remove any of those goods from Mrs Allan's possession without her written permission.

Part 2   Use of Motor Vehicles

4.1   Mr Allan will have the sole use and possession of motor vehicle [*specify*], registration number [*specify*], and Mrs Allan the use and possession of motor vehicle [*specify*], registration number [*specify*].

5.1   Both vehicles are declared to be owned in common by the parties. Neither may be sold, hired, lent or otherwise disposed of without the other party's consent. Each party will be liable for the insurance and maintenance of the vehicle in his or her possession.

Part 3   Succession Rights

6.1   The parties revoke the survivorship destination in respect of the matrimonial home registered in the Land Register of Scotland under Title Number REN 1845 (or disponed in favour of the parties by Disposition dated and recorded in the General Register of Sasines for the County of Renfrew on [*specify*]).

Part 4   The Children

7.1   Annabel and Catherine will live with Mrs Allan and Mr Allan will have contact with them on a residential and non-residential basis as provided herein or as otherwise from time to time agreed by the parties.

7.2   Mrs Allan will be responsible for day to day decisions in relation to the children but will consult with Mr Allan regarding major parenting decisions, and will not reside with the children outside of the United Kingdom without the consent of Mr Allan or in the event of a disagreement in this regard, with obtaining a relevant court order to that effect.

7.3   The children will have their own passports, and Mrs Allan will have custody of the passports. However, Mrs Allan will hand over the passports to Mr Allan if he is taking the children on an agreed trip abroad.

7.4   Mr Allan will have contact with the children one weekend in two between [*specify*], for two weeks in their summer school holidays as agreed each year and each alternate Christmas and Boxing Day commencing. Notwithstanding the generality of this contact, Mrs Allan will have the right to have the children on holiday with her for a period of up to three weeks in total during each year, provided only this does not in any year interfere with Mr Allan's entitlement to contact on Christmas and Boxing Day.

Part 5   Aliment

8.1 Mr Allan will aliment Annabel and Catherine at the rate of FIFTY POUNDS (£50) a week for each child until each child respectively attains the age of 18 years, and make these payments to Mrs Allan for the maintenance of the children. But these obligations will cease from the effective date of any Child Support Agency maintenance assessment, and the parties acknowledge that the Agency may overturn their agreement as to aliment for the children. Further, these sums have been calculated with reference to the scheduled statement of the party's income and outgoings, which they warrant as a full and frank disclosure thereof, and they undertake to disclose to each other annually a full and frank statement of their income and outgoings.

8.2 Mr Allan will aliment Mrs Allan herself at the rate of ONE HUNDRED POUNDS (£100) a week. However, in the event of a Child Support Agency maintenance assessment providing that Mr Allan pay more money than in total agreed under clause 8.1, the amount provided for in this clause will be decreased by the amount of such increase, and if such increase equals or exceeds the amount provided herein, then Mr Allan will pay no aliment for Mrs Allan.

8.3 Payments of aliment for the children and Mrs Allan will commence on and will be made in advance each week by Mr Allan by credit transfer into Mrs Allan's nominated bank or other account.

8.4 Mr Allan will pay interest on each instalment of aliment for its due date until paid at 15% a year.

Part 6   Other Matters

9.1 The parties will maintain separate bank accounts.

9.2 Account number [*specify*] with Bank of Scotland, High Street, Paisley, will be closed within six days of the date of the signing of this agreement, with neither party drawing on the account in the intervening six-day period, except existing direct debits or standing orders, and:
   (a)   the amount at credit will be paid over to Mrs Allan;
   (b)   Mr Allan renounces any further claim on this money.

9.3 Account number [*specify*] with Bank of Scotland, High Street, Paisley will remain in Mr Allan's name.

10.1 The family dog 'Hugo' will stay with Mrs Allan and the children.

Part 7   Termination of This Agreement

11.1 This agreement ceases to have effect on divorce or on the parties entering into a formal agreement renouncing this agreement, and registered for preservation in the books of council and session and is not an agreement as to financial provision on divorce. It will revive if the parties separate after any reconciliation.

Part 8   Final Provisions

12.1 Mrs Allan's solicitor will register this agreement, and obtain two extracts. Mr Allan's solicitor will reimburse Mrs Allan's solicitor one half of the cost of registration and obtaining extracts whereupon he will be entitled immediately to receive one of the extracts. Except for these costs, each party will bear his or her own legal costs for this agreement.

13.1 This agreement will be governed by and construed in accordance with the law of Scotland.

14.1 The parties consent to registration of this agreement for execution in the books of council and session:

IN WITNESS WHEREOF

Notes to Style 2

Occupancy of the matrimonial home

1   The formulation 'Mrs Allan has the right to occupy' the matrimonial home does not oblige her to do so. It and the three clauses generally are designed to secure to her the right solely to use the matrimonial home and the household goods within it. As an alternative to Mr Allan paying household accounts etc these might be transferred to Mrs Allan, and the amount of aliment increased.

Use of motor vehicles

2   This is a practical expediency, settling possession rather than defining ownership. An additional clause might be added (if appropriate) about who is to pay any hire purchase instalments. Clause 5.1 depends on who owns the vehicles, and is given as an example only.

Succession rights

3   Mrs Allan still gets her legal and prior rights, but the house gets divided equally between the deceased spouse's estate and the surviving spouse. This might be qualified to operate only in favour of Mrs Allan. It is by no means always right or advisable to have it.

The children

4   See note 8 to Style 1. Here the situation envisaged by the parties is non-residential contact, but it could be anything.

Aliment

5   See note 9 to Style 1. Here there is no need for a periodical allowance. The Family Law (Scotland) Act 1985, s 7 allows the court to vary on a material change of circumstances and there is no need to 'contract' in. But an interim variation is not possible: *Woolley v Strachan* 1997 FLR 95.

Other matters

6   These are substantive matters of a miscellaneous nature and may be of varying significance or importance. Only two examples are given.

Termination

7   An agreement will usually terminate on reconciliation. It is made clear that it will revive if the parties separate after a reconciliation, and that it ceases to have effect on divorce and is not intended to regulate financial provision on divorce. It will also cease to have effect if the parties so agree, but to prevent any disputes and to allow the parties a chance to reflect on matters, only a formal agreement registered for preservation in the books of council and session will do.

Final provisions

8   Such of the final provisions in style 1 that are appropriate to this agreement are repeated here.

Style 3

Pension sharing agreement (pension arrangement)

19.03

AGREEMENT

BETWEEN

PERCIVAL PROSPERO, 5 Prince's Castle, Stirling

and

HELEN HERALD or PROSPERO, 4 Knight's Way, Falkirk

WHEREAS:

The parties married at Glasgow on 15 December 1990; have no children of their marriage; and separated on 12 July 2000, the 'relevant date' for the purposes of sections 9(1)(a) and 10(3) of the Family Law (Scotland) Act 1985 ('the 1985 Act').

Mr Prospero has the right to benefits under a personal pension scheme with (specify) and those rights are shareable with Mrs Prospero within the meaning of s 27(2) of the Welfare Reform and Pensions Act 1999 ('the 1999 Act') (hereinafter 'shareable pension rights').

The parties agree: that their marriage has broken down irretrievably, and that there is no prospect of them reconciling; wish to enter into an agreement concerning their matrimonial and other property in contemplation of them divorcing; and wish the agreement to determine (1) Mrs Prospero's financial provision on divorce including provision for Mrs Prospero (the transferee) sharing in Mr Prospero's (the transferor's) shareable pension rights; and (2) other related matters.

On [*specify date*] Mr Prospero, the transferor, intimated to [*specify*], the person responsible for his personal pension scheme, prior to him and Mrs Prospero, the transferee, making this agreement, the intention to have his pension rights under the pension scheme shared with the transferee.

Mr Prospero had relevant benefits valued at [*specify*] in respect of his pension scheme on [*specify date*], the valuation day in respect of those rights.

This agreement is to be registered in the books of council and session.

THEREFORE the parties AGREE as follows:

Part 1   Financial Provision

1.1   Mrs Prospero is to receive a (*specify percentage*) share of Mr Prospero's shareable pension rights as provided for by the separable annex to this agreement.

2.1   The pension sharing provision made by the separable annex is to take effect on the grant of a decree of divorce under the Divorce (Scotland) Act 1976 or declarator of nullity of marriage in relation to the parties' marriage.

Part 2   Succession Rights

3.1   The parties renounce and discharge their prior rights and legal rights, and claims to mournings, or ailment *ex jure representationis,* in the other's estate, and hereby discharge each other's executors accordingly. This does not apply to Mrs Prospero's entitlement to a pension credit in accordance with this agreement.

3.2   The parties renounce their rights as surviving spouse under any pension scheme save to the extent provided in Part 1 hereof.

Part 3   Divorce

4.1   Either party may after a period of two years in which the parties have not cohabited as husband and wife raise an action of divorce in Scotland on the ground that the marriage has broken down irretrievably as established by that non-cohabitation and the other party's consent.

4.2   The other party will give his or her consent to the divorce.

4.3   The party who has not raised the divorce proceedings will be obliged to pay to the party who has one half of his or her legal costs and outlays involved in the raising of such proceedings, subject to taxation of the costs and outlays for the action in the event of disagreement as to the amount.

4.4   The obligation referred to in clause 4.3 does not arise until after the court has issued the extract decree of divorce. Neither party, or that party's solicitor, may insist on the other party contributing to the costs of his or her divorce proceedings until after those proceedings have been concluded and the extract decree of divorce has been issued. The party raising the proceedings must in the first instance bear the costs of doing so.

Part 4   Final Provisions

5.1   The cost of registering this agreement and obtaining two extracts will be borne equally by the parties. Mrs Prospero's solicitors will attend to the registration and obtaining two extracts of the agreement. Mr Prospero's solicitors will reimburse one half of the cost involved to Mrs Prospero's solicitors whereupon Mrs Prospero's solicitors will send one of the extracts to Mr Prospero's solicitors.

6.1   Except as provided for in clauses 4.3 and 5.1, each party will be responsible for his or her own legal costs and outlays in respect of the negotiation, preparation, execution and implementation of this agreement, but excluding any costs of litigation arising in connection with the implementation of this agreement. The following costs in respect of the pension sharing provision in the separable annex will be borne as follows: [*specify*].

7.1   The parties acknowledge and agree:

(a)   That except as provided by this agreement, (and without prejudice to an application for a pension sharing order under s 8(1)(baa) of the 1985 Act, or any order incidental thereto, or other legislation, required to give effect to Part 1 of this agreement), the terms of this agreement represent a full and final settlement of all claims that either party has against the other for financial provision arising on divorce or annulment and that it comprises all the express terms of their contract.

(b)   That this agreement operates to discharge each party (including that party's estate) of the obligation to aliment the other party, including aliment *pendente lite* and interim aliment.

(c)   That in reaching the terms of this agreement both parties have had the opportunity and benefit of separate legal advice and in particular that they have been fully advised about the terms of the 1985 Act and Parts III and IV of the 1999 Act.

(d)   That in reaching the terms of this agreement Mrs Prospero has had the opportunity and benefit of independent financial advice in respect of the pension sharing provision made by this agreement and in particular in regard to the options available to her for her pension credit under Schedule 5 to the 1999 Act.

(e)   That having regard to the whole circumstances prevailing at the date of execution of this agreement, the terms of settlement set out in this agreement are fair and reasonable.

(f)   That without prejudice to the provisions of any other part of this agreement, the parties will sign and deliver to the other party or that party's solicitor all deeds, documents, agreements, or forms and will take such steps, necessary to give effect to the terms of this agreement, including the provision for pension sharing, and to enable [*specify name of pension provider*] to implement the pension sharing provisions in the separable annex on time in accordance with section 34 of the 1999 Act.

8.1 Mr Prospero is not entitled to withhold performance of an obligation owed to Mrs Prospero under this agreement by reason of her non-performance of any obligation owed to him.

9.1 This agreement will continue to have effect after the parties are divorced.

10.1 This agreement will be governed by and construed in accordance with the Law of Scotland.

11.1 The expression 'date of signature' or 'signature' in relation to this agreement means the later of the two days on which it has been signed by the parties.

11.2 The provisions and definitions in the introduction and separable annex to this agreement are integral parts of it.

11.3 Expressions used in this agreement or its annex in relation to Mr Prospero's shareable pension rights have the same meaning as in the 1999 Act or regulations made thereunder.

11.4 References in this Agreement to any enactment are to that enactment as re-enacted or amended at any date after the date of execution of this agreement.

12.1 The parties consent to the registration of this agreement and its annex in the books of council and session for execution:

IN WITNESS WHEREOF

ANNEX TO AGREEMENT

between

PERCIVAL PROSPERO, 5 Prince's Castle, Stirling

And

HELEN HERALD or PROSPERO, 4 Knight's Way, Falkirk

This is the annex to the agreement between Percival Prospero and Helen Herald or Prospero signed at [*specify*] on [*specify*].

1.1 Information in relation to the transferor (Mr Prospero):
  (a) all names by which the transferor has been known;
  (b) date of birth;
  (c) address;
  (d) national insurance number;
  (e) the name and address of the pension arrangement to which the pension sharing provision relates;
  (f) the transferor's membership number or policy number in that pension arrangement.

2.1 Information in relation to the transferee (Mrs Prospero):
  (a) all names by which the transferee has been known;

(b)   date of birth;

(c)   address;

(d)   national insurance number; and

(e)   if the transferee is a member of the pension arrangement from which a pension credit is derived, her membership number in that pension arrangement.

3.1   The specified percentage of the cash equivalent of the relevant benefits on the valuation day to be transferred to the transferee (Mrs Prospero) is [*specify*] (together with interest from the date of this agreement of [*specify percentage*] to the date of the transfer).

4.1   Where the transferee has given her consent, in accordance with paragraphs 1(3)(c), 3(3)(c) or 4(2)(c) of Schedule 5 to the 1999 Act (mode of discharge of liability for a pension credit), to the payment of a pension credit to the person responsible for a qualifying agreement:

(a)   the full name of that qualifying arrangement;

(b)   its address;

(c)   if known, the transferee's membership number or policy number in that arrangement; and

(d)   the name or title, business address, business telephone number and, where available, the business facsimile number and electronic mail address of a person who may be contacted in respect of the discharge of liability for the pension credit;

5.1   Details of the provision about the apportionment (if any) made by the transferor and the transferee of liability for any charges levied by the person responsible for the pension arrangement in relation to pension sharing under Chapter I of Part IV of the 1999 Act (*eg provide these should be shared equally or in other specified proportions*);

5.2   The transferor intimated to the pension arrangement his intention with respect to pension sharing on [*specify*]. The pension arrangement acknowledged receipt of the intimation on [*specify*].

Notes to Style 3

Instance

1   This identifies the parties to the agreement, but it is preferable in the actual agreement to refer to them as 'Mr Prospero' and 'Mrs Prospero' to avoid confusion or mistakes.

Preamble

2   This recites essential facts which should be stated. It helps to avoid disputes, eg about the date of the parties' separation (which is important for fixing the relevant date under the Family Law (Scotland) Act 1985). It also defines the purposes and intended scope of the agreement and contains confirmation of the information needed for it to be a qualifying agreement under the Welfare Reform and Pensions Act 1999, s 28(1)(f) (as prescribed by the Pensions on Divorce etc (Pension Sharing) (Scotland) Regulations

2000 (SI 2000/1051), reg 3). Note that pension sharing in respect of non-state scheme rights is in relation to the various 'pension arrangements', specified in s 26(1) of the 1999 Act. This style selects a personal pension scheme.

Headings

3   These are useful in identifying the different parts of the agreement and what each is about.

Financial Provision

4   This part is all about pension sharing, but might be expanded if there are other matters.

   Note that pension sharing may be either by reference to a percentage value or an amount to be transferred: Family Law (Scotland) Act 1985, s 27(1)(b). This style chooses a percentage value as an example, but it could equally be an amount that the parties chose to agree upon.

   The Welfare Reform and Pensions Act 1999, s 28(1)(f)(i) allows for pension sharing by means of a qualifying agreement. A 'qualifying agreement' is one which has been entered into in such circumstances as prescribed by the Secretary of State and is registered in the books of council and session: Welfare Reform and Pensions Act 1999, s 28(3). See note 2 regarding these circumstances. By virtue of s 28(1)(f)(ii), the qualifying agreement must be in a form prescribed by the Secretary of State: see SI 2000/1051, reg 2, which requires particular information to be set out in a separable annex to the agreement. By s 28(1)(f)(iii) of the 1999 Act the agreement must take effect, in relation to the marriage, on the grant of decree of divorce under the Divorce (Scotland) Act 1976 or of a declarator of nullity. Clauses 1.1 and 2.1 attempt to comply with the requirements of s 28(1)(f), (3) of the 1999 Act and SI 2000/1051.

Succession rights

5   See note 7 to Style 1. This had been adapted, however, to take into account the specialities of pension sharing.

Divorce

6   Clauses 4.1–4.4 are suggested as a non-binding but useful way of achieving a non-contentious divorce in Scotland such as to allow for activation of the pension sharing provisions in the annex.

Final provisions

7   See note 11 to Style 1 for comments in relation to similar final provisions for that style. These have been varied as seem suitable for pension sharing provision. Reference has been made to the important provisions of the Welfare Reform and Pensions Act 1999, Sch 5.

Annex

8   Clause 4.1 might alternatively refer to a specified amount to be transferred instead of a percentage amount: see note 4, second paragraph.

9   Copies of relevant matrimonial documents and certain prescribed information must be given to the person responsible for the pension scheme within two months of the date of the extract decree of divorce or declarator of nullity of marriage otherwise the pension sharing provision is deemed never to have had effect: Welfare Reform and Pensions Act 1999, s 28(7)–(9), and the Pensions on Divorce etc (Provision of Information) Regulations (SI 2000/1048), reg 5. However, application can be made to the sheriff to extend this period, although it is submitted good cause would need to be shown to persuade the sheriff to exercise this power: see s 28(10) of the 1999 Act. The application under s 28(10) is made by minute in the divorce process of the sheriff court: OCR 1993, r 33.51(3)(c). If the divorce was granted in the Court of Session or the court granted decree of declarator of nullity of marriage, application to extend the two-month period would be made by summary application to the sheriff.

10   Pension sharing provision may not be made where an earmarking order has been made under the Family Law (Scotland) Act 1985, s 12A: see Welfare Reform and Pensions Act 1999, s 28(6).

Style 4

Pension sharing agreement (state scheme rights)

19.04

AGREEMENT

between

PERCIVAL PROSPERO, 5 Prince's Castle, Stirling

and

HELEN HERALD or PROSPERO, 4 Knight's Way, Falkirk

WHEREAS:

The parties married at Glasgow on 15 December 1990; have no children of their marriage; and separated on 12 July 2000, the 'relevant date' for the purposes of ss 9(1)(a) and 10(3) of the Family Law (Scotland) Act 1985 ('the 1985 Act').

Mr Prospero has the right to benefits under a state pension scheme and those rights are shareable with Mrs Prospero within the meaning of s 47(2) of the Welfare Reform and Pensions Act 1999 ('the 1999 Act') (hereinafter 'shareable state scheme rights').

The parties agree: that their marriage has broken down irretrievably, and that there is no prospect of them reconciling; wish to enter into an agreement concerning their matrimonial and other property in anticipation of them divorcing; and wish the agreement to determine (1) Mrs Prospero's financial provision on divorce including provision for Mrs Prospero (the transferee) sharing in Mr Prospero's (the transferor's) shareable state scheme rights; and (2) other related matters.

On [*specify date*] the parties received confirmation from the Secretary of State that shareable state scheme rights are held in the name of Mr Prospero, the transferor.

The separable annex to this agreement makes provision corresponding to a pension sharing order under s 8(1)(baa) of the 1985 Act.

This agreement is to be registered in the books of council and session.

THEREFORE the parties AGREE as follows:

Part 1   Financial Provision

1.1   Mrs Prospero is to receive a [*specify percentage*] share of Mr Prospero's shareable state scheme rights as provided for by the separable annex to this agreement.

2.1   The pension sharing provision made by the separable annex is to take effect on the grant of a Decree of Divorce under the Divorce (Scotland) Act 1976 or declarator or nullity of marriage in relation to the parties' marriage.

Part 2   Succession Rights

3.1   The parties hereby renounce and discharge all succession rights, including their prior rights and legal rights, and claims to mournings, or aliment *ex jure representationis* in the other's estate, and hereby discharge each other's executors accordingly. This does not apply to Mr Prospero's entitlement to pension sharing in accordance with this agreement.

Part 3   Divorce

4.1   Either party may after a period of two years in which the parties have not cohabited as husband and wife raise an action of divorce in Scotland on the ground that the marriage has broken down irretrievably as established by that non-cohabitation and the other party's consent.

4.2   The other party will give his or her consent to the divorce.

4.3   The party who has not raised the divorce proceedings will be obliged to pay to the party who has one half of his or her legal costs and outlays involved in the raising of such proceedings, subject to taxation of the costs and outlays for the action in the event of disagreement as to the amount.

4.4   The obligation referred to in clause 4.3 does not arise until after the court has issued the extract decree of divorce. Neither party, nor that party's solicitor, may insist on the other party contributing to the costs of his or her divorce proceedings until after those proceedings have been concluded and the extract decree of divorce has been issued. The party raising the proceedings must in the first instance bear the cost of doing so.

Part 4   Final Provisions

5.1   The cost of registering this agreement and obtaining two extracts will be borne equally by the parties. Mrs Prospero's solicitors will attend to the registration and obtaining two extracts of the agreement. Mr Prospero's solicitors will reimburse one half of the cost involved to Mrs Prospero's solicitors whereupon Mrs Prospero's solicitors will send one of the extracts to Mr Prospero's solicitors.

6.1   Except as provided for in clauses 4.3 and 5.1, each party will be responsible for his or her own legal costs and outlays in respect of the negotiation, preparation, execution and implementation of this agreement, but excluding any costs of litigation arising in connection with the implementation of this agreement.

7.1   The parties acknowledge and agree:

    (a)   That except as provided by this agreement (and without prejudice to an application for a pension sharing order under s 8(1)(baa) of the 1985 Act, or any other incidental thereto, or other legislation, required to give effect to Part 1 of this agreement), the terms of this agreement represent a full and final settlement of all claims that either party has against the other for financial provision arising on divorce or annulment and that it comprises all the express terms of their contract.

    (b)   That this agreement operates to discharge each party (including that party's estate) of the obligation to aliment the other party, excluding aliment *pendente lite* and interim aliment.

    (c)   That in reaching the terms of this agreement both parties have had the opportunity and benefit of separate legal advice and in particular that they have been fully advised about the terms of the 1985 Act and Parts III and IV of the 1999 Act.

    (d)   That having regard to the whole circumstances prevailing at the date of execution of this agreement, the terms of settlement set out in this agreement are fair and reasonable.

    (e)   That without prejudice to the provisions of any other part of this agreement, the parties will sign and deliver to the other party or that party's solicitor all deeds, documents, agreements, or forms, and will take such steps, necessary to give effect to the terms of this agreement, including the provisions for pension sharing, and to enable the pension sharing provisions in the separable annex to take effect in accordance with section 49 of the 1999 Act.

8.1   Mr Prospero is not entitled to withhold performance of an obligation owed to Mrs Prospero under this agreement by reason of her non-performance of any obligation owed to him.

9.1   This agreement will continue to have effect after the parties are divorced.

10.1   This agreement will be governed by and construed in accordance with the law of Scotland.

11.1   The expression 'date of signature' or 'signature' in relation to this agreement means the later of the two days on which it has been signed by the parties.

11.2   The provisions and definitions in the introduction and separable annex to this agreement are integral parts of it.

11.3   Expressions used in this agreement or in its annex in relation to Mr Prospero's shareable state scheme rights have the same meaning as in the 1999 Act or regulations made thereunder.

11.4   References in this agreement to any enactment are to that enactment as re-enacted or amended at any date after the execution of this agreement.

11.5 The parties consent to registration of this agreement in the books of council and session for execution:

IN WITNESS WHEREOF

ANNEX TO AGREEMENT

between

PERCIVAL PROSPERO, 5 Prince's Castle, Stirling

and

HELEN HERALD or PROSPERO, 4 Knight's Way, Falkirk

This is the annex to the agreement between Percival Prospero and Helen Herald or Prospero signed at [*specify*] on [*specify*].

1.1 Information in relation to the party who is transferor (Mr Prospero):
   (a) full name;
   (b) date of birth;
   (c) address;
   (d) national insurance number; and
   (e) details of the specified amount or, as appropriate, the specified percentage of the cash equivalent on the transfer day of the transferor's relevant state scheme rights immediately before that day.

2.1 Information in relation to the party who is the transferee (Mrs Prospero):
   (a) full name by which the transferee is or will be known;
   (b) date of birth;
   (c) address; and
   (d) national insurance number.

3.1 The transferor and the transferee received confirmation from the Secretary of State on [*specify date*] that shareable state scheme rights are held in the name of the transferor and that on the grant of decree of divorce or declarator of nullity of marriage a pension sharing agreement will be implemented.

Notes to Style 4

General note

1   This style is similar to Style 3 (pension arrangement) but contains subtle differences to reflect the slightly different provisions applying to sharing of state scheme rights.

Instance

2   This identifies the parties to the agreement, but it is preferable in the actual agreement to refer to them as 'Mr Prospero' and 'Mrs Prospero' to avoid confusion or mistakes.

Preamble

3   This recites essential facts which should be stated. It helps to avoid disputes, eg about the date of the parties' separation (which is important for fixing the relevant date under the Family Law (Scotland) Act 1985). It also defines the purposes and intended scope of the agreement and contains confirmation of the information needed for it to be a qualifying agreement under the Welfare Reform and Pensions Act 1999, 48(1)(f) (as prescribed by the Pensions on Divorce etc (Pension Sharing) (Scotland) Regulations 2000 (SI 2000/1051), reg 5).

Headings

4   These are useful in identifying the different parts of the agreement and what each is about.

Financial provision

5   This part is all about pension sharing, but might be expanded if there are other matters.

   Note that pension sharing may be either by reference to a percentage value or an amount to be transferred: Family Law (Scotland) Act 1985, s 27(1)(b). This style chooses a percentage value as an example, but it could equally be an amount that the parties chose to agree upon.

   The Welfare Reform and Pensions Act 1999, s 48(1)(f)(i) allows for pension sharing by means of a qualifying agreement. A 'qualifying agreement' is one which has been entered into in such circumstances as prescribed by the Secretary of State and is registered in the books of council and session: Welfare Reform and Pensions Act 1999, s 48(3). See note 3 regarding these circumstances. By virtue of s 48(1)(f)(ii), the qualifying agreement must be in a form prescribed by the Secretary of State: see SI 2000/1051, reg 4, which requires particular information to be set out in a separable annex to the agreement. By s 48(1)(f)(iii) of the 1999 Act the agreement must take effect, in relation to the marriage, on the grant of decree of divorce under the Divorce (Scotland) Act 1976 or of a declarator of nullity. Clauses 1.1 and 2.1 attempt to comply with the requirements of the Welfare Reform and Pensions Act 1999, s 48(1)(f), (3) and SI 2000/1051.

Succession rights

6   See note 7 to Style 1. This has been adapted, however, to take into account the specialities of pension sharing.

Divorce

7   Clauses 4.1–4.4 are suggested as a non-binding but useful way of achieving a non-contentious divorce in Scotland such as to allow for activation of the pension sharing provisions in the annex.

Final provisions

8   See note 11 to Style 1 for comments in relation to similar financial provisions for that style. These have been varied as seem suitable for pension sharing provision. The Welfare Reform and Pensions Act 1999, Sch 5 (which applies to pension arrangements) does not apply to state scheme rights and references to it are therefore omitted in this style.

Annex

9   Copies of relevant matrimonial documents and certain prescribed information must be given to the Secretary of State within two months of the date of the extract decree of divorce or declarator of nullity of marriage otherwise the pension sharing provision is deemed never to have had effect: Welfare Reform and Pensions Act 1999, s 48(6)–(8), and the Pensions on Divorce etc (Provision of Information) Regulations 2000 (SI 2000/1048), reg 5. However, application can be made to the sheriff to extend this period, although it is submitted good cause would need to be shown to persuade the sheriff to exercise this power: see s 48(9) of the 1999 Act. The application under s 48(9) is made by minute in the divorce process of the sheriff court: OCR 1993, r 33.51(3)(c). If the divorce was granted in the Court of Session, or the court granted decree of declarator of nullity of marriage, application to extend the two-month period would be made by summary application to the sheriff.

Style 5

Arbitration agreement for aliment

19.05

AGREEMENT

between

ANNE DAVIDSON or CHIESLEY, 10 Carnwath Way, Edinburgh

and

JOHN CHIESLEY, 5 Lockhart Avenue, Dalry, Edinburgh

WHEREAS:

The parties married at Edinburgh on 31 March 1996; have three children under the age of 18 years: Anne Chiesley, born 1 August 1997; John Chiesley, born 1 October 1998; and George Chiesley, born 2 December 2000; and separated on 1 August 2002.

The parties have been unable to agree on the amount of aliment which Mr Chiesley is to pay to Mrs Chiesley both for herself and on behalf of the children.

The parties have agreed to submit their dispute to arbitration, and to be bound by the result of that arbitration.

The parties wish to make provision for registration of the arbitral award, and other matters consequent upon the submission of their dispute to arbitration.

THEREFORE the parties AGREE as follows:

Part 1   The Arbitration Agreement

1   The dispute submitted to arbitration
1.1   The arbiter appointed in accordance with this agreement will determine the amount of aliment (if any) which Mr Chiesley is to pay to:
(a)   Mrs Chiesley;
(b)   Mrs Chiesley on behalf of Anne;
(c)   Mrs Chiesley on behalf of John; and

(d)   Mrs Chiesley on behalf of George.

2   The arbiter
2.1   A sole arbiter will be appointed.
2.2   The parties will reach agreement on the person to be appointed arbiter within one month of Mrs Chiesley serving her demand for arbitration on Mr Chiesley.
2.3   Failing agreement within that period, the President of the Law Society of Scotland for the time being will appoint a person to act as sole arbiter under this agreement. The parties will be bound by that nomination.
2.4   These provisions apply *mutatis mutandis* to any replacement arbiter who may require to be appointed, or if the original person nominated does not accept the appointment as arbiter or declines to act.

3   Arbiter not to be called as witness or haver
3.1   The parties agree not to call the arbiter as a witness or expert in any pending or subsequent litigation as to any matter related to the arbitration.
3.2   They will defend the arbiter from any citation as witness or haver from any party as to the subject of the arbitration.

4   Liability and responsibilities of arbiter
4.1   The arbiter is not liable to any party for any act or omission in connection with the arbitration.
4.2   The arbiter is bound by the provisions of this agreement.
4.3   The arbiter must disclose any conflict of interest or other circumstance which would prevent him or her from acting fairly and impartially in the arbitration, and decline to act in any of these circumstances.

5   Seat and place of arbitration
5.1   The seat of the arbitration is Scotland.
5.2   The place of the arbitration will be determined by the arbiter.
5.3   The arbiter will first consult with the parties before determining the place of the arbitration. It need not be in Scotland.

6   Substantive law
6.1   The substantive law of Scotland concerning aliment is applicable to the dispute.

7   Language of the proceedings
7.1   The language of the arbitral proceedings is English.
7.2   The arbiter and the parties may, however, agree to another language as the language of the proceedings.
7.3   The arbiter and both parties must all agree to depart from English as the language of the proceedings.

7.4   If they do so, they must all be agreed on the specific language to be substituted for English. This agreement must be recorded in writing in a memorandum of agreement signed by the arbiter and both parties.

8   Commencement of arbitration
8.1   Mrs Chiesley will serve a demand for arbitration on Mr Chiesley.
8.2   The proceedings will be deemed to have commenced on the date on which Mrs Chiesley's demand for arbitration is served on Mr Chiesley.
8.3   The demand for arbitration must be in the form annexed to this agreement.

9   Scheduling the arbitration
9.1   Within ten days of accepting appointment, the arbiter must schedule the date, time and place of the arbitration and must notify the parties of the schedule.
9.2   The arbiter must first consult with the parties before scheduling the date and time of the arbitration.

10   Evidence
10.1   The arbiter is not required to apply rules of evidence used in judicial proceedings.
10.2   The arbiter may accept evidence in the form of an affidavit, or a signed witness statement.
10.3   The evidence may be recorded by a shorthand writer if the parties agree to this, or if the arbiter in special circumstances determines the evidence should be so recorded.

11   Exchange of arbitration memoranda
11.1   At least ten days prior to the arbitration, each party must provide the other party and the arbiter with an arbitration memorandum.
11.2   The arbitration memorandum must include the following information:
   (a)   a succinct statement of position regarding needs and resources of the parties and the children;
   (b)   a description of any legal issues involved, with citation and copies of legal authority;
   (c)   a schedule of each party's income and outgoings on a calendar month basis;
   (d)   proof of income and resources;
   (e)   vouchers verifying outgoings;
   (f)   a list of proposed witnesses;
   (g)   a list of proposed productions;
   (h)   a list of facts agreed upon;
   (i)   a list of facts which it is proposed the parties agree upon;
   (j)   copies of expert or other reports on which the parties intend to rely; and
   (k)   an estimation of the time the hearing is expected to take.
Failure to comply with these clauses may result in an application for award by default under clause 13.2(f) of this agreement.

12   Attendance at arbitration

12.1 The attendance of the parties at the arbitration is mandatory.

12.2 The arbiter may enter an award against a party who fails to appear at the arbitration.

13   Additional powers of arbiter

13.1 The arbiter has power to order on a provisional or interim basis any relief he or she would have power to grant in a final award, including power to make an award of interim aliment. The arbiter may, on cause shown, excuse a party who has failed to comply with any time limit, or procedural provision, within this agreement, by granting such relief as seems appropriate.

13.2 The arbiter may also:
 (a) order a party to disclose details of his or her income, resources, or outgoings;
 (b) order a party to disclose details of any of the children's income, resources, outgoings or other circumstances (including confidential matters relating to their health or education) considered relevant to their aliment;
 (c) appoint a commissioner (who may be the arbiter) to recover evidence from the parties or a third party haver;
 (d) adjourn the arbitration hearing if necessary for the exercise of any of these powers, or where satisfied special circumstances exist which justify the delay and expense involved in adjourning the hearing;
 (e) apply to any competent court for aid in exercising these powers; and
 (f) grant award by default against any party not complying with the provisions of this agreement.

13.3 The parties agree that in relation to clause 13.2(e) Edinburgh Sheriff Court shall be prorogated a court of competent jurisdiction. This is without prejudice to any other court in Scotland or elsewhere which is competent to exercise jurisdiction to aid the arbiter in the exercise of these additional powers.

13.4 The arbiter may consider applications by a party or the parties under clause 13.2 whether made prior to or subsequent to the arbitration hearing, on a period of notice of two days, or may dispense with notice if it seems justified. An arbiter who proposes to act under clause 13.2(e) should normally schedule a hearing or give the parties an opportunity of commenting before exercising this power.

14   The award

14.1 The award will be in writing signed by the arbiter.

14.2 The arbiter will make the award within two months of closing the arbitration proceedings.

14.3 The award may include interest on arrears of aliment which accrue under the award.

14.4 The interest rate must not exceed 8% a year, or such other percentage directed by act of sederunt for sheriff court decrees by virtue of s 4 of the Administration of Justice (Scotland) Act 1972, in force at the date of the arbitration hearing.

14.5 The award may be back-dated prior to the date of service of the demand for arbitration only in special circumstances.

14.6 The aliment must be in the form of periodical payments either on a weekly or calendar monthly basis, as determined by the arbiter.

14.7 The arbiter has power to award a higher or lower sum than is claimed for aliment. The arbiter must make such award as he or she considers reasonable in all the circumstances, having regard to the resources of the parties.

15 Correction of the award

15.1 The correction of any errors in computation, clerical or typographical errors, or any errors of a similar nature, is within the sole discretion of the arbiter.

15.2 A party seeking correction of the award must apply to the arbiter for its correction within 30 days of the date of the award. The party will use the 'form of Request for Correction of the award' in the annex to this agreement and will serve a copy on the other party.

15.3 Any correction must take the form of a separate memorandum dated and signed by the arbiter.

15.4 The memorandum of correction forms part of the award.

16 Variation of the award

16.1 Either party, or the parties acting jointly, may seek variation, recall or termination of the award on a material change of circumstances.

16.2 Such application must proceed as a separate arbitration, to which all the provisions of this agreement will apply. A different arbiter may be appointed. It must be commenced by one party serving a demand for variation, recall or termination in the 'Form of Demand for Variation' specified in the annex to this agreement.

17 Exclusion of recourse to the courts and exceptions

17.1 The dispute to be submitted to arbitration under this agreement or variation of any award may not be referred to a court in Scotland or elsewhere, except to the extent of a party or the arbiter:
   (a) seeks aid from the court in compelling the parties', or the other party's, compliance with the agreement, or enforcement of an arbitral award, including provisional and interim awards made by the arbiter and awards as varied or corrected by the arbiter;
   (b) seeks the attendance of witnesses or havers at the arbitration hearing, any adjournment of that hearing, or a commission under clause 13.2(c); or
   (c) to the extent a party seeks provisional or protective measures from the court.

17.2 Provisional or protective measures under clause 17.1(c) include these measures:
   (a) making an order under s 1(1) or (1A) of the Administration of Justice (Scotland) Act 1972;
   (b) making an order, or granting warrant, under ss 18, 19 or 20 of the Family Law (Scotland) Act 1985 on the same basis as if an action of aliment had been raised before the court.

17.3 The court may make provisional or protective measures under clause 17.1(c) whether before or after the commencement of the arbitration proceedings. It may do so only to the extent it would have power to make those orders, or grant those warrants, in an action of aliment brought or likely to be brought before it. Such orders may only be made after the commencement of the arbitration with the consent of the arbiter. A party may apply to the arbiter for his consent *ex parte* if giving notice to the other party would be likely to defeat the object of applying to the court for the provisional or protective measure in question. The arbiter should refuse consent only where the proposed application seems unnecessary, or if it would be appropriate for the arbiter to exercise powers under clauses 13.2(a)–13.2(e) of this agreement, or to grant award by default under clause 12.2 or 13.2(f) of this agreement.

17.4 Section 3 of the Administration of Justice (Scotland) Act 1972 does not apply to an arbitration under this agreement.

18   Service of notices and representation of parties

18.1 Notices may be served on Mrs Chiesley at 10 Carnwath Way, Edinburgh and on Mr Chiesley at 5 Lockhart Avenue, Dalry, Edinburgh or on their solicitors on their behalf.

18.2 The parties are under an obligation to notify the other party if their address changes at any time after the date of signature of this agreement. The party whose address changes must with ten days of a change of address notify the other party of a new address for service of notices under this agreement. If this is not done, notices will be properly served if served at the address referred to in clause 18.1.

18.3 Notices will be sufficiently served if served by first class recorded delivery letter posted at any post office in the United Kingdom, or by any equivalent method if posted elsewhere. If this method of service is not successful, service may be effected by delivery of the notice to the party's address, or previous address if the final sentence of clause 18.2 applies.

18.4 References to the parties in this agreement include their solicitors.

19   Expenses of the arbitration

19.1 The arbiter in his award must fix the costs of the arbitration and apportion these between the parties as seems reasonable in the whole circumstances.

19.2 The costs of the arbitration include:
   (a)   The fees and expenses of the arbiter;
   (b)   The costs of meeting and hearing facilities; and
   (c)   The fees and expenses of any shorthand writer appointed for the arbitration.

19.3 The parties will each be initially responsible for payment of one half of any costs of meeting and hearing facilities, and any fees and expenses of a shorthand writer. Mrs Chiesley will be responsible for booking and instructing the meeting and hearing facilities, and the shorthand writer, expect in an arbitration for variation, recall or termination of an arbitral award in which case the party seeking the variation, recall or termination of the award will be responsible for booking and instructing the meeting and hearing facilities, and the shorthand writer if appointed.

19.4 The parties will each be initially responsible for payment of an equal share of the fees and expenses of the arbiter.

19.5 The arbiter will be paid £350 on accepting appointment as an initial fee for scheduling the arbitration hearing, and notifying the parties of the hearing.

19.6 This fee is not refundable if the parties cancel or settle the arbitration.

19.7 The arbiter will be paid £400 for conducting the arbitration hearing for up to two hours. If the hearing exceeds two hours, he or she will be paid a fee of £30 for each additional quarter hour the hearing exceeds two hours.

19.8 The arbiter will be paid £100 an hour for all other work reasonably carried out in connection with the arbitration.

19.9 The arbiter is entitled to charge fees in advance of the hearing, or for any other work needed to be carried out in connection with the arbitration, by giving the parties ten days' notice of the estimated fees.

19.10   The arbiter need not pay expenses reasonably incurred in connection with the arbitration, unless the parties agree to reimburse these expenses within ten days of the arbiter notifying the parties that those expenses have been incurred.

19.11   Any decision which the arbiter makes under clause 19.8, 19.9 or 19.10 may not be challenged by the parties and must be complied with. However, if the parties or either of them disagrees with any such decision, they may give notice of their disagreement to the arbiter. Within three months after conclusion of the arbitration, the parties, or party disagreeing with the arbiter's decision, may refer their disagreement to the Auditor of the Court of Session for determination, if it has not previously been resolved by discussion or negotiation between the arbiter and the parties. No such disagreement may be the subject of court proceedings.

19.12   The arbiter may add VAT to the fees if registered for VAT or, if charging on behalf of his or her firm, the firm is registered for VAT.

Part 2   Provisions Concerning This Agreement

20   Costs of registration

20.1 The cost of registering this agreement and obtaining two extracts will be borne equally by the parties. Mrs Chiesley's solicitors will attend to the registration and obtaining two extracts of the agreement. Mr Chiesley's solicitors will reimburse one half of the costs involved to Mrs Chiesley's solicitors whereupon Mrs Chiesley's solicitors will send one of the extracts to Mr Chiesley's solicitors.

21   Costs of agreement

21.1 Each party is responsible for his or her own legal costs and outlays in respect of the negotiation, preparation and signature of this agreement. The costs of any subsequent arbitration are to be dealt with in accordance with clauses 19.1–19.12 of this agreement.

22   Effect of subsequent divorce, and of this agreement, on obligations of aliment

22.1 This agreement for arbitration concerns Mr Chiesley's obligations to aliment Mrs Chiesley and the children by virtue of the Family Law (Scotland) Act 1985, s 1. Any award for Mrs Chiesley ceases to have effect on the parties' divorce or Mrs Chiesley's death. Any award to Mrs Chiesley on behalf of the children ceases when the child for whom the award is made attains the age of 18 years, but this is without prejudice to any continuing obligation of aliment either Mrs Chiesley or Mr Chiesley may have for the children at that time. The children will be expected to pursue any claim for aliment themselves after they attain the age of 18. Mrs Chiesley may not submit a demand for her own aliment after her divorce from Mr Chiesley, but may continue to do so on behalf of each of the children until each of the children concerned attains the age of 18 years.

22.2 This agreement does not prejudice any claim Mrs Chiesley has for divorce or nullity of marriage, or financial provision on divorce or nullity of marriage, including periodical allowance, or a separate agreement between the parties for financial provision on divorce or nullity of marriage, including for periodical allowance if desired by them. The parties' divorce, or the annulment of their marriage, will not affect any award of aliment made on behalf of the children by an arbiter acting under this agreement.

23   Duty to co-operate to make this agreement effective

23.1 The parties will sign and deliver to the other party or that party's solicitor all documents, and will take such steps necessary to give effect to this agreement.

24   Governing law of agreement

24.1 This agreement will be governed by and construed in accordance with the law of Scotland.

25   Interpretation

25.1 The expression 'date of signature' or 'signature' in relation to this agreement means the later of the two dates on which it has been signed by the parties, or the date on which it has been signed by the parties if they sign the agreement on the same date.

25.2 'Aliment' in this agreement means a final award of aliment or a provisional or interim award of aliment made by the arbiter under clause 13.1. The arbiter's power to order provisional or interim relief under clause 13.1 includes power to make a provisional or interim variation or suspension of payment of aliment in relation to an award in an arbitration under clauses 16.1 and 16.2 of this agreement. 'Aliment' does not include a periodical allowance payable on divorce or nullity of marriage.

25.3 'Award' includes a decree-arbitral, and any correction, variation, suspension or termination of an award.

25.4 These provisions supplement provisions for interpretation contained elsewhere in this agreement.

26 Revocation

26.1 This agreement may only be revoked by mutual agreement of the parties recorded in writing.

Part 3   Registration

27 Registration of the award and the agreement

27.1 The parties consent to registration in the books of council and session for execution of:

(a) any award or awards made under this agreement; and

(b) this agreement:

IN WITNESS WHEREOF

ANNEX

1 Clause 8.3 – form of demand for arbitration

1.1 I, Ann Davidson or Chiesley, 10 Carnwath Way, Edinburgh [*or any new address*] hereby require John Chiesley, 5 Lockhart Avenue, Edinburgh [*or any new address*] to submit to arbitration the amount of aliment he is to pay for:

(a) me [*specify amount and whether on a monthly or weekly basis*]

(b) For our daughter Anne – [*specify amount and whether on a monthly or weekly basis*]

(c) For our son John – [*specify amount and whether on a monthly or weekly basis*]

(d) For our son George – [*specify amount and whether on a monthly or weekly basis*]

Signed
Party/Solicitor
Date

2 Clause 15.2 – form of request for correction of the award

2.1 I, [*name and address of party*], hereby request the arbiter to correct the following error in his award:

> [*specify the error in computation, clerical error, typographical error or error of a similar nature it is alleged to have been made, and how it may be corrected*].

Signed
Party/Solicitor
Date

3 Clause 16.2 – form of demand for variation

3.1 I, [*name and address of party*], hereby require [*name and address of party*] to submit to arbitration the [*variation/recall/termination*] of the arbiter's award dated [*specify*].

I wish the aliment changed as follows:

For whom aliment paid	Present amount paid	Amount to which payment is sought to be varied
Mrs Chiesley		
Anne		
John		
George		

Signed
Party/Solicitor
Date

Notes to Style 5

Agreement

1   Whatever the parties are entitled to contract about, they may refer to arbitration: *Bankton* I, 23, 17. Since husband and wife are entitled to make agreement in relation to aliment, they are entitled to refer any dispute concerning the amount of aliment to arbitration: *Shand v Shand* (1832) 10 S 334.

2   The preamble narrates the parties' marriage and who their children are. Spouses have an obligation to aliment each other, and parents their children, by virtue of the Family Law (Scotland) Act 1985, s 1. For this reason, the agreement does not constitute alimentary obligations (and nor need it do so), but rather submits to arbitration any dispute of the amount of aliment to be paid by Mr Chiesley to Mrs Chiesley.

3   The agreement assumes the husband will aliment the wife, and pay to her aliment on behalf of the children. His obligation to pay aliment to his wife will end on their divorce or her death; his obligation to pay aliment to his wife on behalf of the children ends when each of the children reach 18.

4   This agreement does not prejudice the children, if in further education, or vocational training, after 18 and up to 25, from seeking aliment on their own behalf from their parents, or indeed entering into an arbitration agreement with their parents to determine the amount of such aliment.

5   The submission has been drafted with reference to the Scottish Arbitration Code 1999, reproduced in Davidson *Arbitration* (2000), Appendix A.

6   See Jamieson, 'Arbitration and Conciliation for Aliment' (2003) SLT (News) 47 for further information in relation to arbitration for aliment.

Annex

7   These forms may be varied to suit the circumstances. If a form is signed by a solicitor on behalf of a party, the solicitor must add his business address, fax number and telephone number.

Style 6

Cohabitation agreement

19.06

AGREEMENT

BETWEEN

HAROLD LETTERMAN, 3 CONFLICT WAY, PAISLEY

AND

RHONA McGINTY, 7 CANAL ROAD, JOHNSTONE

WHEREAS:

The parties have been cohabiting with each other since 31 August 1996.

The parties wish to derive from their relationship, so far as possible, certain benefits they would obtain if they were married to each other.

THEREFORE the parties AGREE as follows:

1   Rights arising from the parties' relationship:

1.1   Each party has the right to:
    (a)   aliment from the other party during the period of their relationship and for up to three years after the date of the termination of their relationship;
    (b)   an equal share in the household goods;
    (c)   financial provision on the termination of their relationship; and
    (d)   an equal share in money and property derived from a house keeping allowance.

1.2   This agreement does not have retrospective effect for the purposes of clause 1.1(a). The extent of the parties' rights under clause 1.1(b)–1.1(d) are to be determined from the date of their cohabitation with each other on 31 August 1996.

1.3   'Aliment' in clause 1.1(a) and this agreement includes interim aliment.

1.4   'Household goods' in clause 1.1(b) and this agreement has the same meaning as in section 25 of the Family Law (Scotland) Act 1985 ('the 1985 Act'). For the avoidance of doubt, Mr Letterman's collection of Shakespeare plays, including his eighteenth century editions of 'Julius Caesar', 'The Merchant of Venice' and 'MacBeth' are his sole property and are not to be considered 'household goods' to which the provisions of this agreement apply (*or adapt to suit the circumstances, for either or both of Mr*

Letterman and Ms McGinty – if very detailed refer to and add an appropriate schedule to the agreement).

2   Extent of parties' rights, and corresponding obligations, under Part 1 of this agreement

2.1   The following provisions of the 1985 Act apply, with necessary modifications, in determining the extent of the party's rights or, obligations to the other party, under Part 1 of this agreement:

(a)   To aliment – sections 1(2), 2(6)–(9) and 3–6.

(b)   Equal share in household goods – section 25.

(c)   Financial provision on termination of relationship:
   (i)   section 8(1)(a);
   (ii)   section 8(2)(b);
   (iii) section 9(1)(a) in respect of the family home only and section 8(2)(a) so far as it applies thereto;
   (iv)   section 9(1)(b) and section 8(2)(a) so far as it applies thereto;
   (v)   section 10(1)–(4), (6) and (7);
   (vi)   section 11(2) and (7);
   (vii) section 12(2)–(4);
   (viii) section 14(2)(a)–(c), (f), (j), and (k) and section 8(1)(c) so far as it applies thereto;
   (ix)   section 14(4).

(d)   Equal share in money and property derived from a house keeping allowance – section 26.

2.2   'Family Home' in clause 2.1(c)(iii) means the heritable property owned by Mr Letterman known as 3 Conflict Way, Paisley registered under title number REN 12356 in the Land Register for Scotland.

2.3   'Family home' also means any other heritable property which the parties or either of them may subsequently own and which is or has been acquired for the purpose of them living together there.

3   Children

3.1   Mr Letterman will obtain parental responsibilities and rights in relation to any children to be born of the parties' relationship. Ms McGinty will enter into an agreement with him to this effect under s 4 of the Children (Scotland) Act 1995.

3.2   Mr Letterman has the right to give the children his surname.

3.3   Ms McGinty may only change the children's names with Mr Letterman's consent.

3.4   Neither party will change any child's name after the child attains the age of 12. The child him or herself may, however, consent to the change of his or her name after attaining the age of 12.

4   Arbitration

4.1   The parties agree to submit disputes arising between them to arbitration. Such disputes concern:

(a)   Rights to property arising under Part 1 of this agreement, or otherwise.

(b)   A party's right to aliment, interim aliment, or financial provision on the termination of the parties' relationship, arising under Part 1 of this agreement.

(c)   The extent, breach, or enforcement of any obligation owed by one party to the other, whether arising under Part 1 of this agreement, or otherwise.

4.2   Arbitration does not apply in relation to disputes between the parties concerning the obtaining or exercise of parental responsibilities and rights for any children of the parties' relationship, or in respect of the children's names or change of names. However, it applies to any dispute concerning one party's obligation to aliment any children of the parties' relationship (and, if appropriate, children of one party accepted by the other as the child of the relationship). A party claiming aliment or interim aliment on behalf of any such children under Part 1 of the Family Law (Scotland) Act 1985 may submit the claim to arbitration in accordance with the provisions of this agreement.

4.3   A single arbiter will be appointed by agreement of the parties or failing their agreement within one month by the Dean of the Faculty of Procurators in Paisley for the time being.

4.4   The place of arbitration will be determined by the arbiter in consultation with the parties. It need not be in Scotland.

4.5   The seat of the arbitration will be in Scotland.

4.6   The language of the arbitration will be English.

4.7   The arbitration will be carried out in accordance with the arbitration rules of the Netherlands Arbitration Institute (English version). The arbiter, in determining the dispute, must apply the provisions of Part 2 of this agreement in the adjudication of the parties' rights and obligations under Part 1 of this agreement. This does not otherwise limit his or her powers in an arbitration under this part of this agreement, whether conferred by this part or otherwise.

4.8   The arbiter is empowered to make provisional and interim awards except in relation to an order for payment of a capital sum on termination of the parties' relationship. The arbiter may make the incidental orders referred to at clause 2.1(c)(viii) either in the course of an arbitration pending before him or her, on the making of the final arbitral award or, subject to clause 4.9 of this agreement, after the making of the arbitral award. The arbiter may vary, recall or terminate any provisional or interim award or incidental order made in the course of an arbitration on an application made in the process of that arbitration by either or both parties at any time up to the date of the final arbitral award. The matters referred to in clause 4.9 of this agreement must be dealt with by way of a subsequent arbitration, as provided for by that clause.

4.9   The following matters must be dealt with in a subsequent arbitration, carried out in accordance with the provisions of this agreement:

(a) An application by either or both of the parties for a variation, recall or termination of an award of aliment (not, in this instance, including an award of interim aliment in a pending arbitration) made in a previous arbitration.

(b) An application by either or both parties for an incidental order referred to in clause 2.1(c)(viii) of this agreement where the application is made after an arbiter has made a final award in a dispute concerning either or both parties' entitlement to financial provision on the termination of their relationship.

(c) An application by either or both parties for variation or recall of an incidental order referred to in clause 2.1(c)(viii) of this agreement, where the application is made after an arbiter has made a final award in a dispute concerning either or both parties' entitlement to financial provision on the termination of their relationship.

(d) An application by either or both parties to vary the date or method of payment of a capital sum awarded in a previous arbitration.

4.10 In no case may an award of aliment or interim aliment for one of the parties' own benefit subsist for more than three years after the date of termination of the parties' relationship. An award of aliment or interim aliment made on behalf of the parties' children will subsist until the child concerned attains the age of eighteen, or its subsequent variation, recall or termination under clause 4.10.

4.11 The arbiter may determine the date of the termination of the parties' relationship, if that is disputed, and will determine the period for which aliment is to continue after the date of termination of the parties' relationship up to a maximum of three years after that date.

4.12 Recourse to the courts except to aid in the arbitration process or to enforce any award is excluded in relation to the matters which may be referred to arbitration under this agreement.

4.13 Arbitration is compulsory for the disputes mentioned in clause 4.1, and for the matters referred to in clause 4.9. Arbitration is not compulsory for the disputes mentioned in clause 4.2 which are referable to arbitration, but either party may opt for arbitration, without prior agreement of the other party, in relation to the disputes mentioned in clause 4.2 of this agreement and, if that is done, the jurisdiction of the court to determine the issue submitted to arbitration is excluded.

4.14 Where an arbiter has made an award of aliment in a dispute referred to him under clause 4.2 of this agreement, the subsequent variation or recall of that award must be submitted to arbitration (to the exclusion of the jurisdiction of the court to determine the issue) in accordance with clause 4.9 of this agreement.

4.15 Section 3 of the Administration of Justice (Scotland) Act 1972 does not apply to an arbitration under the provisions of this agreement.

5 Mediation and conciliation

5.1 Disputes concerning the parties' parental responsibilities and rights to their children, or the children's names, will be resolved by mediation. Failing this, a conciliator will be appointed who will have power to issue recommendations to the parties. Only if these recommendations are not accepted by both parties may either of them resort to litigation. However, the party or parties rejecting the recommendations must explain to the court the just reasons he or she or they had for not doing so.

5.2   The parties will not call any mediator as a witness or haver in any subsequent litigation in relation to the matters referred to mediation. His mediation summary will be confidential and may not be disclosed to the court by either party.

5.3   If a conciliator is appointed, the parties will not call the conciliator as a witness or haver in any subsequent litigation in relation to the matters involving the subject matter of the conciliation. However, the conciliator's recommendations may be disclosed by both or either parties to the court.

5.4   Where it is necessary to proceed to conciliation, a conciliator will be appointed by mutual agreement of the parties, failing which within one month, the Dean of the Faculty of Procurators in Paisley for the time being. The conciliator will determine his or her own procedure in relation to the conciliation process, and will be expected to complete the conciliation within a period of six weeks from the date of appointment as conciliator.

5.5   The parties will co-operate fully with any mediator, or with any conciliator appointed under provisions of this agreement.

5.6   Neither party may refuse to co-operate with the mediator or conciliator on the ground that he or she denies the existence of a dispute between the parties, or on any other ground. If a party does so in breach of this clause, then he or she will be liable to the other party for the expenses incurred by that party in raising any court proceedings for resolution of the matter in dispute which ought to have been submitted to mediation or conciliation in accordance with this agreement.

6   Revocation and suspension of this agreement

6.1   This agreement may only be revoked or suspended (whether for a definite or indefinite period) by the mutual agreement of the parties recorded in writing. It will be revoked if they subsequently marry each other, from the date of their marriage, but without prejudice to any rights which either or both parties have acquired under this agreement to the date of their marriage.

7   Registration

7.1   The parties hereby consent to the registration in the books of council and session for execution of:

(a)   any arbitral awards under this agreement; and

(b)   this agreement:

IN WITNESS WHEREOF

Notes to Style 6

Cohabitation

1   It is unlikely that a cohabitation agreement between a heterosexual couple, or even nowadays a homosexual couple, would be regarded as *contra bona mores* and therefore unenforceable: see Recommendation R(88)3 on the validity of contracts between persons living together as an unmarried couple and their testamentary dispositions, at para 18.115. Such parties are entitled to enter into an agreement to aliment each other, but it will not be subject to the statutory regime in the Family Law (Scotland) Act 1985 and they must therefore make their own contractual provision for determining disputes and varying awards of aliment: see *Drummond v Drummond* 1995 SC 321.

Aliment and financial provision

2   The purpose of this agreement is to confer on the cohabiting parties the right to obtain aliment from the other party for up to three years after the date of termination of their relationship. It allows for a limited form of financial provision on termination of their relationship based on the principles set out in the Family Law (Scotland) Act 1985, s 9(1)(a), in respect of the family home only; and in s 9(1)(b) of the Act. It applies the provisions of that Act to the parties, so far as possible; but, in particular, it does not apply the provisions of the Act to pension earmarking or pension sharing. The reason for this is that these orders usually require to be confirmed by a court granting a divorce or decree of declarator of nullity of marriage and that cannot happen where parties merely cohabit and do not marry each other. Furthermore, such orders require to be implemented by a third party. The parties to a cohabitation agreement cannot contract in such a way that the third party would be bound by their agreement.

Children

3   Provision is made in Part 3 of the agreement for Mr Letterman to share in parental responsibilities and rights for any children of their relationship, and it deals with the names to be given to any children of their relationship.

Arbitration

4   Part 4 of the agreement provides for arbitration of disputes in connection with the parties' property rights and obligations as set out in Parts 1 and 2. However, it is wider than this for in clause 4.1 all other property disputes are to be submitted to arbitration and in clause 4.2 all disputes concerning aliment for any children of the parties' relationship may also be submitted to arbitration. Clause 2.1(c)(vii) applies the Family Law (Scotland) Act 1985, s 14(2)(c) to an arbitration under the provisions of this agreement and therefore allows the arbiter to make a declarator as to the parties' property rights.

5   The arbitration provisions of this agreement are simpler than those set out in Style 5. The main difference is that instead of setting out the procedural rules of the arbitration in detail, as is done in that style, the procedural rules are incorporated by reference to

the rules of the Netherlands Arbitration Institute. These are available in English and can be found at www.nai–nl.org/english/info2.html. Clause 4.5 provides that the seat of the arbitration will be in Scotland. This refers to the juridical seat of the arbitration: the physical place where the arbitration is to be conducted may be anywhere in the world. For example, if the parties move to England, and one of them seeks a variation of the award, it may be more convenient to them to have the arbitration there: see clause 4.4.

Mediation and conciliation
6   Provision is made for mediation and conciliation of any disputes concerning the children (not including their aliment) or a child's name since such disputes may be referred to arbitration. There is no mechanism provided in this agreement for the appointment of a mediator as the parties must either agree on who the mediator will be, failing which a conciliator will require to be appointed – see clause 5.1, second sentence.

Revocation and suspension of this agreement
7   Part 6 of the agreement provides that it may only be revoked or suspended by the mutual agreement of the parties recorded in writing.

Registration
8   Finally, the agreement provides for its registration in the books of council and session for execution and also for the subsequent registration for execution in those books of any arbitral award or variation of an arbitral award (see clause 4.9) made under the agreement.

Parental responsibilities and conciliation agreement

19.07

AGREEMENT

between

ARTHUR KING, 1 High Street, Camelot

and

AMANDA HUGHES, 10 High Street, Porthmadog

WHEREAS:

The parties (who are not married to each other or to anyone else) intend to cohabit with one another in Scotland.

The parties both wish to have parental responsibilities and rights in relation to any children born of their relationship.

The parties wish to enter into a parental responsibilities and parenting agreement in respect of those children.

The parties wish to provide for conciliation of any disputes which may arise between them in respect of this or their parenting agreement.

THEREFORE the parties AGREE as follows:

1   Parental responsibilities and rights
1.1   Ms Hughes will confer on Mr King parental responsibilities and rights for each child of their relationship by entering into an agreement with him to that effect under the Children (Scotland) Act 1995, section 4.

2   The children's names
2.1   The parties will jointly agree on the children's first name or names.
2.2   Mr King has the right to give the children his surname.
2.3   Ms Hughes may only change the children's names with Mr King's consent. Neither party may change any of the children's names after the child attains the age of 12,

unless the child himself, or court acting under clause 8.12 of this agreement, agrees to this.

3   The children's education

3.1   The parties will jointly agree the school or schools which the children will attend during their childhood.

3.2   Neither party may make a placing request in respect of any of the children without first informing the other party and obtaining his or her agreement.

4   The children's religious upbringing

4.1   The children will be brought up in the (Christian) religion.

4.2   Either parent has the right to have the children attend the [*specify name of church*] each week for such services, instruction and other observations as are customary within the church.

5   Recording agreement ('parenting agreement')

5.1   The parties will record in a parenting agreement their agreement in relation to the children's:

(a)   name;

(b)   education;

(c)   religious upbringing; and

(d)   any other matters relating to the children's upbringing which they wish to reach agreement about.

5.2   The parties may make use of the form of parenting agreement provided by the Department for Constitutional Affairs ('DCA') for the purpose of recording their parenting agreement made in accordance with clause 5.1. They may, however, choose to make use of any other document they deem suitable in place of the DCA's parenting agreement.

5.3   If the parties enter into a parenting agreement, they will each sign it, and they will each keep a copy of it.

6   Changing this agreement or a parenting agreement

6.1   The parties may enter into a new parenting agreement at any time. It may alter any of the provisions of clauses 1.1–4.2 of this agreement, or any parenting agreement.

6.2   To change any part of this or a parenting agreement itself requires agreement of the parties.

6.3   Any change which the parties agree will be recorded as provided for in Part 5 of this agreement. If appropriate, they will enter into a new parenting agreement in accordance with clause 5.2 of this agreement. Whether or not they do this, they will make a written record of any change and will sign it. Clause 5.3 will apply to any such record of change of agreement.

7 Preservation of agreements

7.1 Neither party may act contrary to this agreement or any parenting agreement they subsequently sign.

7.2 A party doing so, or threatening to do so, accepts that a competent court may interdict him or her from continuing to do so, or carrying out his or her threats to do so. This includes interim interdict.

7.3 The court may award expenses against the party breaking any agreement.

8 Conciliation

8.1 If the parties cannot agree on any part of their parenting agreement or changing it, or on changing any part of clauses 1.1–4.2 of this agreement then they must seek to resolve their dispute by conciliation in accordance with this agreement. If their child, having attained the age of 12, does not agree to either or both parties changing his or her name, then the parties, or either of them, may, but is not required to, refer that dispute to conciliation in accordance with the provisions of this agreement.

8.2 A conciliation will be commenced by one party giving to the other written notice of his or her intention that their dispute be referred to conciliation. This will not be necessary in the case where both parties wish to change the child's name, but the child has attained the age of 12 and objects to his or her name being changed.

8.3 The party or parties desiring conciliation must within ten days of giving the notice under clause 8.2 (if required) ask the President of the Law Society of Scotland for the time being to nominate a conciliator. In the case of a dispute in which both parties wish to change the child's name but the child has attained the age of 12 and does not agree to his or her name being changed, the parties may, at any time, in the course of that dispute, ask the President to nominate a conciliator. If a party who is required to do so fails to comply with the ten-day time limit then he or she may cure that defect by serving a further notice to the other party of his or her intention that their dispute be referred to conciliation.

8.4 The parties are bound to accept as conciliator the person nominated by the President, and to take part in conciliation.

8.5 It is not permissible for either party to refuse to accept the person nominated as conciliator by the President, or to refuse to take part in the conciliation, on the ground he or she denies the existence of a dispute between the parties, or on any other ground.

8.6 A sole conciliator is to be appointed by the President. On the conciliator's acceptance of appointment, the parties will each pay the conciliator one half of the fee for the conciliation. The fee will be a fixed amount calculated at 100 units or such lesser sum chosen by the conciliator. A unit is the unit provided for by the Law Society of Scotland in its recommended Table of Fees for General Business at the date of appointment of the conciliator. The conciliator is entitled to add VAT to the fee if his or her fees are chargeable to VAT, and may also add a sum of up to £100 for out of pocket expenses such as a travelling allowance, or such other necessary sums if the parties do not live near each other, as determined by the President in the absence of agreement between the parties and the conciliator. These additional amounts are in the discretion of the conciliator and are not open to challenge by the parties.

8.7   The parties agree that the conciliator may not be cited as a witness or haver in relation to any litigation or commission concerning the parties' dispute. They will take all possible steps to prevent this happening.

8.8   In accepting appointment, the conciliator will be bound by the provisions of this agreement.

8.9   In any conciliation other than a conciliation involving change of a child's name where the child has attained the age of 12, the conciliator will meet with each party separately, at least twice. Without prejudice to this he or she has the power to arrange a joint meeting or meetings of the parties. The conciliator will seek to ascertain the facts relevant to the determination of the dispute and record these in a memorandum for consideration of the parties, and will give the parties an opportunity of commenting on the memorandum. Thereafter the conciliator will seek to facilitate an amicable resolution of the dispute. If this cannot be achieved, the conciliator will issue a final report with recommendations to the parties and reasons for those recommendations. He or she will attempt to complete the conciliation within a period of six weeks of his nomination as conciliator.

8.10   The conciliator's recommendations in a conciliation governed by the procedures in clause 8.9 are not binding on the parties. However, a party may refer to the conciliator's memorandum, report or recommendations in the course of any litigation brought in connection with the dispute. The party must give to the court his reasons showing why he or she had just cause not to accept the conciliator's recommendations. The court may award expenses against a party who did not have just cause for not accepting the conciliator's recommendations.

8.11   In the case of a conciliation involving the change of name of a child having attained the age of 12, the conciliator may adopt such procedure as seems appropriate to meet the circumstances of the case. The conciliator must seek to ascertain the facts relevant to the determination of the dispute, but will dispense with the preparation of a memorandum for consideration of the parties and the child. He or she will seek to reconcile the views of the parties, or the party referring the dispute to conciliation, with the views of the child in order to obtain an amicable resolution of the dispute. If this cannot be achieved the conciliator will issue a report with recommendations to the parties and his reasons for those recommendations.

8.12   In the case of conciliation involving the change of a name of a child having attained the age of 12, the parties agree not to proceed further with their proposals for changing the child's name if the conciliator recommends against this course of action. If the conciliator recommends that the child's name should be changed, it is the duty of the parties or the party referring the dispute to conciliation, to make an application to court seeking authority to change the child's name. The parties, or the party referring the dispute to conciliation, may in that case refer to the conciliator's report and recommendations in support of their or his or her application for authority to change the child's name.

9 Duty to consult

The parties

9.1 The parties will not enter into any agreement concerning any of their children unless they first consult with the child to be affected by the agreement, provided the child is of an age and degree of maturity to understand the implications of the decision.

9.2 Clause 9.1 normally applies where any of the parties' children have attained the age of 12.

9.3 In exceptional circumstances, where it would be harmful to the child's interests, or impracticable to do so, the parties may dispense with their duty to consult the child.

9.4 The parties' duty to consult with their children applies to any matter, whether or not referred to in this agreement or a parenting agreement, unless it is a matter of minor importance not having a significant effect on the child's upbringing.

Conciliator

9.5 A conciliator may, after consulting with the parties, seek to ascertain the views of the child, not having attained the age of 12, in relation to the matter about which the parties are in dispute. He or she may take those views into account in the conciliation or in making any recommendations to the parties.

9.6 The conciliator must attempt to ascertain the views of a child who has attained the age of 12, unless it is not practicable to do so.

10 Marriage, divorce and separation

10.1 This agreement will continue in force if the parties marry each other. It will remain in force if they marry and then divorce, including if they re-marry a third party, or if they separate whether or not they are married at the date of separation.

11 Revocation or suspension

11.1 This agreement or a parenting agreement, can only be revoked or suspended in its application (whether for a definite or indefinite period) by mutual agreement of the parties recorded in writing or by the court acting under s 11 of the Children (Scotland) Act 1995.

12 Registration

12.1 This agreement will be registered in the books of council and session for preservation:

IN WITNESS WHEREOF

Notes to Style 7

Use of agreement

1   This agreement may well form part of a larger cohabitation agreement between unmarried persons.

Preamble

2   The preamble will be altered in accordance with the circumstances in which the parties enter into, or require to enter into, the agreement.

Parental responsibilities and rights

3   The agreement is a parental responsibilities and conciliation agreement. The first function of the agreement is to confer parental responsibilities on the unmarried father of the children and to regulate certain major issues which, in the context of this draft, could be anticipated even prior to the children's births. The issues chosen for consideration in Parts 1–4 are the children's names, education and religious upbringing, but the parties may wish to alter these to reflect their own individual circumstances.

Parenting agreements

4   The agreement makes provision at Parts 5–7 for recording agreements, changing agreements, and preserving agreements. Parts 2–4 of the agreement in particular set out a framework upon which the parties will base subsequent agreement in relation to the children's names, education and religious upbringing. Part 5 allows the specific choices which the parties make to be recorded in a separate, less formal, document which is referred to in this draft as a parenting agreement. The parties are free to make use of whatever form of parenting agreement they wish, provided they sign it, but provision is made for them on an optional basis to use the parenting agreement provided by the Lord Chancellor's Department. The latter document was drafted in accordance with the practice in England and Wales but is useful for adoption and adaptation in Scotland. Part 7 of the agreement recognises that there will be circumstances in which the parties may require urgently to proceed to court and seeks to build in sanctions for breach of agreement.

Concilliation

5   Conciliation, as a process, may be viewed as a halfway house between mediation and arbitration. The parties can never totally exclude the jurisdiction of the court because of the court's overriding duty to make orders in relation to the children where that is in accordance with the children's welfare. Nevertheless, the parties may seek to resolve disputes by means of alternative dispute resolution (in this case, conciliation) and provision is made in Part 8 for conciliation in relation to the matters covered by the parental responsibilities agreement itself, and any subsequent parenting agreement. Conciliation is not really intended for major disputes such as residence or contact, but for discrete disputes involving issues such as change of name, education or changes in

the child's religious upbringing. Detailed provisions are made about the appointment of the conciliator, payment of his fees, and procedure in relation to the conciliation. These are designed to ensure that as soon as one party wishes to conciliate, a conciliator will be appointed without opportunity on the part of the other party to obstruct that happening and the subsequent conciliation taking place. So as to minimise the possibility of dispute later, the parties would be wise to agree in advance to proceed to conciliation, if necessary, and even to agree on a particular conciliator. They could also negotiate his fee and they could present a joint application for the President of the Law Society of Scotland to appoint that person on that basis. None of that is intended to be precluded by this draft agreement.

6 The procedures for conciliation are divided into two types. The first involves all disputes other than those concerning the change of name of a child who has attained the age of 12. The style adopts a provision in clause 2.3 that a child should have the right to consent to the change of his name. This had been modelled on legal provisions existing in the Netherlands. A different procedure has been adopted against the background of Scottish conditions for resolution of change of name disputes where the child has attained the age of 12. The idea is that the parties in this situation only would bind themselves not to proceed with the change of name if the conciliator recommended against that. On the other hand if he did make such recommendation then the parties could proceed to the court to authorise the change of name. The final decision would lie with the court but it would have available for its consideration the conciliator's report recommending why a change of name would be appropriate. In this case, conciliation would be an optional procedure and the parties could if they wished make a direct application to court.

Duties to consult the child
7 The agreement in Part 9 makes general provision about the duty of the parties and the conciliator to consult with the child in appropriate circumstances.

Ancillary provisions
8 Parts 10, 11 and 12 of the agreement make ancillary provision for the matters referred to in clauses 10.1, 11.1 and 12.1. It is debatable whether either of the parties, upon separation, could seek to revoke the parties' agreement in the same way that a spouse could revoke a separation agreement: see *Shand v Shand* (1832) 10 S 334. Clause 11.1 is intended to make it plain that this agreement may only be revoked (or suspended) by mutual agreement of the parties recorded in writing or the court acting under the Children (Scotland) Act 1995, s 11.

Registration
9 The subject matter of this agreement is not subject to enforcement by summary diligence and therefore it would not be appropriate to have a clause consenting to registration for execution. The clause consenting to registration for preservation (only)

is not, strictly speaking, required but it is a useful provision, and a reminder, to the parties, that the agreement should be registered.

Execution

10   The agreement should be executed and witnessed in accordance with the formalities of the Requirements of Writing (Scotland) Act 1995 in order that it would be a self-proving document to enable it to be registered for preservation in the books of council and session.

Style 8

Provisions in a separation agreement referring to a separate parenting agreement

19.08

Part 5   The Children

9.1   The parties will record in a parenting agreement their agreement in relation to the children's:
   (a)   name;
   (b)   education;
   (c)   religious upbringing; and
   (d)   any other matters relating to the children's upbringing which they wish to reach agreement about.

9.2   The parties may make use of the form of parenting agreement provided by the Department of Constitutional Affairs for the purpose of recording their parenting agreement made in accordance with clause 9.1. They may, however, choose to make use of any other document they deem suitable in place of that form.

9.3   If the parties enter into a parenting agreement they will each sign it. They will each keep a copy of it or, in relation to an agreement registered for preservation in the books of council and session or sheriff court books, they will each obtain an extract of the registered agreement.

9.4   The parties may enter into a new parenting agreement at any time. Clauses 9.1–9.3 of this agreement apply in relation to the making of a new parenting agreement.

9.5   Neither party may act contrary to any parenting agreement which they sign. A party doing so, or threatening to do so, accepts that a competent court may interdict him or her from continuing to do so, or carrying out his or her threats to do so. This includes interim interdict.

9.6   The court may award expenses against any party breaking a parenting agreement, according to the discretion of the court.

Notes to Style 8
1   These provisions replace Part 5 of Style 1, at para 19.01. They are modelled, however, on the equivalent clauses in Style 7 (see notes 3 and 4 to that style, at para 19.07), but omitting mention of major parenting issues, such as residence and contact. All these matters, and others besides, are placed in a separate parenting agreement: see Style 9 at para 19.09.

2   The reasons for proceeding in this way are explained in paras 7.22–7.25; but it may also be thought that, if there is an informal, unregistered agreement, that would better preserve the parties' and the children's privacy.

3   It may be that the formal, or informal parenting agreement will be signed on the same day as the main separation agreement.

Style 9

Parenting agreement: legitimate children

19.09

AGREEMENT

BETWEEN

MRS ANNABEL LEE OR ALLAN, 5 RUE MORGUE, PAISLEY

AND

EDGAR ALLAN, 'THE RAVEN', WILLIAM WILSON ROAD, PAISLEY

WHEREAS:

The parties married at Edinburgh on 1 July 1990; have two children under the age of 16 years: Annabel Allan, born 14 February 1992; and Catherine Allan, born 26 August 1994; and separated on 2 May 1997.

The parties wish to enter into an agreement concerning the children.

THEREFORE the parties AGREE as follows:

1 Residence and contact

1.1 Annabel and Catherine will live with Mrs Allan.
1.2 Mr Allan will have contact with them one weekend in two between [*specify*], for two weeks in their summer school holidays as agreed each year and each alternative Christmas and Boxing Day commencing [*specify*]. These rights are subject to Mrs Allan's holiday entitlements in clause 1.3 of this agreement.
1.3 Mrs Allan will have the right to have the children on holiday with her for a period of up to three weeks in total during each year, providing only this does not in any year interfere with Mr Allan's entitlement to contact on Christmas and Boxing Day.

2 Day-to-day and major parenting decisions
2.1 Mrs Allan will be responsible for day-to-day decisions in relation to the children, but will consult with Mr Allan regarding any major parenting decisions.
2.2 Major parenting decisions include those in respect of the children's:
  (a) names;

    (b)   school;

    (c)   religious upbringing;

    (d)   health, except for routine doctors, hospital and dentist appointments, minor healthcare issues, and major emergencies;

    (e)   acting as the children's legal representative;

    (f)   administering the children's property; and

    (g)   taking or sending the children out of the United Kingdom.

2.3   Where the parenting decision involves the children's:

    (a)   names;

    (b)   school; or

    (c)   religious upbringing,

    Mrs Allan must also obtain Mr Allan's consent to the decision in accordance with the provisions of clauses 3.1–5.2 of this agreement.

2.4   Mr and Mrs Allan need to obtain the agreement of the other parent where the parenting decision involves taking the children outside the United Kingdom, in accordance with the provisions of clauses 6.1–6.3 of this agreement.

3   The children's names

3.1   Mrs Allan may not change the children's Christian or surname without Mr Allan's consent to the proposed change.

3.2   Neither party may change any of the children's names after the child obtains the age of 12, unless the child herself, or the court, agrees to this.

4   The children's education

4.1   Annabel and Catherine will both attend [*specify*] primary school and [*specify*] secondary school.

4.2   Mr Allan must agree if Mrs Allan proposes to change these schools in respect of either or both children's attendance at them.

4.3   Neither party may make a placing request in respect of either of the children without first informing the other party and obtaining his or her agreement.

5   The children's religious upbringing

5.1   The children will continue to be brought up in the Roman Catholic faith.

5.2   Mrs Allan is responsible for the children's religious instruction, and attendance at church services on a regular basis. She may not take any step to change the faith in which the children are being brought up without Mr Allan's consent.

6   Taking or sending the children outside the United Kingdom

6.1   The parties may only take or send the children out of the United Kingdom in accordance with their holiday entitlements with the children recorded at clauses 1.2 and 1.3 of this agreement.

6.2   Mrs Allan's right to have the children live with her in accordance with clause 1.1 of this agreement does not entitle her to reside with the children outside of the United

Kingdom without the consent of Mr Allan, or in the event of disagreement in this regard, without obtaining a relevant court order to that effect.

6.3 The children will have their own passports, and Mrs Allan will have custody of the passports. However, she will hand over the passports to Mr Allan for the period he is taking the children on holiday abroad in accordance with clause 6.1 of this agreement. Mr Allan must return the passports to Mrs Allan within seven days of arriving home with the children.

7 Legal representation and administration of children's property

7.1 Mrs Allan will have the right to act as the children's legal representative, without Mr Allan's consent, and to administer their property, except in case of her incapacity or insolvency.

7.2 Mr Allan will not act as the children's legal representative, or administer their property, without Mrs Allan's consent.

7.3 Mr Allan retains the right to apply to court for an order concerning the administration of the children's property, on the appointment of a judicial factor.

8 Consultation with the children

8.1 The parties will not take any decision concerning the children unless they first consult with the child to be affected by the decision, provided the child is of an age and degree of maturity to understand the implications of the decision.

8.2 Clause 8.1 normally applies when either child has attained the age of 12.

8.3 In exceptional circumstances, where it would be harmful to the child's interests, or impracticable to do so, the parties may dispense with their duty to consult the child.

8.4 The parties' duty to consult the children applies to any matter, whether or not referred to in this or any other agreement between the parties, unless it is a matter of minor importance not having a significant effect on the child's upbringing.

8.5 The duty to consult is subject to clause 3.2 of this agreement.

9 Breach of this agreement

9.1 Neither party may act contrary to this agreement or any other agreement between them concerning the children.

9.2 A party doing so, or threatening to do so, accepts that a competent court may interdict him or her from continuing to do so, or carrying out his or her threats to do so.

9.3 The court may award expenses against the party breaking this or any other agreement between the parties concerning the children.

10 Continuing effect of this agreement

10.1 This agreement will continue in force after the parties' divorce.

10.2 It will be suspended during any period of reconciliation, but will revive again if the parties separate again.

11   Revocation of agreement

11.1 This agreement can be revoked only by the mutual agreement of the parties recorded in writing, or by order of the court.

12   Definitions

12.1 References in clauses 8.4 and 9.3 of this agreement to other agreements are to agreements between the parties, or to which they are a party, concerning any aspect of the children's upbringing, or the administration of their property, whether entered into before, after, or at the same time as this agreement, and whether or not in writing.

12.2 Such agreements may only be in respect of matters not dealt with in this agreement, or in respect of any additional agreement made to implement particular provisions of this agreement.

12.2 Other expressions used in this agreement have the following meaning:

   (a) 'United Kingdom': this does not include the Isle of Man or Channel Islands;
   (b) 'taking' or 'sending', in relation to the taking or sending of the children outside of the United Kingdom, has the same meaning as in section 6 of the Child Abduction Act 1984.

13   Registration for preservation

13.1 The parties consent to preservation of this agreement for registration in the books of council and session.

13.2 Mrs Allan's solicitors will obtain two extracts of this agreement, and send one of them to Mr Allan's solicitors within seven days of obtaining it. Upon receipt of that extract, Mr Allan's solicitors will immediately reimburse Mrs Allan's solicitors one half of the cost of registration and of the two extracts.

IN WITNESS WHEREOF

Notes to Style 9

Purpose of the agreement

1   This is intended to be a formal parenting agreement, in the context of the parents' separation, registered for preservation in the books of council and session, but without prejudice to informal agreement about any matter not covered in this agreement, for example attendance at school events such as parents' nights and sports days, and informal agreements reached in accordance with the provisions of this agreement, for example, changing the children's names or schools (clauses 3.1 and 4.2). It is hoped this balance between formality, and informality, will encourage the flexibility often needed in relation to a child's upbringing.

The sharing of parental responsibilities and rights

2   The effect of the agreement is to confer on Mrs Allan, as the parent with whom the children are to live, responsibility for parenting decisions in connection with the children's upbringing, *acting* as their legal representative, and administering their property, subject to (a) a duty to consult with Mr Allan on 'major parenting decisions'; (b) a duty to obtain his agreement, or consent, to certain of those major decisions; and (c) Mr Allan's entitlements to (i) contact with the children and (ii) to apply to court if he has any concerns as to Mrs Allan's administration of any property the children may have, or acquire. Although Mrs Allan has sole right to act as the children's representative, she will be obliged to consult with Mr Allan on whether she should, for example, raise court proceedings on their behalf. Both parents have a duty to consult the children about parenting decisions (clauses 8.1–8.5), and to obtain the agreement of either child, age 12 or over, to a change of any of her names (clause 3.2).

3   There is no exclusive definition of 'major parenting decisions', but some of these are listed in clause 2.2. Taking the children outside the United Kingdom is included as a major parenting decision, and regulated by the provisions of clauses 6.1–6.3. Other options would be to schedule the countries to which the children can be taken, either by reference to considerations of health or danger in the country concerned, or only to countries in respect of which there are reciprocal provisions for return of abducted children. The 'United Kingdom' is defined for the benefit of the parties to the agreement, as they may not be aware that the Isle of Man and Channel Islands are not part of the United Kingdom. 'Taking' and 'sending' are also defined as meaning taking or sending by either parent, or that parent causing or inducing the child to be taken from the United Kingdom, as defined in the Child Abduction Act 1984, s 6.

Ancillary provisions

4   Provision is made for breach of the agreement, its continued effect after the divorce, suspension on reconciliation, revocation by subsequent agreement or court order, and registering it for preservation in the books of council and session.

Style 10

Parenting agreement: homosexual couples

19.10

AGREEMENT

BETWEEN

SAMANTHA MOOR, KNOWN AS SAM MOOR, 1 HIGH STREET, STAIR, AYRSHIRE, SCOTLAND

AND

RHODA HARRIET GOOD, KNOWN AS R H GOOD, 1 HIGH STREET, STAIR, AYRSHIRE, SCOTLAND

AND

HENDRIK VAN DER WORTELS, 1A HUGO DE GROOT PLEIN, DELFT, SOUTH HOLLAND, THE NETHERLANDS

AND

WILLEM HURKMANS, KNOWN AS WILLEM VAN DER WORTELS, 1A HUGO DE GROOT PLEIN, DELFT, SOUTH HOLLAND, THE NETHERLANDS

WHEREAS:

Sam and Rhoda are lesbians in a committed long-term relationship.

Sam and Rhoda were desirous of having a child.

Hendrik and Willem are gay men in a long-term committed relationship.

Hendrik and Willem wanted a child in whose upbringing they could participate.

Sam conceived a child through confused artificial insemination of Hendrik's and Willem's sperm.

Sam gave birth to her son Henry Willem van der Wortels Good-Moor, born in Scotland on 25 July 2001.

Henry is now being cared for by Sam and Rhoda.

Sam and Rhoda wish Hendrik and Willem to be known to Henry as his fathers.

All the parties wish to enter into an agreement for the discharge of parental responsibilities and rights in relation to Henry.

THEREFORE the parties AGREE as follows:

1   Parental responsibilities and rights
1.1   Sam retains her parental responsibilities and rights in relation to Henry's upbringing, to act as his legal representative, and to administer his property, subject to any court order made pursuant to clauses 4.1 or 4.3 of this agreement.
1.2   However, she agrees to discharge her parental responsibilities and rights in relation to Henry's upbringing in conjunction with Rhoda, Hendrik and Willem in accordance with the provisions of this agreement.

2   Residence and contact
2.1   Henry will live with Sam and Rhoda in their common household in Scotland. He will be brought up by them as his mothers, and have regular visiting contact from Hendrik and Willem as his fathers.
2.2   Hendrik and Willem will have contact with Henry:
       (a)   for one weekend in six, between [*specify*];
       (b)   for two weeks in Henry's summer school holidays as agreed each year, once he begins attending school; and
       (c)   each alternative New Year (from 28 December–3 January, or such other dates as are agreed between the parties), commencing 28 December 2007 or such other date as agreed between the parties.

3   Day-to-day and major parenting decisions
3.1   Sam and Rhoda will be responsible for day-to-day decisions in relation to Henry's upbringing, but will consult with Hendrik and Willem regarding:
       (a)   any proposed change of Henry's name;
       (b)   if Henry is to have any religious upbringing; and
       (c)   a permanent change of residence for themselves and Henry.
3.2   Sam and Rhoda will inform Hendrik and Willem of any significant decisions, or developments, in relation to Henry's upbringing. They will regularly supply them with photographs of Henry, and encourage Henry to speak on the telephone with them. They will keep them informed about Henry's progress at school when he has

started attending school, and consent to Hendrik and Willem having access to Henry's school and health records.

3.3   Sam and Rhoda will take all practical steps to teach Henry the Dutch language (*Nederlands*), both written and spoken. Hendrik and Willem will give them, and Henry, all reasonable assistance in this regard.

3.4   Once Henry is of school age, Hendrik and Willem will have the right to take Henry on summer and New Year holidays with them in accordance with clauses 2.2(b) and 2.2(c) of this agreement to any country that is a member state of the European Union. Sam and Rhoda will sign any necessary consents to this effect, and will allow Hendrik and Willem use of Henry's passport to allow him to travel on holiday with them.

3.5   Clause 3.4 is without prejudice to any additional contact arrangements the parties may agree between themselves from time to time.

4   Applications to court

4.1   Sam may agree to Rhoda applying to a competent court to be awarded parental responsibilities and rights in relation to Henry in addition to her.

4.2   If such an application is made, and granted by the court, Rhoda will exercise parental responsibilities and rights for Henry as well as Sam. In that case, subject to the court order, both Sam and Rhoda can exercise those rights independently of the other, but they will endeavour to consult with each other, and agree in all matters concerning Henry and his property (if Rhoda is appointed his legal representative as well), where possible.

4.3   It is not considered necessary at this stage for Hendrik and Willem to have parental responsibilities and rights in relation to Henry (other than the responsibilities and rights set out in this agreement), but in the event of a change of circumstances, the parties recognise that an application to a competent court might be made also to give Hendrik and Willem parental responsibilities and rights in relation to Henry.

4.4   If such an application is made, and granted, but subject to the court order, Hendrik and Willem may only exercise those parental responsibilities and rights in relation to Henry if Sam, or in the event Rhoda has been granted parental responsibilities and rights, all the parties to this agreement, agree to the decision in question. This does not apply to Hendrik and Willem's right to contact with Henry and their other responsibilities and rights, in relation to Henry imposed upon, or given to them by this agreement.

4.5   An application may be made to the court by any of the parties to this agreement to resolve any question concerning the granting, continued existence, or exercise of parental responsibilities and rights by any of the parties to this agreement, or their rights under this agreement, in the event:

(a)   Sam and Rhoda separate from each other;

(b)   Hendrik and Willem separate from each other;

(c)   any dispute arises between the parties (or any of them) which they cannot amicably resolve in some other manner; or

(d) Henry's presumed capacity to understand decisions affecting him does not in fact exist when he attains the age of 12 years (see clause 5.1 of this agreement); or

(e) Henry refuses to consent to change of his name under clause 5.2 of this agreement.

5 Duty to consult Henry, and obtain his consent

5.1 All parties with parental responsibilities in relation to Henry will consult him in relation to any decision affecting him when he is of an age and degree of maturity to understand the implications of the decision in question, unless to do so would clearly not be in his best interests. He will be presumed to be of such an age when he attains the age of 12, unless the court decides to the contrary in an application made under clause 4.5(d) of this agreement.

5.2 Henry's name cannot be changed by the parties when Henry attains the age of 12 unless Henry, or the court, agrees to the change.

6 Breach of this agreement

6.1 No party may act contrary to this agreement.

6.2 A party doing so, or threatening to do so, accepts that a competent court may interdict him or her from continuing to do so, or carrying out his or her threat to do so.

6.3 The court may award expenses against a party breaching this agreement.

7 Continuing effect and revocation of this agreement

7.1 This agreement continues in effect even if Sam and Rhoda, or Hendrik and Willem separate from each other.

7.2 Clause 7.1 is subject to any order made by the court in pursuance of clause 4.5 of this agreement.

7.3 This agreement may be revoked only by mutual agreement of all the parties in writing, or by order of the court.

8 Applicable law and language

8.1 This agreement is governed by and is to be construed in accordance with Scots Law.

8.2 It is drawn up solely in the English language.

8.3 A certified Dutch translation will be made in four copies at Hendrik and Willem's expense within four months of the last date of signature of this agreement, but it will not be authoritative in relation to the construction of this agreement.

8.4 Hendrik and Willem will send to each of Sam and Rhoda one of the certified translations into Dutch within seven days of Hendrik and Willem receiving the translations. Hendrik and Willem will retain one copy each for their own records.

9 Registration of agreement

9.1 This agreement will be registered in the books of council and session for preservation only at Sam's expense, including the expense of obtaining four extracts.

9.2 Each of the parties to the agreement must receive an extract of it within seven days of the four extracts being issued to Sam's solicitors. This does not prejudice each of the other parties, on a voluntary basis, refunding Sam a quarter share of the costs of registration, and the extracts.

IN WITNESS WHEREOF

Notes to Style 10

1   The fictional story of Henry Carrots, told in this agreement in the context of a cohabiting lesbian couple, is based on a real life story narrated in the Dutch paper *De Telegraaf* (see 'Meer dan Genetisch Pretpakketje' (2003) 21 June). In the scenario of this agreement, however, Henry's birth is set in Scotland and confused artificial insemination of both men was used to impregnate Sam. The author is indebted to Ms Cary MacMahon, Paisley for her role in Henry's intellectual conception. For more information, see:www.coc.nl-meerdangewnest; www.kidkids.nl; and www.homo-ouders.nl.

2   An agreement such as this is unenforceable and does not confer any parental responsibilities and rights on any party to it who does not have those rights in relation to Henry. As Henry is illegitimate and Sam is his mother, she alone has parental responsibilities and rights in relation to him. Nonetheless, the court, if called upon to adjudicate in any dispute as to Henry's upbringing can take the agreement into consideration, though ultimately it will have regard to what is in Henry's best interests: *C v S* 1996 SLT 1387.

3   The agreement attempts to deal with what might be a number of practical issues in an arrangement of this sort. Sam reserves her parental responsibilities and rights in relation to acting as Henry's legal representative, and administering his property, but agrees to share the rest with Rhoda and the two men. Provision is made for the other parties to the agreement to acquire parental responsibilities and rights for Henry, including rights to act as his legal representative.

Style 11

Provisions in a Separation Agreement Referring to a Separate Agreement on Aliment for Children

19.11

Part 6   Aliment and Periodical Allowance

10.1 This Part makes provision for Mrs Allan's maintenance by Mr Allan by way of aliment during their marriage, and thereafter by way of periodical allowance for a period of three years from the date of the parties' divorce. It also makes provisions for the payment and revision of the aliment payable by Mr Allan to Mrs Allan for the maintenance of the children set out in any separate agreement between Mr and Mrs Allan.

10.2 Mr Allan will pay Mrs Allan aliment for herself at the rate of ONE HUNDRED POUNDS (£100) a week until the date of the parties' divorce. Thereafter, he will pay her a periodical allowance of SEVENTY-FIVE POUNDS (£75.00) a week for a period of three years from the date of the parties' divorce. However, in the event of a Child Support Agency maintenance assessment providing that Mr Allan pay more money than in total agreed under any separate agreement between Mr and Mrs Allan providing for aliment for the children, the amounts in this clause will be decreased by the amount of such increase, and if such increase equals or exceeds the amounts provided herein, then Mr Allan will pay no aliment for or periodical allowance to Mrs Allan.

10.3 The following apply in respect of aliment and periodical allowance:

(a) All payments of aliment and of periodical allowance will be in advance each week.

(b) They will be made by credit transfer into such bank or other account as Mrs Allan may from time to time nominate or by any other method designated by her.

(c) Payments of aliment will commence on [*specify*].

(d) Payments of aliment for Annabel and Catherine will be made to Mrs Allan for the maintenance of the children, and will be increased each year as the children get older and in line with inflation, subject to the parties' respective incomes and resources and obligations. Such increase will be agreed each year, and failing agreement either party may make application to the Child Support Agency, failing which either party may apply to the President of the Law Society of Scotland to nominate an arbiter to determine whether any increase is justified and, if so, how much. It will be in the option of either party whether to apply for the nomination of an arbiter, but on an arbiter being nominated both parties will be bound to arbitrate. If, however, the parties reach agreement on an increase, such agreement will be recorded in a formal writing registered for execution in the books of council and session. The decision of any arbiter will be registered for execution in the books of council and session, and the parties will pay the arbiter's costs equally, with neither being found liable for the expenses of the other.

10.4 Mr Allan will pay interest on each instalment of aliment and periodical allowance from its due date until paid at 15% a year.

10.5 Subject to clause 10.3(d), a competent court exercising jurisdiction and the power to do so may vary the foregoing amounts of aliment and periodical allowance on there being a material change of circumstances, not including the transfer or sale of the matrimonial home. In this regard, the parties prorogate the non-exclusive jurisdiction of the sheriff of North Strathclyde at Paisley.

10.6 The sums calculated with reference to Mrs Allan's maintenance have been calculated with reference to the scheduled statement of the parties' income and outgoings, which they warrant is a full and frank disclosure thereof, and they undertake to disclose to each other annually, both in connection with Mrs Allan's maintenance, and the aliment of the children, a full and frank statement of their incomes and outgoings.

10.7 Any separate agreement between Mr and Mrs Allan for the aliment of the children will form an integral part of this agreement, for the period that it is in force, and will be construed and enforced accordingly. It will be registered for execution in the books of council and session.

Notes to Style 11
1   These provisions replace Part 6 of Style 1, at para 19.01; paras 9.17 and 9.18 explain why.

Style 12

Separate agreement for aliment for the children

19.12

AGREEMENT

BETWEEN

MRS ANNABEL LEE OR ALLAN, 5 RUE MORGUE, PAISLEY

AND

EDGAR ALLAN, 'THE RAVEN', WILLIAM WILSON ROAD, PAISLEY

WHEREAS:

The parties married at Edinburgh on 1 July 1990; have two children under the age of 16 years: Annabel Allan, born 14 February 1992; and Catherine Allan, born 26 August 1994; and separated on 2 May 1997.

The parties entered into a separation agreement dated [*specify*] and registered in the books of council and session on [*specify*] ('the separation agreement').

Clause 10.1 of that agreement contemplates that the parties might enter into a separate agreement between them providing for aliment of the children.

The parties now wish to enter into such an agreement.

THEREFORE the parties AGREE as follows:

1   Alimentary obligations
1.1   Mr Allan will aliment Annabel at the rate of FIFTY POUNDS (£50) a week until she attains the age of 18 years.
1.2   Mr Allan will aliment Catherine at the rate of FIFTY POUNDS (£50) a week until she attains the age of 18 years.
1.3   These obligations will commence on [*specify*] and will cease from the effective date of any Child Support Agency maintenance calculation made in respect of the children, or either of them.

2   Relationship to the separation agreement

2.1   This agreement forms an integral part of the separation agreement, for the period this agreement is in force, and will be construed and enforced accordingly.

3   Duration of this agreement

3.1   This agreement will continue in force until revoked by a subsequent agreement replacing this one.

3.2   This agreement revokes the previous agreement between the parties dated [*specify*] and registered in the books of council and session on [*specify*] providing for aliment for the children. It does so from the date this agreement is registered for execution in the books of council and session.

4   Final provisions

4.1   The cost of registering this agreement will be borne by Mrs Allan. Her solicitors will register it in the books of council and session immediately after its signature and obtain two extracts. They will send one of these to Mr Allan's solicitors within seven days of obtaining the two extracts from the keeper of the register.

4.2   The parties consent to registration of this agreement for execution in the books of council and session:

IN WITNESS WHEREOF

Notes to Style 12

1   As explained in chapter 9, agreement registered for execution in the books of council and session is a maintenance order which excludes Child Support Agency ('CSA') jurisdiction for a year after its registration. A new agreement will be needed each year if CSA jurisdiction (other than where Mrs Allan receives benefits and is required by the Secretary of State to apply for a maintenance calculation) is to be excluded. To achieve this, the aliment provisions for the children should be removed from the main separation agreement and put into a separate aliment agreement, which can be renewed each year.

2   To achieve this renewal, the original aliment agreement should be signed at the same time as the separation agreement and should remain in force until its revocation by a subsequent agreement, rather than last for just a year. Otherwise, the husband may not renew the agreement the next year and the wife will be left with no alimentary provision for the children at all. The wife will then have the choice, if the husband does not renew the agreement to apply to the CSA for a maintenance calculation, or rely on the provisions of the original aliment agreement. Since the original agreement and the aliment agreement both contain provisions to be construed as a single agreement, the wife can invoke the provisions of the separation agreement to apply for an increase in the amount of aliment for the children, on a material change of circumstances.

3   Clause 3.2 is appropriate only to a second, or subsequent, separate aliment agreement for the children. It revokes the previous agreement from the date the new agreement is registered for execution in the books of council and session.

Appendix 1

Applications and appeals

1. Authentic instruments

A1.01 The following table shows the court or administrative authority to which a maintenance creditor would submit an 'authentic instrument' for enforcement under the procedures referred to in CHAPTER 14. The official language of the State or territory concerned is shown in italics in the first column, together with any useful website which gives further information in English. Additionally, the names of the courts, and the type of final appeal, have been translated here from the original language of the legal instrument concerned.

STATE/TERRITORY	APPLICATION	1ST APPEAL	2ND AND FINAL APPEAL	TYPE OF FINAL APPEAL
Aruba (B) *Dutch*	Court of First Instance	Common Court of Justice of the Netherlands Antilles and Aruba	Supreme Court of the Netherlands	Appeal in cassation
Austria (R) *German*	District Court	District Court	Supreme Federal Court of Appeal	Appeal on a point of law
Belgium (R) creditor *Dutch; French; German*	Court of First Instance	Court of Appeal	Court of Cassation	Appeal in cassation
debtor	—	Court of First Instance	Court of Cassation	Appeal in cassation
Cyprus (R) *Greek*	Family Court	Family Court	Supreme Court	Appeal
Czech Republic (R) *Czech*	District Court or the court bailiff	District Court	Supreme Court	Application for annulment

STATE/TERRITORY	APPLICATION	1ST APPEAL	2ND AND FINAL APPEAL	TYPE OF FINAL APPEAL
Denmark (B) *Danish* www.domstol.dk	County Court	High Court	Supreme Court	Appeal with leave of the Minister of Justice
Estonia (R) *Estonian* www.just.ee	County or City Court	Court of Appeal	Supreme Court	Appeal in cassation
Finland (R) *Swedish*: Åland Islands; *Finnish and Swedish:* Rest of Finland; www.oikeus.fi	District Court	Court of Appeal	Supreme Court	Appeal
France[1] (R) *French*	The Presiding Judge of the Tribunal de Grande Instance	Court of Appeal	Court of Cassation	Appeal in cassation
Germany (R) *German*	A notary in a procedure of enforceability of an authentic instrument	Higher Lander Court of Appeal	Federal Court of Appeal	Appeal
Gibraltar (B) *English*	Magistrates' Court, on transmission by the Attorney General of Gibraltar	Magistrates' Court	Supreme Court	Appeal on a point of law
Greece (R) *Greek*	Court of First Instance	Court of Appeal	Court of Cassation	Appeal in cassation
Hungary (R) *Hungarian* other than Budapest	District Judge of the County Court	County Court	Supreme Court	Appeal
Budapest	Central District Court	Court of the Capital City	Supreme Court	Appeal
Iceland (L) *Icelandic*	District Court	District Court	Supreme Court	Appeal
Ireland (Rep.)(R) *English; Irish*	High Court	High Court	Supreme Court	Appeal on a point of law
Italy (R) *Italian; French* (Valle d'Aosta); *German* (Alto Adige)	Court of Appeal	Court of Appeal	Supreme Court	Appeal in cassation

STATE/TERRITORY	APPLICATION	1ST APPEAL	2ND AND FINAL APPEAL	TYPE OF FINAL APPEAL
Latvia (R) *Latvian* www.tiesas.lv	District Court	Regional Court	Supreme Court	Appeal
Lithuania (R) *Lithuanian* www.teismai.lt	Court of Appeal	Supreme Court	—	Retrial, in cases prescribed by statute
Luxembourg (R) *French*; *German*; *Luxembourgish*	The Presiding Judge of the Tribunal d'Arrondissement	Superior Court of Justice, sitting as a Court of Civil Appeal	Superior Court of Justice, sitting as a Court of Cassation	Appeal in cassation
Malta (R) *English*; *Maltese* www.justice.gov.mt	The Registrar of the Court, on transmission by the Minister of Justice	Magistrates' Court	Court of Appeal	Appeal
Netherlands (Kingdom in Europe) (R) *Dutch*				
creditor	Presiding Judge of the District Court	Court of Appeal	Supreme Court of the Netherlands	Appeal in cassation
debtor	—	District Court	Supreme Court of the Netherlands	Appeal in cassation
Norway (L) *Norwegian* odin.dep.no	District Court	Court of Appeal	Supreme Court	Appeal
Poland (R) *Polish*	District Court	Appeal Court	Supreme Court	Appeal in cassation
Portugal[2] (R) *Portuguese*	District Court	Court of Appeal	Supreme Court	Appeal on a point of law
Slovakia (R) *Slovakian*	District Court or exekutor	Regional Court District Court	— Regional Court	— Appeal
Slovenia (R) *Slovenian*; *Italian*; *Hungarian*	District Court	Supreme Court	—	Retrial, in cases prescribed by statute
Spain[3] (R) *Spanish* (plus regional languages)	Judge of First Instance	Provincial Court	Supreme Court	Appeal in cassation
Sweden (R) *Swedish*	Court of Appeal	Court of Appeal	Supreme Court	Appeal

State/Territory	Application	1st Appeal	2nd and Final Appeal	Type of Final Appeal
Switzerland (L)[4] *French; German; Italian*	The Cantonal Court having jurisdiction to enforce judgments	Cantonal Tribunal	Federal Tribunal[5]	Appeal in cassation
United Kingdom[6]: England and Wales[7] *English; Welsh*	Magistrates' Court, on transmission by the Lord Chancellor[9]	Magistrates' Court	High Court	Appeal on a point of law by way of case stated under Magistrates' Court Act 1980, s 111
Northern Ireland[7] *English*	Magistrates' Court, on transmission by the Lord Chancellor[9]	Magistrates' Court	Court of Appeal	Appeal on a point of law
Scotland[8] *English*	Sheriff Court, on transmission by the Scottish Ministers	Sheriff	Inner House of the Court of Session	Appeal on a point of law

(B) = Brussels Convention
(L) = Lugano Convention
(R)= Council Regulation on Jurisdiction and Judgments

1   Includes overseas départements: Guadeloupe, Guyane, Martinique, Réunion.
2   Includes the Azores and Madeira.
3   Includes the Canary Islands.
4   In Switzerland, legislation in the field of civil law and civil procedure is a federal matter, but each has canton its own system of courts, and appeals. A final appeal lies to the Federal Tribunal.
5   Appeals are assigned to the 'Cour de droit public' which, *inter alia*, has jurisdiction to examine violations of international agreements in the field of judicial cooperation: see www.tribunal-federal.ch.
6   Intra-UK enforcement is not possible: an authentic instrument must be registered separately for enforcement in each of the three jurisdictions.
7   Not available in respect of Scottish authentic instruments.
8   Relevant only to foreign authentic instruments.
9   This function is likely to be transferred to the Secretary of State on the possible abolition of the office of Lord Chancellor by the intended Constitutional Reform Act 2004.

2. Final appeals

A1.02   As will be noted, final appeals are in some countries limited to a point of law. An appeal in cassation, where that exists, involves the Supreme Court in question reviewing errors of law on the part of the lower appeal court. The procedure is one for annulment of the lower court decision as the Supreme Court, if finding an error of law, remits to and does not substitute its own judgment for that of the lower court.

Further research

A1.03   See the 'European Judicial Atlas in civil matters' and 'European Judicial Network in civil and commercial matters' at the 'Justice and Home Affairs' site, available at:
— www.europa.eu.int.

A1.04   The European Court of Justice's website also gives links to national 'institutional and legal internet sites', at:
— www.curia.eu.int.

Also, the Polish Supreme Court's website has a number of useful links to other Supreme Court websites (these links are available in English); see:
— www.sn.pl.

A1.05   Interpol's website gives useful information on the court systems in Europe, at:
— www.interpol.int, under 'regional activities' (Europe) and then 'police and judicial systems'.

A1.06   Other useful websites are:
— www.eurolegal.org; and
— www.iasaj.org.

A1.07   Also of assistance is the publication entitled *Judicial Organisation in Europe* (Council of Europe Publishing, May 2000).

Appendix 2

Case law on the Brussels and Lugano conventions

Further research

A2.01 The attention of practitioners and other interested parties is drawn to the fact that the full text of recent rulings handed down by the European Court of Justice and national courts concerning the Conventions on jurisdiction and the enforcements of judgments in civil and commercial matters (the Brussels and Lugano Conventions) are available on-line at www.curia.eu.int, by following the link to 'Brussels and Lugano Conventions' and choosing the French or English text.

A2.02 Under art 3 of Protocol 2 on the uniform application of the Lugano Convention, a Standing Committee meets on a periodic basis to exchange views on the functioning of the Lugano Convention. In recent years, individual members of that Committee have produced reports which give an overview of the case law in this area. The reports compiled in 1999–2002 are available to download from:
— www.bj.admin.ch/themen/v-lugue/intro-e.htm.

A2.03 Information as to the status of the Conventions is obtainable at:
— Brussels Convention: www.fco.gov.uk (search on 'Brussels convention status'); and
— Lugano Convention: www.bj.admin.ch/themen/v-lugue/intro-e.htm.

Index

Action for aliment	18.14
Action of adjudication	15.15–15.16
Action of separation	1.07, 1.09
Adjudication	15.15–15.16
Admissibility	17.14–17.17, 18.11, 18.29
Adoption	
civil partnership	12.03, 12.07
CSA jurisdiction	9.16
generally	7.13
registered partnerships	
in Europe	13.01–13.08
Adoption order	
annulment	7.06
common law recognition	7.06
parental responsibilities	
and rights	7.04, 7.05, 7.06
Adult, meaning	2.11
Adultery	1.08, 19.01
Advice	
investment	2.17
solicitor's duty	2.13, 17.10
sources	2.02
Agreements, generally	
alterations	3.30
annexations	3.29
best interests	2.09
blind granter	3.30
capacity to contract	2.10–2.11, 6.04, 7.02
challenges	16.01–16.04
clauses	3.09
common law challenge	16.01
cross-references	3.10
drafting	2.12, 3.01–3.23
enforcement measures	15.01
execution	3.24–3.30
extract	3.35, 3.36
final provisions	3.04

Agreements, generally – *contd*	
foreign	
protective measures	15.19–15.23
form of	3.03
forms of warrant of execution	3.36
grammatical rules	3.15–3.22
indented lists	3.07–3.08
inventories	3.29
language	3.05
lists	3.07–3.08
marriage *see* marriage contract	
negotiating	2.05–2.06
numbering	3.10
obligations	3.11–3.14
paragraphs	3.09, 3.10
performance, time of	3.13
pronouns	3.17–3.22
protective measures	15.19–15.23
punctuation	3.23
recitals	3.03, 3.05
reference to	3.05
schedules	3.29
sections	3.09
set aside	16.02, 16.03
statutory challenge	16.02–16.04
structure	3.06–3.08
styles	3.01–3.05, 19.01–19.12
subscription	3.24–3.30
testing clause	3.31–3.33
time of performance	3.13, 3.14
under duress	2.09
validity of signature	3.25
variation	16.02, 16.03
witness	3.24–3.28
Agreements registered for execution	
payment of money	15.02–15.04
recall of inhibition	17.24–17.26

Agreements registered for execution – *contd*
registration process   3.34–3.36
suspension of charge   17.24
warrant   3.36, 15.02
Aliment
action for   18.14
agreement to vary   8.09
arbitration agreement for
aliment, style   19.05
arbitration for aliment   17.20, 17.21
civil imprisonment for
non-payment   15.17
cohabiting parties   19.06
de facto separation   5.01
forum non conveniens   8.05
future liability exclusion   8.06
jurisdiction   8.05
material change   8.04
non-payment   15.17
periodical allowance,
distinction between   8.02
separate agreements for
children, in   19.11, 19.12
separation agreements, in   19.01, 19.02
unilateral obligation   8.03
variation   8.04–8.06, 8.09, 19.05, 19.06
Aliment agreement
children
provisions referring to separate
agreement   19.11
separate agreement   19.12
CSA jurisdiction exclusion   9.17, 19.12
date of registration   9.15
decree for payment   15.01
legislation   18.15
payment arrears   15.01
registration for execution   3.35
separate obligations   9.18
styles
aliment for children   19.11, 19.12
variation   9.11–9.13
Alimentary bond   5.09, 8.03, 18.17
Alterations   3.30
Animals   19.01, 19.02
Annexations   3.29
Annulment of marriage
effect on will   1.19
Arbitration   17.11, 17.20–17.21
cohabitation agreement, in   19.06
Arbitration agreement for
aliment, style   19.05
Arbitration for aliment   2.07, 17.20, 17.21
Aruba   14.04, 14.36
Assurance policy
civil partners   12.10
marriage contract   4.07
Authentic instruments
admissibility   18.11, 18.29

Authentic instruments – *contd*
appeals   18.08, 18.29
application for inhibition   15.06
Benelux   14.08
certificate
of authenticity   14.11, 14.12, 14.25
of judgment   18.12
of writ registered for execution   18.31
challenge to   14.28
conditions for establishing   14.08–14.09
copies   14.10, 18.12
costs exemption   14.30–14.31
court settlements   18.81, 18.112
currency of payment   18.10, 18.29
Denmark   14.04, 14.08
documents needed   14.10, 14.14,
14.15–14.16
proof and admissibility   18.11, 18.29
domicile   14.07
enforceability   14.06–14.07
enforcement
mutual enforcement in EU   14.01
partial   14.29
procedural rules   14.01
enforcement abroad of Scottish   14.34–
14.35
enforcement under Brussels or Lugano
Conventions   18.30
enforcement under EC regulation   18.64
form of certificate   18.71
European Enforcement Order   14.37
form of certificate,
writ registered for execution   18.31
France   14.08
further appeal   14.24
Germany   14.08
interest   18.09, 18.29
legal aid   14.14, 14.15, 14.30–14.33
legal provisions   14.02
meaning   14.01
mutual enforcement in EU   14.01
partial enforcement   14.29
payment of maintenance
under registered   15.05–15.06
currency   18.10
procedural rules for enforcement   14.01
procedure, sheriff court   14.19–14.23
proof and admissibility   18.11, 18.29
protective measures   15.23
public policy   14.26
recognition and enforcement   18.07
registration
ground for refusal   14.26
registration procedure
further appeal   14.24–14.28
Scottish Ministers   14.10–14.18
sheriff court   14.19–14.23

Authentic instruments – *contd*
  Scottish Ministers,
    application to   14.10–14.18
    service   14.26–14.27, 14.36
    sheriff court procedure   14.19–14.23
    territorial scope   14.03
    translation   14.14, 14.15
    validity   14.26

Balearic Islands   13.08
Bank account   19.01, 19.02
Belgium
  civil partnership   11.06
  same sex marriage   1.16, 11.02,
                                    11.03, 11.04, 11.14
  statutory cohabitation   12.05, 13.06
Benefit, meaning   9.08
Benefit Agency   2.02
Benefit sharing
  activation   18.21
  qualifying agreement, meaning   18.21
Benelux countries   14.08
Brussels Convention   18.72–18.92
  see also authentic measures

CALM   17.14
Canada   11.02, 11.11, 12.07
Capacity   2.10–2.11, 6.04, 7.02
Capital sum   19.01
Certificate
  of authenticity   14.11, 14.12, 14.25
  of judgment   18.12
  of writ registered for execution   18.31
Channel Islands   7.06
Child
  abduction issues   7.20, 7.21
  civil partnerships   12.03, 12.07, 12.08
  consultation with   19.07, 19.09, 19.10
  definition   7.02
  education   19.07, 19.08, 19.09, 19.10
  foster   7.14
  name   19.06, 19.07, 19.08, 19.09
  passports   19.01, 19.02
  property   7.11, 19.09
  religious upbringing   19.07, 19.08, 19.09,
    19.10
  residence and contact 19.01, 19.02, 19.09,
    19.10
  sex assigned at birth   1.15
  step   9.16, 12.03, 12.08
Child care arrangements   15.01
Child Support Act 1991
  maintenance agreements   9.14
  s4 application   9.02, 9.03, 9.08, 9.10, 9.11
  s6 application   9.08, 9.09, 9.11
  s7 application   9.07, 9.08, 9.10, 9.11
  s8(5) order   9.04, 9.05, 9.09

Child Support Agency   9.01
Child Support Agency jurisdiction
  adopted child   9.16
  benefit cases   9.08–9.09
  consent order   9.05, 9.06
  exclusion   2.12, 9.10, 9.16, 19.12
  maintenance calculation   9.02, 9.03, 9.11
  maintenance order   9.04–9.06
  non-benefit cases   9.02–9.07, 9.17
  step-child   9.16
  written maintenance agreements
    before 5 April 1993   9.10
Civil imprisonment
  non-payment of aliment   15.17
  periodical allowance   15.18
Civil partnership   1.12, 1.13, 1.16, 6.01
  see also same sex marriage
  adoption   12.03, 12.07
  children   12.03, 12.07, 12.08
  definition   12.02
  dissolution   12.03, 12.08
  earmarking order   12.09
  effect of 2004 Act   11.05–11.08
  eligibility   12.02
  family law agreements   12.08–12.10
  family mediation   17.15
  family relations   12.03
  household goods   12.03
  married women's assurance   12.10
  obligations   12.03
  overseas relationship   12.04–12.07
  pensions   12.03, 12.09
  property   12.03
  registered overseas relationship   12.04–
    12.07
  registered partnership   12.01
    Europe   13.01–13.04
    United Kingdom   12.02–12.03
  statutory challenge   16.02–16.04
  statutory cohabitation   12.01, 13.05–13.08
Cohabitation
  marriage, compared with   1.02–1.04
  parental rights and responsibilities   1.04
  past   6.07
  revocation of will   1.20
  same sex   1.12, 1.13
Cohabitation agreement
  competence   6.05
  disposal of property   6.03
  duly attested   1.23
  generally   1.05–1.06, 6.01–6.06
  past   6.07
  same sex   1.12, 1.16, 6.08, 19.06
  style   19.06
  unenforceable   6.02, 6.04
Cohabitation contract   1.12, 1.13
Colourable case   15.22
Common law challenge   16.01

Common law wife   1.02
Conciliation   17.11, 17.18–17.19, 19.07
Conditio si testator sine liberis decesserit 1.20
Consent order
    CSA jurisdiction   9.05, 9.06, 9.09
Contact agreement   15.01
Council of Europe
    Fifth European Conference on Family
        Law 1999   13.09
    recommendation on validity of contracts,
        unmarried couple   18.115
Council Regulation on jurisdiction and
    enforcement of judgments 18.44–18.71
    see also authentic instruments
Criminal property, definition   2.18
Cross-references   3.10
CSA *see* Child Support Agency
Current maintenance, meaning   18.16

Data
    processing   2.21
    registration   2.23
    sensitive personal   2.20, 2.22
Data protection   2.20–2.23
Death
    appointment of guardian
        by will   1.18, 7.09
    parental responsibilities and rights   7.05
    separation agreement   5.21
    wife 18.04
Denmark
    authentic instruments 14.04, 14.08, 14.36
    registered partnership   12.05, 13.01
Diligence   17.24–17.26
    power to execute   18.06
    registered agreement   3.34, 3.35
Disability working allowance   9.08
Dispute resolution
    anticipation   17.05
    arbitration   17.11, 17.20–17.21
    conciliation   17.11, 17.18–17.19
    drafting techniques   17.02–17.09
    generally   17.01
    litigation   17.11, 17.22–17.26
    mediation   17.11, 17.13–17.17
    negotiation   17.11, 17.12
    solicitor's duty to give
        objective advice   17.10
    time to perform   17.07
Divorce
    effect on will   1.19
    financial provision,
        statutory challenge   16.02–16.03
    provisions in agreements   19.01, 19.03,
        19.04
Drafting   2.12, 3.01–3.23
Durable relationship 'duly attested'   1.23

Duress   2.09

Earmarking order   10.01, 10.05, 10.06
    civil partners   12.09
Earnings arrestment   15.05
Endowment policy   19.01, 19.02
Enforcement measures
    adjudication   15.15–15.16
    civil imprisonment   15.17–15.18
    diligence   15.04
    generally   15.01
    letters of arrestment   15.12–15.14
    letters of inhibition   15.07–15.11
    maintenance arrears   15.03
    money obligations   15.01
    protective measures,
        foreign agreements   15.19–15.23
England and Wales   7.06, 15.21
Europe   11.09
European Enforcement Order   14.37
European Union
    family member   1.22, 1.23
    free movement of persons   1.22–1.27
    spouse   1.22
Evrigenis and Kerameus Report   14.01
Execution
    meaning   3.14, 17.06
    title to land   18.05
Extract   3.35, 3.36

Family home, meaning   19.06
Family Mediation Scotland   17.14
Family member, definition   1.22, 1.23
Faroe Islands   13.01
Father, unmarried   7.01, 7.03, 7.08
Financial Services Authority   2.17
Finland   12.05, 13.01
FMS   17.14
Foreign agreements
    petition   15.22
    proceedings in
        other jurisdictions   15.19–15.22
    protective measures   15.19–15.23
Forum non conveniens   8.05
Foster child
    definition   7.14
    private arrangements   7.14
France
    authentic instruments   14.08
    civil solidarity pact   12.05
    statutory cohabitation   13.05
Free movement of persons   1.22–1.27
FSA   2.17

Germany
    authentic instruments   14.08

Germany – *contd*
  registered lifepartnership   12.05, 13.04
Gibraltar   14.36
Gift
  marriage contract   4.06
Grammatical rules   3.15–3.22
Greenland   13.01
Guardian   1.18, 7.09–7.12

Hague Convention on the Recognition
  and Enforcement of Decisions
  authentic instruments   14.02
Heritable property
  stamp duty land tax   5.14
  title   1.21
Hermaphrodites   1.15, 1.16
Hire-purchase goods   19.01
Homosexual couples
  see also same sex
  parenting agreement, style   19.10
House, common ownership   1.03
Household goods   12.03, 19.01, 19.02, 19.06
House-keeping arrangements   15.01

Iceland
  confirmed cohabitation   12.05, 13.01
  free movement of persons   1.22
  Lugano Convention   14.05
  service of documents   14.36
Inadmissibility rule   17.14, 17,15
  exceptions   17.16–17.17
Income support   9.08
Information Commission
  registration   2.23
Inheritance tax
  marriage contract   4.06
Inhibition
  recall   17.24–17.26
Inhibition and arrestment on
  dependence of the action   1.11
Inhibitions in security   15.10, 15.11
Interdict   1.11
Interim exclusion order   1.11
Interim interdict   1.11
Interim residence order   1.11
International Commission
  on Civil Status   13.10
Inventories   3.29
Investment advice   2.17, 10.08
Isle of Man   7.06

Jenard and Moller Report   14.01, 14.08
Jobseekers' allowance, income-based   9.08
Judgments, jurisdiction and enforcement of
  see also authentic instruments
  Brussels Convention   18.72–18.92

Judgments, jurisdiction and
  enforcement of – *contd*
  Council Regulation
    EC/44/2001   18.44–18.71
  Lugano Convention   18.93–18.114

Language   3.05, 14.14, 14.15
Law Society of Scotland   17.14
  guidelines   2.03, 2.04, 2.06,
    2.14, 2.15, 2.16, 2.17
  pension sharing   10.08
Legal advice and assistance   2.04
  separation agreement   5.15–5.17
Legal aid   2.04
  authentic instruments   14.14, 14.15,
    14.30–14.33
  separation agreement   5.15–5.17
Legal capacity   2.10–2.11, 6.04, 7.02
Legal drafting   2.12, 3.01–3.23
Legal representative   7.09, 7.11
Legal separation   1.07
Legitim   4.05
Leichtenstein   1.22
Letters of arrestment   15.12–15.14
Letters of inhibition   15.07–15.11
Litigation   17.11 , 17.22–17.26
Lugano Convention   18.93–18.114
  see also authentic instruments

Maintenance
  arrears   15.03
  definitions   18.16–18.17
  enforcement   15.03
Maintenance agreement
  Child Support Act 1991   9.14
  legislation   18.18
Maintenance calculation
  child aged 12 or over   9.07
  court orders and   18.19
  CSA jurisdiction   9.02
  relationship between court orders and
    18.19
  restrictions   9.06, 9.07, 9.14
Maintenance obligations
  authentic instrument, *see* authentic
    instruments
Maintenance order   9.14, 9.15
  appeals   18.40–18.41
  application   18.33
    under s5   18.37, 18.39
  enforcement of registered   18.42
  incoming orders, 1982 Act   18.37–18.42
  jurisdiction   9.02
  meaning   18.17
  notice of determination
    of application   18.39
    form   18.43

Maintenance order – *contd*
    prescribed officer   18.34
    service   18.38
    written agreement,
      non-resident parent   9.04
Maintenance Orders Register   15.05, 18.35
    inspection   18.36
Maintenance payments
    tax relief   5.13
Marriage
    cohabitation, compared with   1.02–1.04
    generally   1.01
    legislation   18.01–18.03
    nullity   16.04
Marriage contract
    advisability of   4.03–4.04
    assurance policies   4.07
    gifts   4.06
    inheritance tax   4.06
    legitim   4.05
    purpose   4.02
    terminology   4.01
Massachusetts   12.07
Matrimonial home
    sale   2.15–2.16
    separation agreement,
      provisions in   19.01, 19.02
Matrimonial property, pensions   10.07
Maxwell Report   14.01, 14.08, 14.26
Mediation   2.07, 2.08, 17.11, 17.13–17.17
    accredited organisations   17.14
    inadmissibility rule   17.14–17.17
Mediation and conciliation
    cohabitation agreement   19.06
Mental disorder, definition   2.11
Money laundering   2.18–2.19
Money obligations   15.01
Motor vehicles   19.02

National Criminal Intelligence
    Service (NCIS)   2.18
negative obligations   15.01
negotiation   2.05–2.06, 17.11, 17.12
Netherlands
    civil partnership   11.06
    registered partnership   12.05, 13.02–13.03
    same sex marriage   11.02, 11.03, 11.04,
                   11.14, 11.17
    surrogacy   7.28
Netherlands Private International
    Law Commission   11.04
North America
    civil union   12.05
    same sex marriage   11.03, 11.10–11.11,
                   11.15, 12.07
Northern Ireland   7.06

Norway
    free movement of persons   1.22
    Lugano Convention   14.05
    registered partnership   12.05
    service of documents   14.36
Notice of litigiosity   15.15
Nullity of marriage
    financial provision
      statutory challenge   16.04

Obligations   3.11–3.14
Ordinary debt, meaning   18.16
Overseas relationships
    civil partnerships in UK, as   12.04–12.07

Parent, definition   7.01
Parental order   7.03, 7.05
Parental responsibilities, definition   7.22
Parental responsibilities and
    conciliation agreement, style   19.07
Parental responsibilities and rights
    acquisition   7.03
    care arrangements   7.15
    cohabitation   1.04
    conferred by court   7.05, 7.07
    deprivation of   7.05
    exercise of   7.04–7.05
    guardian   7.09, 7.10, 7.11
    person not habitually resident
      in Scotland   7.06
    transfer   7.04
    unmarried fathers   7.08
Parenting agreement
    abduction issues   7.20
    authentic instrument   7.22, 7.24, 7.25
    child taken out of UK   7.21
    contents   7.16, 7.17
    enforceable in European Union   7.22–7.25
    enforceable instrument   7.22–7.25
    examples   7.17–7.19
    styles
      homosexual couples   19.10
      legitimate children   19.09
      provisions in a separation
        agreement   19.08
Parenting plan, *see* parenting agreement
Paternity, presumption of   7.01
Payment
    arrears   15.01
    currency   18.10, 18.29
    decree   15.01
    interest   18.09, 18.29
    suspending charge for   17.24–17.26
Pension sharing   10.02–10.07
    activation   18.20
    actuarial advice   10.06
    challenge to agreement   16.02

Pension sharing – *contd*
civil partners 12.03, 12.09
competency 10.05
investment advice 10.08
pension arrangement
rights 18.23–18.24, 19.03
prescribed form of provision
rights under pension arrangement, 18.23
state scheme rights 18.24
state scheme rights 18.25–18.26, 19.04
valuation of pensions 10.07
Pension sharing agreement, styles
pension arrangement 19.03
state scheme rights 19.04
Performance, time of 3.13
Periodical allowance
agreement to vary 8.07–8.08, 8.10–8.12
aliment, distinction between 8.02
civil imprisonment 15.18
jurisdiction 8.07
material change 8.08
post-decree 8.12, 8.13
separation agreements, in 19.01, 19.11
variation 8.07–8.08, 8.10–8.13
Personal data 2.20, 2.21, 2.22
Poland 14.05
Precedents, *see* styles
Presumed revocation of the will 1.20
Presumption *pater est quem*
nuptiae demonstrant 7.01
Pronouns 3.17–3.22
Proof and admissibility 18.11, 18.29
Property
civil partnership 12.03
Property recovered or preserved 5.15–5.17
Public policy, contrary to 14.26
Punctuation 3.23

Qualifying agreement, meaning 18.21

Recognition and enforcement of judgments
see also authentic instruments
Brussels Convention 18.72–18.92
Council Regulation
EC/44/2001 18.44–18.71
Lugano Convention 18.93–18.114
Reconciliation 1.10–1.11
Register of Births 1.15
Registered partnership
see also civil partnership
Belgium 1.16, 13.06
free movement of persons 1.23, 1.25
generally 12.01
Germany 13.04
meaning 12.01
Netherlands 1.16, 13.02

Registered partnership – *contd*
Nordic countries 13.01
opposite sex 13.02
same sex 13.01
status and rights 13.01
statutory cohabitation 13.05–13.08
UK, definition 12.02
Residence agreement 15.01
Retention 17.03–17.04

Same sex
cohabitation agreement 1.12, 1.16, 6.08
parenting 7.27
parenting agreement, style 19.10
Same sex marriage
see also civil partnership
Canada 11.02, 11.11, 12.07
Civil Partnership Act 2004,
effect of 11.05–11.08
current position 11.01–11.04
Europe 11.09
North America 11.03, 11.10–11.11,
11.15, 12.07
recognition abroad 11.02–11.04
recognition in Scotland 11.03, 11.05–11.08
spouse 1.23
statistics 1.16
Schedules 3.29
Schlosser Report 14.01
Scottish Legal Aid Board 5.16, 5.17
Sensitive personal data 2.22
definition 2.20
Separation
action of 1.09
decree *a mensa et thoro,*
property of wife 18.04
generally 1.07–1.08, 1.16
Separation agreement
aliment 8.02, 8.03
alimentary bond 5.09
child support and, *see* Child Support
Agency jurisdiction
cohabitation after 5.01, 5.18
contract rules 5.12
death of spouse 5.21
definition 5.04–5.06
form 5.07–5.10
generally 5.01–5.06
legal aid priorities 5.15
maintenance payments 5.13
pension sharing provisions 5.10
periodical allowance 8.02
property law rules 5.12
property recovered
or preserved 5.15–5.17
property rights 5.05
reconciliation 1.10–1.11

Separation agreement – *contd*
  revocation   5.01, 5.02, 5.18–5.21
  scope and form   5.07–5.10
  separation after reconciliation   5.20
  stamp duty land tax   5.14
  styles
      continuing after divorce   19.01
      generally   5.11
      terminating on divorce   19.02
  tax relief, maintenance payments   5.13
  trial reconciliation   5.02
  unilateral obligation   8.03
  variation   5.19
Service   14.26–14.17, 14.36, 19.05
Shares   19.01
Solicitor
  advice, duty to give objective   2.13
  agreements   2.05–2.12
  conflict of interest   2.14–2.16
  data protection   2.20–2.23
  fees   2.04
  investment advice   2.17
  matrimonial home, sale of   2.15–2.16
  money laundering   2.18–2.19
  professional responsibility   2.13–2.17
  taking instructions   2.01–2.12
  terms of engagement letter   2.03
Spain   13.07–13.08
Spouse
  death   5.21, 18.04
  free movement of persons   1.22–1.25
  same sex   1.23
Stamp duty land tax   5.14
State scheme rights
  activation   18.21
  pension sharing   18.25–18.26
  pension sharing agreement   19.04
Statutory challenge   16.02–16.04
Statutory cohabitation
  see also registered partnerships
  Belgium   12.05, 13.06
  France   13.05
  meaning   12.01
  Spain   13.07–13.08
Step-child
  civil partnership   12.03, 12.08
  CSA jurisdiction exclusion   9.16
Step-parents   7.03
Styles
  arbitration agreement for aliment   19.05
  cohabitation agreement   19.06
  generally   3.01–3.05
  parental responsibilities and conciliation
      agreement   19.07
  parenting agreement
      homosexual couples   19.10
      legitimate children   19.09

Styles – *contd*
  pension sharing agreement
      pension arrangement   19.03
      state scheme rights   19.04
  provisions in a separation agreement,
      referring to a separate agreement on
          aliment for children   19.11
      referring to a separate parenting
          agreement   19.08
  separate agreement for aliment for the
      children   19.12
  separation agreement,
      continuing after divorce   19.01
      terminating on divorce   19.02
Subscription   3.24–3.30
Succession rights
  generally   1.17–1.20
  pension sharing agreement   19.03, 19.04
  separation agreement   19.01, 19.02
Summary application   17.24
Surrogacy arrangements   7.03, 7.13, 7.15
Survivorship destination   1.21
Suspension of charge   17.24–17.26
Sweden   12.05, 13.01
Switzerland   14.05, 14.36

Taxation
  inheritance tax   4.06
  maintenance   5.13
Terms of engagement letter   2.03
Testing clause   3.31–3.33
Title
  to heritable property   1.21
  to land   18.05
Translation   14.14, 14.15
Transsexuals   1.14, 1.16

United States of America
  civil union   12.05
  same sex marriage   11.03, 11.10–11.11,
                                     11.15, 12.07
Unmarried couples, validity of contracts
  Council of Europe
      Recommendation   18.115, 19.06
Unmarried fathers   7.03, 7.08

Variation
  of agreement, 16.02, 16.03, 19.01, 19.02
  of aliment, 8.04–8.06, 8.09, 9.11–9.13,
      19.05, 19.06

Will
  annulment decree   1.19
  child born subsequent to existing   1.20
  divorce   1.19

family law agreements	1.17–1.20
presumed revocation	1.20
Withholding performance	
of obligations	17.03, 17.04
Witness	3.24–3.28